EARLY CHILDHOOD SOCIAL STUDIES

Cynthia S. Sunal
The University of Alabama

Merrill Publishing Company
A Bell & Howell Information Company
Columbus ■ **Toronto** ■ **London** ■ **Melbourne**

Cover Photo: Mary Kate Denny/Photo Editor

Published by Merrill Publishing Company
A Bell & Howell Information Company
Columbus, Ohio 43216

This book was set in Zapf

Administrative Editor: David Faherty
Production Coordinator: Victoria M. Althoff
Art Coordinator: Gilda Edwards
Cover Designer: Brian Deep
Photo Editor: Terry Tietz

Photo Credits: pp. 3, 53, 145, 234 by Barbara Hatcher; pp. 6, 23, 39, 60, 111, 136,
179, 203, by Dennis Sunal; pp. 14, 65, 87, 95, 100, 120, 141, 172, 186, 190, 207,
227 by Barbara Warash.

Library of Congress Catalog Card Number: 89–061334
International Standard Book Number: 0–675–20960–9
Printed in the United States of America
1 2 3 4 5 6 7 8 9—92 91 90

To Dennis, who has always offered unceasing support and love

To Alisa and Paul, who brought the joys of early childhood home

To Joseph A. Szymanski and Sophie Bartnik Szymanski, who stimulated an interest in thinking, talking, and learning about the social world

PREFACE

Early Childhood Social Studies takes a developmental viewpoint in considering social studies education for young children. Young children have many opportunities to experience social studies. Their understanding and their capabilities develop and change as they actively explore the social environment.

Because the social world affects all parts of our lives, social studies education should be an integral part of the early childhood curriculum, not be separated from other curricula. As part of the integrated day, social studies affects all that occurs throughout that day. Truly the core of the early childhood curriculum, the social studies define how the child learns to become an active, positive, contributing member of human society.

This book presents three models for teaching social studies to young children, each of which is based on use of the senses, concrete experiences, and opportunities to discuss observations. Although each model addresses a particular level of development, the models can be used as needed with children at differing levels. A model normally appropriate for less mature children may be appropriate for all in an unfamiliar situation, while a model usually appropriate for more mature children may be used for all in a highly familiar situation.

This book focuses on a cognitive developmental approach but incorporates the valuable knowledge derived from social learning theory and behavioral learning theory. It addresses the reality that children grow, change, and think differently as they acquire more and more experience with the world. Research related to a range of social, emotional, and intellectual development theories is incorporated. The eclectic view that most teachers employ—"use what can help"—is important in this book. Although a cognitive developmental approach is the focus of the book, teachers will also want to consider the effects of modeling and behavior modification upon children, as well as other approaches.

v

Examples are provided for teaching social studies in such traditional subjects as history and geography, as well as in newer themes such as economics and multicultural education. Rather than covering all of the social studies areas, *Early Childhood Social Studies* suggests ways that selected themes within the social studies may be approached in early childhood. Using this framework, teachers should be able to adapt approaches and apply them to other themes within social studies education. Each chapter gives useful and practical ideas for integrating social studies into the entire early childhood program.

This book also recognizes teachers' concerns about teaching social studies to mainstreamed special education students, to children from a variety of ethnic backgrounds, and to children who are first being introduced to large groups of peers in day-care settings, preschools, and primary-grade classrooms. Each contributor has many years' experience teaching young children both in North America and overseas and has experienced many of the same concerns. The ideas in this book are derived from those personal, practical experiences. The contributors and I hope you find this book theoretically sound and practically useful. Most of all, we hope that in trying these ideas you and the children will learn more about your social world and will have fun doing so.

ACKNOWLEDGMENTS

Many thanks to Mrs. Barbara Warash and the West Virginia University Nursery School for encouraging the use of the school to develop social studies education program ideas and for allowing the use of pictures of the children at the school.

The suggestions and comments of the reviewers were most helpful. The extensive amount of time each devoted to reviewing drafts of this book is much appreciated. I would like to thank Mona Lane, Oklahoma State University; Rosalie Allison, Valdosta State College; Kenneth Campbell, Auburn University at Montgomery; Sandra Styer, Northeastern Illinois University; Dale Rice, Auburn University; Robert Thurman, University of Tennessee; Richard Needham, University of Northern Colorado; Mary Verhoeven, Kent State University; Max Ferguson, Southern Utah State College; and Marie Sandler, Canada College.

CONTENTS

6

THE CONCEPT ATTAINMENT MODEL

7

PLANNING FOR TEACHING

Sandra Bradford DeCosta

1

THE SOCIAL STUDIES AND THE CHILD

When you think of "social studies" from your own preschool and elementary school days, what memory surfaces first? Some preservice early childhood teachers have said:

- Making maps. "In the third grade I made a map out of plaster of paris. It was so heavy I staggered around trying to move it over to the table where we displayed our maps, but I was so proud of it."
- Making projects. "Remember the igloo out of sugar cubes Johnnie built in the second grade?"
- Thick social studies books with lots of questions to answer. "When you got to the end of a unit you dreaded all those questions in the review section."
- Field trips. "I really liked going to visit the newspaper offices and seeing the presses printing that afternoon's paper. For a long time I really wanted to be a printing press operator when I grew up."
- Reports. "Beginning in the second grade I had to write a report on Abraham Lincoln, year after year."
- Community helpers. "I was so impressed by the fire engine and the firefighter driving it. They visited our school when we were studying about firefighters in kindergarten."
- Discussions. "My third grade teacher liked having discussions about current events and people in the news. We sometimes got on far-off tangents but it was really interesting."

"Social studies" was fun sometimes and boring at others. It involved doing as well as reading, visiting and visitors, talking and thinking. It was about people— Abraham Lincoln (over and over again!), the firefighter, the printing press operator, people in the news—what they did and maps of where they lived.

WHAT THE SOCIAL STUDIES ARE

The social studies were and are "social" because they deal with our social lives. They investigate the ways in which we adapt to each other and come to understand ourselves. All of the many definitions of the social studies reflect our roles as member–citizens of our society (Barr, Barth, & Shermis, 1977, p. 69; Engle, 1976, p. 234; Kenworthy, 1980, p. 6; Michaelis, 1985, p. 2). In 1983 the Task Force on Scope and Sequence of the National Council for the Social Studies developed this definition:

> The social studies may be defined as an area of the curriculum that
> derives goals from the nature of citizenship in a democratic society
> and links to other societies, draws content from the social sciences
> and other disciplines, and reflects personal, social, and cultural expe-
> riences of students.

This definition highlights the function of the social studies as developing students' understanding of the society in which they live. It will serve as the definition on which this book is based. In this book the early childhood years will be defined as the years from birth to age 8, a span recognized by the National Association for the Education of Young Children (1982, p. xii).

A definition of the social studies is abstract. It requires a wide range of concrete experiences if we are to understand it. Each of us will tend to define it in terms of our own experiences. Our remembrances of social studies activities when we were children help us to make the abstract definition concrete.

Because each of us has different memories and different experiences, it's important to begin with a formal definition so we all have the same reference point. Using this reference point we can evaluate the kinds of experiences we have had and plan experiences for our students. If we remember our social studies experiences as being centered on reading a thick text and answering questions, we can wonder whether we weren't just shuffling words around and perhaps never really did "do" social studies. How can we ensure that our students will have concrete social studies experiences that encourage them to explore their social world? If we have pleasant memories of a lingering interest in newspapers following a field trip, for example, we will want to concretize our definition by making sure our students have experiences in the social world that will generate similar enthusiasm in them. The social studies for young children must be concrete, involving children in doing and experiencing. The social studies must help children become active, competent members of their family, community, nation, and world (see Figure 1–1).

FIGURE 1–1
The social studies help us understand how we all depend on one another.

CHARACTERISTICS OF THE SOCIAL STUDIES

Examining the characteristics of the social studies can help us to concretize our definition. The social studies have the following characteristics:

- They involve a search for patterns in our lives.
- They are a natural human activity, a naturally occurring part of our lives.
- They involve both content and processes of learning.
- They are based on information.

- They require information processing.
- They require decision making and problem solving.
- They are concerned with the development and analysis of one's own values.

A Search for Patterns

A pattern is a regular activity that has occurred in the past and can be expected to occur again in the future. The world is full of patterns, such as these:

- People wear more, and heavier, clothes in winter.
- As groups of people get larger, specialization of occupations occurs.
- People try to understand their environment by making a mental map of it.
- People are satisfied when their needs are met.

Children are inundated by information about the world. They must organize it in order to make sense of it and to be able to use it. Children look for patterns. Very young children often badger adults with "why" questions. "Why didn't you say 'Hello' back to Mrs. Greenbaum?" "Why is that boy blind?" In order to understand their social world children must identify the patterns existing in that world. These patterns may be accepted or challenged but first they must be discovered. In social studies we try to help children find these patterns in our social world, understand them, and analyze them. We build the foundation upon which children can eventually make a rational decision to accept, reject, or modify a pattern.

A Basis in Natural Human Activity

The search for patterns in our social world is a naturally occurring part of everyday life. For many, the social studies conjure up pictures of historians pouring over dusty documents. Historians often work with dusty documents searching for patterns in events past, but this is not an accurate picture of the search exemplified by the social studies.

Social studies are built on the human tendency continuously to structure our experience, to search for and impose patterns on the social world around us. This search begins at an early age and continues through life. The young child trying to understand family relationships such as "grandmother" and "uncle" is involved in a search just as difficult as that of the historian. The older child, trying to understand the role of appointed officials in local government, is also involved in a search for patterns. The effort to understand through finding patterns in the information we have is constant. The social studies assist children in this effort as it addresses the social world they live in.

A Two-Sided Role: Content and Processes

Identifying the search for patterns in the social world as a characteristic of the social studies implies a two-sided role for the social studies. On the one hand, the social studies are a search, a continuing activity. This is the *process* part of the social studies. In searching for patterns, people use certain processes, such as observing and inferring (Michaelis, 1985). On the other hand, the products of the search must be considered. These products are facts, concepts, and generalizations. These are the *content* of the social studies (Oliner, 1976). This dual role of the social studies is so interrelated that each aspect is sometimes confused.

One way to distinguish between process and content is to think of the process aspect as "doing." For example, four children are working with a learning center that displays items of children's clothing dating from 1860 to 1890. The clothes are tried on and closely examined. The children complain about how hard it is to get the clothes on. So much buttoning is required! They realize that none of the clothes have zippers and conclude that zippers weren't used in clothes from 1860 to 1890. They wonder why not, because buttons are much harder to use and take more time to fasten. One child suggests, "Maybe buttons were in style and zippers weren't." Another child thinks zippers weren't invented until later. A check of an encyclopedia confirms that zippers hadn't been invented when these clothes were made.

Several processes are occurring during this activity. The children are observing; they notice that there are many buttons but no zippers on the clothes. They are hypothesizing, giving reasons for the lack of zippers. They are inferring; the child aware of fads and styles in clothing infers that no zippers were used because they were not in style, thus developing a hypothesis to explain their absence.

Content is being acquired during this activity as a product of the processes occurring. The children have learned a fact: zippers were not invented until after 1890. They have learned another fact: an item can be closed faster with a zipper than with buttons. They develop a generalization: dressing in pre-zipper clothes is more difficult than in modern clothes. The facts and generalizations developed during this activity are part of the content of the social studies. The actual forming of a pattern involves the process side of the social studies. The pattern, once formed, is called the product, or content.

Children discover the content of the social studies through their search for patterns in the social world. The content of the social studies is large and is derived from several social sciences. As children acquire content in the social studies and have many concrete experiences with the processes used to discover facts, concepts, and generalizations, they become able to understand the abstract presentations of content in sources such as social studies textbooks. Once children have understood the family relationships represented by concepts such as "grandfather" in their own lives, they can begin to read about and discuss similar relationships in other cultures.

A Core of Academic Disciplines

The social studies content to be explored, read about, discussed, and acquired is huge. The social sciences forming the core of the social studies are history, political science, geography, psychology, sociology, economics, and anthropology. All are similar in their focus on understanding and explaining human behavior and relationships, although each focuses on a different aspect. Each carefully uses scientific processes to collect facts on which to base concepts and generalizations.

History.   Past events are the focus of history. Historians describe events and try to piece together known facts into patterns that identify the causes of events (see Figure 1–2). Often, facts are missing and must be searched for. When data cannot be found, historians make inferences from what is available. Sometimes the data

FIGURE 1–2
The social studies help us make friends with famous people from the past.

are conflicting and historians must try to reconcile them or determine which is most likely to be accurate.

Political Science. The management, or governance, of both small social units such as neighborhoods and large social units such as nations is the focus of political science. Governance requires the use of power to organize the unit and to enforce decisions. Political scientists identify the organization of social units. They also examine the patterns in which power is distributed throughout the social unit and among different units.

Geography. Geographers focus on place. Place can refer to the location in which people live, the routes they travel along, the area in which the minerals they use are found, or the regions in which favorable and unfavorable climates exist. Geographers also try to explain the reasons that places are favorable or unfavorable for human settlement or travel.

Psychology. Human mental processes and behavior make up the focus of psychology. Learning, emotions, and the formation of attitudes are some of the areas studied by psychologists. The identification of patterns to predict and explain the behavior of individuals is a major aspect of psychology.

Sociology. The social groups we live in are the focus of sociology. Human beings generally belong to many social groups. We may be family members, students, voters, teachers, renters, and skiers all at the same time. Sociologists study the many social groups people form and the relationships among these groups. They look for patterns in the groups to which we belong and in the ways they are structured.

Economics. The patterns by which human beings satisfy their needs and wants with the limited resources they have available are the focus of economics. Each human group develops systems for satisfying needs and wants. Economists study these systems and try to predict and explain the effects of various means of production, consumption, and exchange of goods and services.

Anthropology. The focus of anthropology is culture and the manner in which people develop it, maintain it, live in it, and change it. Anthropologists search for patterns related to ways people shape their environment into the culture they inhabit. Only human beings have culture. All of the other social sciences study some aspect of human life, whether the study of place by geographers or of motivation by psychologists. Anthropology studies culture as a concept encompassing the focuses of the other social sciences.

An Information Basis

The patterns formed in the social studies are based on information, that is, on collected facts. This contrasts with conclusions based on opinion, feelings, superstition, or authority. The children in the old clothes activity described earlier used observable information they had collected by examining and trying on old clothes. They also used a reference work that reported the date of the zipper's invention—an observable piece of information because this invention was recorded in the patent office in 1893. The patterns they identified, the facts they learned, and the generalizations they developed were based on information.

In the absence of enough information, tentative generalizations can be formed, but the validity of these patterns may be questioned. The questioning will continue until enough information has been collected to give greater support to the generalization or to withdraw support from it.

An Information Processing Requirement

The social studies are characterized by a search for patterns based on information. Single items of information are gathered. These are then put together and summarized. Finally, they are transformed into patterns that are more usable than are the isolated pieces themselves. This activity is called information processing.

People learn to process information efficiently through practice. Unfortunately, in some schools children are often required to learn patterns (concepts and generalizations) through rote memorization rather than allowed to form the patterns through their own processing (Ryan, 1977). Forming patterns through processing information helps children develop the capability to understand and live competently in their social world.

A Decision-Making and Problem-Solving Purpose

What is the point of being able to recognize patterns in our lives? Is it to make decisions based on information? Yes. Is it to process information? Yes. Is it to use decision making and information processing to solve problems? Yes. All these abilities help us to solve the problems that confront us. Solving them requires refusing to avoid them and refusing to jump to a partial solution. It may require waiting to reach a conclusion that will help us choose the best solution. The social studies focus on decision making and problem solving. The problem may be economics related, it may have historical roots, or it may be related to several social science disciplines. In any case, the social studies try to help us make decisions and solve problems arising from social issues.

A Concern With the Development of Values

Decision making, problem solving, and all the other major characteristics of the social studies lead toward the development and analysis of one's own values. Our values define our responses to the social world we live in.

Children today have, and must confront, many more choices than did children of previous generations. The alternatives are so varied as to be overwhelming. The choice is difficult because of the numbers of alternatives but also because of the complexity of the world in which we live. Each choice affects many other aspects of our lives. The social studies help children learn how to keep control of their lives in this confusing world (Sunal, 1981).

Children need to be trained to analyze their values, to be consciously aware of them. They need to recognize alternative values. The teacher models some values, and helps students think about their own values. She does not automatically dispense the right answer. Instead she may ask a leading question so that students' value decisions become truly their own.

A decision is made through the way in which the problem is solved. It is also made through the choice to observe events, people, and things to obtain information and to process it. All the other characteristics of the social studies are, therefore, incorporated and used when a value decision is made.

Young children are not able to make abstract value decisions. Therefore, they need to be helped to use all the other characteristics of the social studies competently. This assistance will enable them to gain the expertise needed to eventually become persons who are conscious of the reasoning by which a particular decision is made.

SUMMARY

Early childhood social studies are hands-on and concrete. Several distinguishing characteristics begin with a naturally occurring search for patterns in our lives and lead to the processing of information to help us solve problems, make decisions, and develop and analyze our values.

REFERENCES

BARR, R., BARTH, J., & SHERMIS, S. (1977). *Defining the social studies* (Bulletin 51). Washington, DC: National Council for the Social Studies.

ENGLE, S. (1976). Exploring the meaning of the social studies. In P. Martorella (Ed.), *Social studies strategies: Theory into practice.* New York: Harper & Row.

KENWORTHY, L. (1980). *Social studies for the eighties in elementary and middle schools* (3rd ed.). New York: Wiley.

MICHAELIS, J. (1985). *Social studies for children: A guide to basic instruction.* Englewood Cliffs, NJ: Prentice-Hall.

NATIONAL ASSOCIATION FOR THE EDUCATION OF YOUNG CHILDREN. (1982). *Early childhood teacher education guidelines.* Washington, DC: NAEYC.

OLINER, P. (1976). *Teaching elementary social studies: A rational and humanistic approach.* New York: Harcourt Brace Jovanovich.

RYAN, F. L. (1977). Implementing the hidden curriculum of the social studies. In B. Joyce & F. Ryan (Eds.), *Social studies and the elementary teacher: Promises and practices* (pp. 152–156). (Bulletin 53). Washington, DC: National Council for the Social Studies.

SUNAL, C. S. (1981). The child and the concept of change. *Social Education, 45,* 438–441.

2

AN INTRODUCTION TO YOUNG CHILDREN AND THE CURRICULUM

S ocial studies programs for children develop a background of experiences related to the social world. This background:

1. Builds a foundation of facts that children can use to develop concepts
2. Enables children to understand the concepts represented by these facts
3. Helps children integrate the concepts they understand to develop the generalizations that make up the content of the social studies
4. Encourages an understanding of the social studies and their role in our everyday lives

GOALS OF THE SOCIAL STUDIES PROGRAM

One goal of a social studies program is to enable children to learn content, the patterns of the social studies. Content is the result of information processing. It exists in the forms of concepts and generalizations describing our social world. Concepts and generalizations are the patterns of the social world. Before concepts and generalizations are formed, a learner must have a background of experiences to draw from when processing information (Fraenkel, 1977). This background exists in the form of facts.

A second goal of a social studies program is to help children learn content through using intellectual process skills such as observation and inference. When children learn content by processing information-using skills such as inference, they do more than acquire facts, concepts, and generalizations. They learn how to learn. By processing information, children practice learning skills that are used not only in the social studies but also in all areas of the curriculum. These skills are referred to as processes.

Achieving Goal One: Learning Content

Facts.   Facts are content acquired through the five senses. They are learned whenever we make observations of both the social and physical world around us. Facts are gathered either through our own direct, sensory experiences or through the experiences of others.

Facts are important because they provide the information necessary to form the patterns (concepts and generalizations) that make up the major content of the social studies. Without a sufficient number of facts, children may not be able to form patterns at all; they may only memorize strings of words that are unrelated to experience. Without an adequate background of facts based on concrete experiences, children's understandings of concepts such as "river" are vague, if not totally absent. Facts form an important link between the learner and the surrounding world. Because facts are reports of sensory experiences, they provide reference points for the concepts and generalizations children form.

Social studies content can be viewed hierarchically:

- First, facts are acquired through interacting with the social and physical environment.
- Next, groups of facts are used to create concepts.
- Finally, concepts are combined into generalizations.

Because the social and physical environment surrounds us, the facts we obtain through experiences with it are the most numerous and least abstract of what we learn. Facts are gathered, analyzed, and integrated into the more abstract concepts. At the most abstract level, concepts are integrated to form generalizations.

Concepts.   Abstractions or ideas that people form to better understand their social and physical world are called concepts (Beyer & Penna, 1971). Concepts are formed by grouping facts into categories. When the categories are formed similarities between the facts are temporarily emphasized while differences are ignored. For example, "baby" is a concept. In forming the concept we focus on similarities found in most babies. These include short legs, crying, no teeth, a large round stomach, and no waist. By emphasizing similarities we ignore other characteristics such as color, temperament, and amount of hair.

In forming concepts we typically see a number of examples and nonexamples of the concept (Eggen, Kauchak, & Harder, 1979). Concepts are called abstractions because they represent this process of pulling out and combining similar aspects of our actual concrete experiences. Although based on facts, they go beyond facts. The concept is a mental image distilled from all the concrete examples we have known (Bruner, Goodnow, & Austin, 1956).

Concepts differ from facts in several ways. First, facts are acquired through seeing, hearing, tasting, feeling, or smelling. Concepts, though based on the observations through which the facts were acquired, go beyond this initial contact. Concept formation requires more than simple observation. Second, concepts summarize our observations into patterns. The essence of concept learning is the grouping of facts, which all differ somewhat individually, on the basis of similar characteristics. The concept summarizes information on similarities and indicates the pattern formed by the similarities; for example, "all buttons are round."

The concept may be inaccurate—some buttons are square, some are oval, and so forth. The individual has formed the concept on the basis of the facts available to him. A narrow range of facts can result in an inaccurate concept. Or the individual may have inaccurately abstracted similar features. Although the concept is inaccurate, it does represent an effort by the individual to abstract similarities. As more facts are acquired, or when the individual reviews the repertoire of facts, the concept may be changed if it is found to be inaccurate.

The summarizing capability of a concept is important. If we did not summarize we would find it difficult to use all the facts we learn. For example, people use many kinds of buildings, big and small, brick and wood, white and blue. To remember each of these with a name would leave little room for anything else. So we form concepts, grouping together similar buildings by a shared characteristic, and talk about "houses," "barns," "fire stations."

Concepts are interrelated, with two concepts often sharing some of the same facts. For example, a "house" might also be a "beauty salon" if its owner operates a business as a beautician in the basement. People are flexible in the concepts they form. We develop the ability to recognize that a fact may belong to several concepts. This flexibility allows us to account for the range of diversity in our social world (see Figure 2–1).

Similar summarizing occurs in all areas of the social studies. We think of political science in terms of broad categories such as power, leadership, loyalty, government, and compromise. This not only allows us to summarize our experiences but also provides us with a means of storing information for later use. Each of these terms is an abstraction. It can be described using key characteristics. It is used to summarize large amounts of information.

Generalizations.   Generalizations further summarize our experiences by relating concepts to each other. In this discussion, Lee uses both concepts and a generalization:

> There are special clothes and play clothes. There are different kinds
> of clothes for different times. Special clothes and play clothes are the
> same for big and little kids.

Lee has been talking about the concepts "special clothes" and "play clothes." Both concepts summarize his experiences with clothes. For Lee, jeans may be play clothes and a suit "special clothes." Lee makes a generalization that goes further

FIGURE 2–1
Children often learn together such concepts as measurement.

than the concepts he was working with. He relates the type of clothing to children's age and size: "big kids" and "little kids."

Generalizations are even more useful than concepts because they are capable of summarizing more information and of describing our social world even more accurately.

Sometimes people mistake generalizations for facts. For example, "Wealth means you have a lot of money" is a generalization, not a fact. It is a generalization for several reasons. First, we haven't formed the statement from observation alone.

Second, the information in the statement is a summarization, not a report of a single event. Generalizations summarize relevant characteristics of observations that have been made. Because we have not seen all possible cases, we generalized from what we did see to make a statement. For that reason it is a generalization from what we did observe. We believe the statement because we have never observed a contradictory case. If a contradictory case is observed, we can change the generalization.

In addition to organizing facts and concepts, generalizations allow us to predict events. Using the generalization about wealth, we can predict that a bank customer who has several accounts totaling a million dollars would be considered wealthy by others in the community. This has important implications because most of social studies education is concerned with helping students learn to predict and control events as citizens of their society.

Achieving Goal Two: Learning Processes

Facts, concepts, and generalizations are acquired by each person through learning processes including making observations and inferences.

Observation.　This is the starting point for all the social studies. Through observation, facts are gathered that can then be processed to form concepts and generalizations. Without the process of observation no starting point exists for forming patterns, nor is there a way of establishing the validity of the concepts or generalizations formed.

Observations come to us in two ways. First, they can be direct and immediate. For example, we observe someone wearing a bright red sari or we hear our neighbors arguing. Second, observations can be vicarious or indirect. We observe on a printed page (read) that George Washington was the first President of the United States. In this case we observe vicariously the direct observations of those who were alive in Washington's time. Such observations form an important part of our learning because they broaden the scope of our experiences to include the experiences of people in other times and places.

The process of observation can take many forms. Psychologists use sight to gather information about the children they are studying. The historian uses touch to identify textures in clay pots or cloth. The political scientist uses hearing to identify the issues being discussed during a debate between two politicians.

Observation is an important process to both social scientists and children. Observations provide the starting point for school activities by bringing children into contact with their world. They also provide the facts needed for subsequent information processing. In addition, children who have the opportunity to develop their observational abilities are practicing a skill that will be useful throughout their lives.

Providing children with opportunities to make many observations in their learning activities is important for two reasons. First, through the process of observation, children are able to gather facts that can be processed into concepts and generalizations. Second, observation-oriented activities provide the opportunity to practice and further develop observational skills.

As important as the process of observation is to social studies education, it is only the beginning point. The acquisition of facts by children will not make them knowledgeable in the social studies unless they are helped to process this information into usable form. Information that is usable is information resulting from observations that have been processed into concepts and generalizations. This processing occurs through making inferences.

Inferences.   In making information usable, people go beyond immediate observations to:

1. Construct patterns
2. Predict future observations
3. Explain the events observed

These extensions and interpretations of observations are called inferences. Through the process of inferring much of our understanding of the world is built. Because inferences help us understand and interpret the world, the ability of a person to make inferences and to decide on the validity of others' inferences is an essential thinking skill (Martin, 1972).

Inferences are statements that are based on observations but include more than the observations themselves. Inferences are extensions of observations and serve four functions:

1. To group together (classify)
2. To summarize (generalize)
3. To predict
4. To explain (Eggen, Kauchak, & Harder, 1979)

Each of the functions that inferences perform represents unique skills. These four forms of inference can be described as distinct processes, but the four are closely related.

Classifying.   The first function of inferences, classifying, involves grouping two items on the basis of some similarity. For example, young children make a classifying inference when they sort water play toys on the basis of color, shape, or use. The individual first encounters a set of uncategorized items. Then he places these items in groups on the basis of some similarity. The result of the process of inferring through classifying is usually a concept.

Classification activities vary in their difficulty, depending upon the number of items to be classified and the thoroughness of the classification system used. For example, 3 items are easier to classify than 10. Classifying a group of 10 items into two classes is simpler than classifying them into three or four.

For the most part, classifying is an arbitrary process. No one classification scheme is inherently better than another. For example, consider three national flags. These could be classified on the basis of color, or stripes, the year of their design, and so on. For any set of items, any number of groupings can be made, all of which are correct. The only criteria that should be used in judging the quality of a classification scheme are logic and consistency.

Sometimes it is necessary to make an inference using a particular type of classification scheme. In examining city governments, for example, we may need to classify them by the type of major administrator they have, such as mayor, city manager, and so on. The task may dictate the classification scheme used. In developing children's ability to make inferences using classification, however, we should not emphasize specific schemes. We should encourage children to develop their own classification schemes. This skill develops most completely when children invent their own schemes and evaluate their logical consistency.

Generalizing. The second function of making inferences is generalizing. Inferences are produced that are statements summarizing and extending a large number of separate observations. They accomplish two activities:

1. They summarize information to simplify it and make it easier to remember.
2. They extend the summary to include cases not yet observed.

A generalizing inference is used to condense a set of observations into usable form. It is also used to extend this summarization to a larger set of observations.

Generalizing inferences differ from classifying inferences in two ways:

1. They extend beyond the immediate objects at hand.
2. They are often not arbitrary.

As an illustration of these differences, consider a father trying to teach his young child the concept of "hat." The father has gathered a number of hats around them on the floor. He starts out by placing several hats together and saying, "These are hats." Then he puts one on his head and one on the child's head. He takes off the hats and puts another one on his head and a different one on the child's head. After trying on hats for a while, he asks, "Can you find any other hats?" Slowly, through the processes of trial and error, and feedback from the parent, the child starts to get the idea. The concept "hat" has to do with the function, not with the color, size, or shape of the object.

For the most part, the concept that the child learns is nonarbitrary. That is, most people will agree that a given object is a hat. In addition, the definition of the concept is commonly shared by most people in our culture. The nonarbitrariness of the concept is also reflected in the fact that the father was teaching a specific concept. He chose his positive examples and nonexamples accordingly. This concept, once learned, could be used in the future to describe other concepts. A major function of inferences made through generalizing, therefore, is to form concepts and generalizations that can be used afterward to describe and explain the world we live in.

The teacher plays a vital role in this process by selecting important social studies concepts and generalizations to teach. Then the teacher provides children with information to process in forming those patterns, the concepts and generalizations. Parents, too, help their children form generalizing inferences about their world by pointing out situations in which patterns occur, as in this example:

> A father gives his child money to hand to a cashier at the supermarket. The child receives change back and then helps his father push a cart loaded with grocery bags out the door. The father says, "I buy food with money. I go to the store and pick out the food I want. Each item costs a certain amount of money. The cashier tells me how much money all the food together costs. When I give him the money he gives us the food."

By calling attention to this aspect of the social environment, the parent has set the scene for further learning in which the child can determine whether the statement "I buy food with money" applies to other people besides the parent.

Noticing other people at the same store, in other stores, and in restaurants buying food with money, the child summarizes the information by noting that other people also buy food with money. Finally, he can conclude, "All people buy food with money." From a number of separate observations, he generalizes to all possible cases. In making this inference, the child processes information to form generalizations that not only summarize past observations but extend this summary to all people. Because the boy generalized from a relatively few observations to all members of the class of people, we call this a generalizing inference. The term is used to refer to the process of extending observations of events or characteristics to include those that have not yet been observed. The generalizing process transforms facts into concepts and generalizations.

The generalizing process is not always accurate. The boy has not observed people trading services for food, or trading one type of food for another. He may see a child trading the celery from a lunchbox for someone else's apple. Or, he may help make a cake to give to new neighbors. These and other observations he makes will challenge his original inference. He will realize he has generalized from a limited number of observations. He is likely to make a different inference as he accumulates observations challenging his original inference.

Predicting. The third function of making inferences is predicting. Predictive inferences are based upon generalizing inferences. The generalization is used to predict further occurrences of an event, action, or attitude. People make predictive inferences based on other inferences so often that the difference between the two types of inferences often becomes obscured. For example, people hunch up their shoulders as they open outside doors on a cold winter day. This involves performing an action based on a predictive inference. The inference predicts that people will feel cold when they open the door because a blast of cold air will come in. This is based on the generalizing inferences, "opening an outside door in winter will let in cold air" and "cold air makes me shiver and feel cold."

Countless human activities are predicted based on just such relationships between generalizing and predictive inferences.

An important difference between generalizing and predictive inferences should be noted. Generalizing inferences refer to, or summarize, classes of observations. Predictive inferences suggest a single observation will occur under certain conditions.

Explaining. The fourth function of making inferences is explanation. An explanatory inference is used to explain observations. As an example of this process, consider the child who is daily observed playing at the water play table. Through our observations of his daily play habits we notice that he is often splashing water. We could infer that the child likes to play at the water play table because he enjoys the chance to splash water. This inference explains why he frequently chooses to play at the water play table.

Children engaged in process-oriented activities have many opportunities to make explanatory inferences. As they work with materials they infer explanations that link cause and effect. Everyday experiences generate many explanatory inferences such as "It's hard to button my raincoat because it is made out of stuff that is all slippery. . . ." An explanatory inference is used to help understand why a particular observation occurred.

Like observing, inferring is a natural process, but that does not mean that people form inferences efficiently or accurately. People commonly tend to make inferences based on inadequate data. For example, a person is inferring incorrectly when he says, "Red-haired people are short-tempered. I knew a red-haired person and he was short-tempered." An observation has been made, the short temper of the person. Another observation was also made, the short-tempered person had red hair. A generalization was formed based on these two observations.

Children often make inferential leaps without sufficient information. The ability to base inferences on sufficient information and to distinguish a valid from an invalid inference is a powerful thinking skill that social studies programs should work to develop. One way of helping children learn to do this is to give them opportunities to make their own inferences and to judge the validity of the inferences others have made.

SUMMARY

Making inferences is a process involving finding patterns in the observations we make. The most basic type of inference, the classifying inference, groups objects together on the basis of some similarity. Generalizing inferences, which form concepts and generalizations, summarize information and extend this summary to instances not yet encountered. Predictive and explanatory inferences are based on generalizing inferences and are used to predict or explain events. The curriculum for young children includes both content and processes. Later chapters in this book describe ways that specific aspects of a social studies curriculum—

for example, those working with geography—can be built so that both content and processes for learning content are developed.

REFERENCES

BEYER, B., & PENNA, A. (Eds.). (1971). *Concepts in the social studies* (Bulletin 45). Washington, DC: National Council for the Social Studies.

BRUNER, J., GOODNOW, J., & AUSTIN, G. (1956). *A study of thinking.* New York: Wiley.

EGGEN, P., KAUCHAK, D., & HARDER, R. (1979). *Strategies for teachers.* Englewood Cliffs, NJ: Prentice-Hall.

FRAENKEL, J. R. (1977). The importance of learning activities. In B. Joyce & F. Ryan (Eds.), *Social studies and the elementary teacher: Promises and practices* (pp. 37–43). (Bulletin 53). Washington, DC: National Council for the Social Studies.

MARTIN, M. (1972). *Concepts of science education.* Glenview, IL: Scott, Foresman.

3

AN INTRODUCTION TO INSTRUCTING YOUNG CHILDREN

The instruction of young children must be appropriate to their level of development. It must be based on an understanding of how children develop the ability to form concepts and generalizations through observation and inference. These abilities develop with experience over long periods of time. Children differ in how they think. The differences arising from maturation are considered to be *developmental* because they develop during the process of maturation. Jean Piaget has provided a theoretical basis for understanding the way this development occurs. The following section will present those of his ideas most critical in considering the cognitive aspects of implementing a social studies program with children. It discusses his theory, the cognitive developmental theory. Other theories are discussed elsewhere in the book. (See especially Bandura's social modeling theory on children's modeling of others' behavior, which appears later in this chapter, and Kohlberg's theory of moral development in chapter 10.)

COGNITIVE-DEVELOPMENTAL THEORY

All of us are social scientists to some extent. We attempt to make sense out of the social world by processing information into patterns. In forming patterns, people are attempting to make the world understandable. They are also changing old structures that aren't working well and forming new patterns when the old ones don't fit a situation.

When the patterns people have enable them to describe and explain what is going on in their world, they are in a condition Piaget calls *equilibrium*. It exists when people's patterns or mental structures are adequate to understand the world around them. When these patterns are inadequate, people search for ways to change them. Quizzical looks, frowns, and exploratory behavior are all evidences of this inadequacy, or *disequilibrium.*

Equilibrium and disequilibrium both result from two processes that are continually occurring. Piaget calls these processes *adaptation* and *organization.* Adaptation is the individual's constant effort to understand the surrounding world. The individual is always processing information and usually finds that the patterns already formed are adequate. For example, if you look up from this page to the room around you and see familiar sights and objects, the patterns that you have will be adequate to describe or explain what you see. If you should see something out of place or strange, however, for example, if the walls suddenly changed color, then your mind would attempt to form an explanation to account for this ill-fitting piece of information. Adaptation is Piaget's term for these attempts. Adaptation occurs when the individual interacts with the environment and either understands that environment (achieves a state of equilibrium) or is in disequilibrium (Cowan, 1978).

Piaget and Inhelder (1969) use the term *organization* to refer to the products of adaptation. Learning something new changes the organization of the mind. This change may consist of the addition of a new fact, concept, or generalization. Or it could consist of the altering of an old pattern. For example, if a child who has previously thought of money as coins finds out that paper dollar bills are also money and will buy her favorite kind of gum, her concept of money changes. As a result of this change in concept, a change in mental organization occurs, making room for the addition of the category of paper money. Organization and adaptation occur because of experiences the individual has with the environment. An important idea of Piaget's (1958) that has tremendous implications for teaching is that people form structures and change them through an active exchange with the environment. The environment includes the people around them. The focus of the social studies program should be to place children in situations in which they can experience and interact with the world they are learning about.

Adaptation: Assimilating and Accommodating

The concept of adaptation is at the core of intellectual, or cognitive, growth. If the individual's organizational structure (her ideas about the world) does not change, intellectual growth cannot occur. Change is central to learning and growth.

How does change, that is, adaptation, occur? Piaget (1958) describes adaptation as occurring through two processes that work together, *assimilation* and *accommodation.* Assimilation refers to the process of interpreting or viewing the world according to structures (patterns) we already have (see Figure 3–1). For example, when a young child sees something flying in the air and says "Bird," she is assimilating the observations she has made about the thing in the air into her cognitive structure. She has observed that it appears to be small, is overhead in the sky, and is moving through the air above her. Everything is fine for the

FIGURE 3–1
"Have I tasted this before?" is assimilation in action.

child until the object circles around and returns flying lower. Now, it obviously doesn't look like a bird, nor sound like one. Accommodation to these new observations must occur as she thinks about the airplane.

Accommodation refers to the processes of changing existing mental structures or patterns in response to the realities we observe. Accommodation occurs when people learn something new. It occurs when people change their minds because of new information. It also occurs when people change their attitudes about a person or groups of people because of experiences they have had. When accommodation takes place, the content of people's minds changes to become more descriptive of the real world they live in. This content can include concepts, generalizations, attitudes, and views.

The young child had to accommodate when she encountered the airplane flying overhead. According to her past experiences, birds fly, but don't make roaring sounds. Nor do birds have stiff, unmoving wings. In attempting to reconcile or accommodate her mental structures with this new experience, she had two options. First, she could conclude that birds do indeed roar and have wings that don't move. Second, she could conclude that not all flying things are birds.

Implications for Instruction

This view of learning has a number of implications for preschool–primary grades social studies. First, people are natural inquirers, continually trying to make sense out of the world around them by processing information into structures, or patterns. Piaget calls these patterns the organizational structure of the individual. In organizing structures, the individual maintains a close contact with the environment. For very young children, contact is easy as they walk, crawl, smell, touch, and listen their way through the world. Later, when children are frequently required to sit quietly and listen passively, adaptation cannot occur as efficiently. Adaptation implies an active interchange. Without active interchange new information cannot be assimilated into previously formed structures. Accommodation, the restructuring of existing patterns into newer, more realistic, patterns is also made difficult (Singer & Revenson, 1978).

Teachers must plan activities that encourage children to actively interact with the world, including the people around them. Active interaction gives children the chance to practice and strengthen the process skills and concepts and generalizations they already have. It also provides them with new information that is used to further develop process skills and form new abstractions.

In the processes of adapting to the environment and of organizing and reorganizing cognitive structures, children display reasoning patterns that vary in relation to their level of maturation. Children adapt to the environment in different ways at different ages. Piaget has identified unique characteristics of the adaptation process at different ages. He has identified four stages of intellectual development through which children mature.

DEVELOPMENTAL STAGES AND INSTRUCTION

The four stages Piaget noted suggest that, at different levels in their maturation, children find different types of problems meaningful and find different kinds of solutions to these problems. A problem is meaningful if the person understands what the problem is asking her to do. For example, a child of 3 will not find the following type of problem meaningful, but an 8-year-old probably will.

> *Katy, Alisa, and Clare are friends. Clare is taller than Katy. Katy is taller than Alisa. Is Alisa taller than Clare?*

The reason these stages are important to the teacher is that they suggest things that children at different stages will find either interesting and meaningful or uninteresting and confusing. By understanding these stages, teachers will be better able to make judgments about what and how to teach.

Developmental psychologists have defined these stages through making a number of observations of children. These observations have then been processed into patterns—the concepts of the four stages. The stages represent general descriptions of the ways children act at different age levels. Large individual differences exist within each stage. The stages are attempts to describe general patterns of development.

Movement from one stage to another is a slow change over an extended period of time. The individual revises existing structures and adds new ones. Eventually the whole set of patterns that one has identified and used to understand the world becomes very different. When the character of the mind's structures becomes fundamentally different, the person has entered a new stage of intellectual maturity.

The Sensorimotor Stage (birth to about 2 years)

During the sensorimotor stage the individual's attempts at adaptation are largely concerned with coordinating the senses and muscles. The child uses seeing, hearing, touching, and moving to gather information and form structures about the environment (Ginsburg & Opper, 1979).

Children at this stage as well as all other stages possess a natural tendency to adapt to the environment. They do this by gathering information about the environment and by processing this information into organizational structures. At birth, children are immobile and must be content with processing information that happens to come to them. Consequently much of their effort during this period is aimed at developing better ways to process information.

The baby's attention seems to wander with little success at focusing on specific aspects of the environment whereas the 2-year-old is quite capable of such focus. Countless hours of watching and listening are important in the development of this capacity.

In addition to developing a longer, more selective attention span, the infant attains an understanding that an object still exists even though it is out of sight. The term for this is *object permanence*. At about 10 months, most children will actively seek an object placed under a blanket, realizing that out of sight doesn't mean it's gone for good.

Muscular development advances as does coordination of the eyes and ears. During this period children's efforts at adaptation are primarily involved with the refinement of perceptual mechanisms and muscular coordination. Children develop structures concerned with these sensory and motor activities. Hence the name for this stage. Once developed, these structures allow the child to assimilate new information from the environment. As the child applies these structures to the environment, some of them are found to be inadequate. Through trial and error the child seeks to develop new ones, and cognitive growth occurs.

The Preoperational Stage (approximately age 2 to about age 7)

This second period is called preoperational because it precedes the period of concrete operations. The preoperational child takes monumental strides in the development of symbolic behavior. The child begins to develop the idea that symbols stand for objects and classes of objects. For example, 2-year-olds use language symbolically when they say "Milk!" to obtain a white, drinkable substance from the refrigerator. They also use symbolic thought in make-believe play, in pretending to be people or creatures other than themselves (Seifert & Hoffnung, 1987).

Preoperational children imitate other people. They are able to imitate actions after an event when the model is no longer there. A teacher modeling courteous behavior can expect that her students may copy her behavior and use it on another occasion in similar circumstances.

During this period, children are also trying to distinguish what is real from what is not real. They have a tendency to focus on one aspect of the environment and to accept surface appearance as reality. At this stage they have a hard time understanding that water, steam, and ice are different forms of the same substance. An explanation for this type of behavior is *centration*, that is, focusing on one aspect of the environment to the exclusion of others. Centration occurs when, for example, a child thinks that the volume of a glass of milk depends entirely on how tall the glass is and forgets to notice how wide it is. It is almost as if the newly developed ability to pay close attention to something has become too powerful. The child seems to focus completely on one part of a problem while giving no attention to others.

Egocentrism is often a characteristic of young children. It is the inability of a person to distinguish between her own point of view and that of another person. It stems from perceptual dominance or centration. Young children frequently, but not always, think egocentrically. Donaldson (1978) has shown that children do not necessarily think egocentrically in a familiar situation or in one in which they think it is highly interesting to pretend they are someone else and therefore take the other person's perspective. However, egocentrism tends to dominate young children in many situations. Flavell (1977) found preschoolers do recognize the existence of different perspectives and sometimes make allowances for that fact. They judge other people's comprehension separately from their own comprehension on the basis of what people say. However, they often fail to realize just how badly people can misunderstand each other even in simple, ordinary communication.

Preoperational children often express a belief, called *animism*, that non-living objects are alive and have human characteristics. A child may trip over a piece of sidewalk jutting up from the ground and berate the sidewalk for "being mean and waiting for me to walk down the block so you could trip me." They also may express artificialism. This is a belief that all objects, whether living or not, are made in the same way, usually by human beings. A child may believe that cats and dogs are made from clay because she has made many other familiar objects from this substance. To a certain extent animism and artificialism are special forms of egocentrism. In animism, children assume that various objects and events have the same qualities that they themselves have, human and living ones. In artificialism, they assume that their immature, incomplete knowledge of the world is actually complete, and so they overgeneralize from it. As with egocentrism children tend to express animism and artificialism in relatively unfamiliar situations (Laurendeau & Pinard, 1972; Seifert & Hoffnung, 1987).

The process of *classification* involves putting objects in groups or categories according to some standard or criteria. Young children are able to classify objects differing in one dimension or feature, especially if that dimension presents fairly obvious contrasts, such as color (Sigel & Cocking, 1977). Sometimes they can manage more complex classification tasks, but not as reliably. An example of this mixed success occurs with *class inclusion*, the ability to compare a subset of objects with some larger, more inclusive set of objects to which it belongs. Red flowers and white flowers, for example, both belong to the larger, more inclusive (or general) class of flowers. Piaget found that young children can easily compare subsets with each other, but cannot easily compare one subset with the group as a whole (Piaget & Inhelder, 1969). If a preschooler is asked, "Are there more red flowers or more white flowers?" she typically can answer correctly. If asked, "Are there more red flowers or more flowers?" she tends to answer as if she is comparing the red and white groups, in spite of being asked to compare the red group with the whole group. She will say, for example, that a collection of four red flowers and two whites has more red flowers than flowers (incorrect); but she will also say that the collection has more red flowers than white flowers (correct). Piaget suggests the child cannot decenter her thinking; she cannot broaden her focus to take account of more than one dimension at the same time. In the class inclusion flowers task, the child must pay attention to the dimensions of color and of "flowerness." McGarrigle, Grieve, and Hughes (1978) have found that young children can accomplish class inclusion when tasks are carefully described. Language confuses the child if a question is vague or surprising. Preschoolers can be relatively skillful when someone else arranges the conditions properly but they are less able to ask clarifying questions or to find a way to understand a confusing situation (Seifert & Hoffnung, 1987).

Preoperational children often seem to lack *reversibility*, the ability to mentally undo a problem and go back to its beginning. We use reversibility when we walk outside a classroom building into rainy weather and realize we must have left our umbrella somewhere in the building. Before setting off to look for the umbrella, we mentally retrace our steps, trying to remember when we last had the umbrella and where we have been in the building. Reversibility contributes to *conservation*, the ability to perceive that certain properties of an object remain the same or constant in spite of changes in the object's appearance. Conservation is achieved during the concrete operational period.

Children progressing through the preoperational stage have made great strides in symbolic behavior. The notion of an abstraction referring to classes of behavior (concept learning) is now understood. Vocabulary has become impressive. Both developments have implications for instruction:

1. They allow for the inclusion of concepts and generalizations in the curriculum.
2. They make it possible to use verbal means to supplement active experience.

Concrete Operations (approximately age 7 to about age 12)

Students in this stage can perform logical thinking operations *if* these operations are performed on real (concrete) objects (Ginsburg & Opper, 1979). A child who has reached this level of development, when asked if there are more boys or students in the class, will be able to think the problem through. She will refer to concrete objects in the form of students in the class and conclude that there are more students.

Concrete logical operations are particular kinds of mental activities focused on real, tangible objects and events. Concrete operations have three interrelated qualities: decentration, sensitivity to transformations, and reversibility (Piaget, 1965). *Decentration* means attending to more than one feature of a problem. *Sensitivity to transformations* involves noticing and remembering significant changes in objects. *Reversibility* of thought refers to solving problems by mentally going back to their beginning. The thinking of concrete operational children has all three qualities. Their thinking also demonstrates a restriction of animism and artificialism and a growth in the ability to classify and to understand class inclusion (Seifert & Hoffnung, 1987).

The concrete operational child would probably have trouble if asked to solve the following problem.

> *All A is B.*
> *Some B is C.*
> *Is all A, C?*

On the other hand, the child would probably be able to figure out this problem:

> *All coins are round.*
> *Some coins are made of silver.*
> *Are all coins made of silver?*

Growth during the period of concrete operations occurs in a number of areas. The most important may be classification. Children become able to sort items consistently and to develop a classification system that sorts every item. They also are able to use multiple classification schemes, sorting first by one characteristic and then resorting by another (Kofsky, 1966). At about the same time, the child develops the ability to classify items hierarchically; for example, cities, counties, states, and nation.

Another major advance during this period is the development of the ability to conserve. We use conservation to understand that certain properties like weight and volume are not changed by operations like pouring and flattening. The nonconserver focuses only on obvious aspects of a situation. In pouring water from a tall, thin glass to a short, wide one the nonconserver focuses on the height of the tall glass and may say that the short glass has less water than the tall one did. The width of the shorter one is not considered. The conserver realizes that width compensates for height so that both can hold the same amount of water.

Concrete operational children also develop improved sequencing ability, or *seriation;* a better sense of time; and spatial relations that allow them to navigate in complex and unfamiliar spaces, such as a neighborhood shopping mall.

The strengths and limitations of the concrete operational child have direct implications for instruction. Children at this stage can solve problems if tasks are presented in concrete terms. They encounter difficulties in performing the same tasks with abstract verbal problems. The need for concrete activities for students in preschool through 6th grade is obvious.

Formal Thought (age 12 to adulthood)

This stage of thinking has been called the period of abstract thinking (Good, 1977). It involves the ability to think without the need to refer to concrete objects directly. Probably the most important advances that mark this stage are the abilities to do theoretical reasoning and to control variables.

Theoretical reasoning means that the formal operational person can approach a problem in an abstract manner. All possible solutions will be mentally considered before a choice is made. Related to the ability of formal operational people to consider a number of possible explanations is their ability to control variables. Other differences between the formal and concrete operational person are not as central to social studies instruction as these two are. These differences, the ability to reason theoretically and to control variables, permit the person to participate in inquiry activities involving hypothesis formulation and testing.

LEARNING THEORIES

Behavioral learning theorists working with classical conditioning and operant conditioning have defined learning as observable changes in behavior resulting from experiences that establish and reinforce stimulus-response associations. Social learning theories have gone beyond the conditioning theories to consider the effects of role models and children's imitation of them (Bandura, 1977).

Classical conditioning often occurs in situations in which young children are taught. Teachers who smile a lot and speak in soft, pleasant voices cause children to identify the school as a pleasant, nonthreatening environment. Teachers use operant conditioning when they reward appropriate behaviors with enthusiastic verbal praise. Young children enjoy the praise and repeat the behavior. Learning theory is frequently applied in situations in which young children are cared for and learn.

Social learning theory emphasizes the role of modeling, of children's observing and imitating, in learning. Bandura (1977) has described the influence of role models on children and their interest in the consequences of actions performed by models. Children observe models important to them and do what they do. Teachers and children viewed as leaders are important models.

While learning theories have much to offer, cognition is important in the social studies. A developmental approach to teaching the social studies is appropriate because there is so much evidence that children develop, that their thinking changes over time.

A DEVELOPMENTAL APPROACH TO SOCIAL STUDIES INSTRUCTION

Children go through stages as they develop increasingly more sophisticated means of processing information. Piaget named these stages: sensorimotor, preoperational, concrete operational, and formal operational thought. How do these relate to teaching the social studies?

No one way to teach is best. The best teaching approach is one that matches a particular strategy with the goals of instruction and the characteristics of the learners. An effective teacher is someone who understands the goals she is trying to accomplish. Effective teaching also means the teacher is able to select and implement a teaching strategy that is appropriate to:

1. The curricular goals
2. The information-processing capabilities of the students (level of cognitive development)

Fitting the teaching to the goals of instruction and the characteristics of the learners results in a models approach to teaching. This approach was formulated by Joyce and Weil (1972). It has been applied to information processing strategies by Eggen, Kauchak, and Harder (1979). The models approach asserts that there is more than one best way to teach. It also encourages teachers to consider a number of factors before selecting teaching strategies.

Three teaching strategies are appropriate for early childhood and elementary students: the social exploration model, the experiential model, and the concept attainment model.

The Social Exploration Model

The first teaching strategy, the social exploration model, is appropriate for infants and toddlers during the sensorimotor period. Older children in very new situations may also benefit from the model. The model's emphasis is on introducing children to new people and settings and on extending the caregiver–child relationship with new activities. Children's self-confidence is built as their social experience is extended. A detailed description of the model is given in chapter 4.

The Experiential Model

The second teaching strategy, the experiential model, is most appropriate for children in preschool and primary-grades settings. It can be used with older children when they are beginning work in a new, unfamiliar area in which they have little experience. Although it is designed to teach all of the goals of the social studies, its heaviest emphasis is on the development of process skills.

Most children in preschool and primary grades are in the preoperational stage of cognitive development. The experiential model is designed to provide young children with direct experiences in their social environment, hence the name *experiential.* The model is described in detail in chapter 5.

The Concept Attainment Model

The concept attainment model is designed for use with more experienced learners. Its primary focus is the development and formation of concepts and generalizations. It deals with the other goals of social studies instruction as well. This model is designed for a learner at the concrete operational stage of development. It can also be used effectively with preoperational children in an area in which they have much experience. This model is described in detail in chapter 6.

General Guidelines

Use of the experiential model should not be restricted to very young children. Use of the concept attainment model should not be restricted to older students. The models are not rigid prescriptions for teaching at different age levels.

A number of factors should determine the choice of a model in a particular situation. These factors include

- The content to be taught
- The developmental characteristics of the children
- The goals of the social studies activity

However, when working with children, the basic assumption should be that the social exploration model is most appropriate for sensorimotor children, the experiential model is most appropriate for preoperational children, and the concept attainment model for concrete operational children. These guidelines should be observed unless other considerations justify using another model.

A teacher may at times intentionally choose a teaching strategy that is beyond the developmental capabilities of children in order to help them develop more effective processing strategies. Growth occurs as the individual encounters problems that current cognitive structures are unable to solve. When a mismatch occurs, the individual must accommodate these structures. The result is cognitive growth. Teachers can encourage this growth by placing children in situations that are developmentally demanding. Such situations encourage children to develop new structures for understanding the environment.

Most children's groups are heterogeneous. In the typical classroom a teacher finds one group of children at one stage of development, another group in a transition stage, and a third group at a higher stage. The effective teacher uses these differences to encourage cognitive growth. She does this by selecting activities that more developmentally advanced students can handle. The teacher thus provides opportunities for other children to see in action the operations of the advanced children and to learn from them. Cognitive growth occurs when less logical and efficient strategies for processing information are compared to more efficient strategies. If children are placed in heterogeneous groups, with some members functioning at a higher cognitive level than others, some children will act as catalysts for the cognitive growth of others.

Cognitive growth, the transition from one level of thought to another, is a gradual process. It takes place slowly as the individual tries new ways of dealing with the environment. It occurs through trial and error using feedback from the environment. The change from one level of thinking to the next is a gradual process in which the individual tries out new processing patterns to see how they work. Teachers who try to facilitate this growth should recognize it as a gradual process requiring a number of opportunities for trial and error.

The model of teaching most appropriate for children depends upon a number of factors. The most important of these are the content to be taught, children's developmental levels, and the goals of the social studies activity. The goals of the activity may include the encouragement of cognitive growth in the students.

SUMMARY

The social studies involve facts, concepts, and generalizations. These should be taught as developmentally appropriate. Teachers should use instructional models that match teaching strategies to children's developmental level.

REFERENCES

BANDURA, A. (1977). *Social learning theory*. Englewood Cliffs, NJ: Prentice-Hall.

COWAN, P. A. (1978). *Piaget with feeling*. New York: Holt, Rinehart & Winston.

DONALDSON, M. (1978). *Children's minds*. New York: Norton.

EGGEN, P., KAUCHAK, D., & HARDER, R. (1979). *Strategies for teachers*. Englewood Cliffs, NJ: Prentice-Hall.

FLAVELL, J. (1977). *Cognitive development*. Englewood Cliffs, NJ: Prentice-Hall.

GINSBURG, H., & OPPER, S. (1979). *Piaget's theory of intellectual development*. 2nd ed. Englewood Cliffs, NJ: Prentice-Hall.

GOOD, R. (1977). *How children learn science*. New York: Macmillan.

JOYCE, B., & WEIL, M. (1972). *Models of teaching*. Englewood Cliffs, NJ: Prentice-Hall.

KOFSKY, E. (1966). A scalogram study of classificatory development. *Child Development,* 37, 191–204.

LAURENDEAU, M., & PINARD, A. (1972). *Causal thinking in the child.* New York: International Universities Press.

MCGARRIGLE, J., GRIEVE, R., & HUGHES, M. (1978). Interpreting inclusion. *Journal of Experimental Child Psychology, 26,* 528–550.

PIAGET, J. (1958). *The growth of logical thinking from childhood to adolescence.* New York: Basic Books.

PIAGET, J. (1965). *The child's conception of the world.* Totowa, NJ: Littlefield, Adams.

PIAGET, J., & INHELDER, B. (1969). *The psychology of the child.* New York: Basic Books.

SEIFERT, K. L., & HOFFNUNG, R. J. (1987). *Child and adolescent development.* Boston: Houghton Mifflin.

SIGEL, L., & COCKING, R. (1977). *Cognitive development from childhood to adolescence: A constructivist perspective.* New York: Holt, Rinehart & Winston.

SINGER, D. G., & REVENSON, T. A. (1978). *How a child thinks: A Piaget primer.* New York: New American Library.

4

THE SOCIAL
EXPLORATION MODEL

The social exploration model is appropriate for children at the sensorimotor level of development, birth through approximately age 2. The model encourages children to explore social relationships and facilitates their introduction to the social world. The aim of the model is the development of satisfying social relationships through personal experiences. Personal development is enhanced as social relationships are built. The adult serves as a guide to the social world and ensures a secure, stable, encouraging environment. The content of the social studies is introduced through children's contact with a wide range of people in many different settings. This teaching/social interaction model is appropriate for more mature children who have had limited social experience or who find themselves in a very new social situation.

SOCIAL-COGNITIVE DEVELOPMENTAL THEORY

Cognitive developmental theory views social schemas as the bases of an individual's functioning in the social world. Social schemas are internal representations of social experiences. Schemas assist children in organizing and understanding events occurring in their environment. They can be simple or complex. An example of a simple schema is a visual image outline of a friend's face. A more complex, or abstract, schema is the generalization that this friend "is the kind of person who is shy unless someone is picking on others; then he will stand up and fight for them." As children experience the social world their social schemas increase in number and become more sophisticated. Children's social schemas are always limited in some ways and share similarities. These limitations and similarities are a result of underlying thought structures shaping the schemas developed. The thought structures are children's basic ways of processing and organizing information (Perry & Bussey, 1984).

By the end of the sensorimotor stage, about 2 years of age, children have many capabilities:

- They use symbols to represent familiar social objects and simple action sequences.
- They possess a schema of themselves as distinct individuals, enabling them to understand that this is "me" and everyone else is "not me."
- They have formed images of familiar others, such as their mother.
- They know that people continue to exist when out of sight (person permanence).
- They know that objects continue to exist when out of sight (object permanence).
- They possess a basic understanding of instrumentality or means–end relationships. They know that people can do things that cause results in the social and physical environment.

By the end of this stage, children can symbolically represent and mentally store sequences of actions. Their schemas, however, are limited to specific sensorimotor events. They may have a schema that identifies an object as a rattle no matter whether it is upside down, lying on its side, or right side up. Schemas do not yet take the form of general rules such as "people are divided into groups like boys and girls, or into those who wear glasses and those who don't."

Social Relationships in Very Young Children

Children are social creatures. From birth, children are able to cause others to interact with them. For example, the crying response stimulates most adults to react quickly and feed or comfort children. Even though newborn children can stimulate social interaction, their role is limited. A major limitation is that they do not adjust their social behavior according to the identity of the person with whom they are interacting. Most 1- and 2-month-old babies are just as easily soothed by a stranger as by their mother. By 6 months of age, however, they become more discriminating in their social responsiveness. They are able to identify people by voice, facial features, footsteps, and so on. They are also developing different styles of interacting with various people. Individual people come to hold different meanings for them (Perry & Bussey, 1984).

Attachment.   As a result of their social interactions, virtually all infants in the middle of their first year form a special bond with their mother, father, and perhaps one or two other special people. This bond is called attachment. Attachment is defined as the continuing disposition to seek to be near a specific other (Perry & Bussey, 1984). Three criteria are involved:

1. The infant must display responses that bring it closer to other people.
2. The infant must direct its proximity seeking with greater frequency or intensity toward one or more specific others.
3. The infant's preference for the proximity of the specific other(s) should be stable over time (Hay, 1980).

Attachment is related to the infant's underlying cognitive structures (Kagan, 1971; Kohlberg, 1969). Infants cannot form specific attachments to people until they are capable of perceptually discriminating one person from another.

Effects of Temperament.   Children are born with temperamental attributes affecting the quality of their relationships with others. Attributes that can have negative effects in social relationships are often biological in origin. These include irregularity, especially in regard to sleeping, feeding, and elimination cycles; withdrawal and distress reactions to new stimuli such as new foods or strange people; slow adaptability to change; and a general tendency for displaying negative moods. These characteristics influence the way parents and others react to the child. Some adults are able to be patient, tolerant of slowness to adapt, and consistent in their reactions to the child. These adult characteristics tend to help "temperamentally difficult" children develop patterns of behavior that result in satisfying social interactions (Chess, Thomas, & Birch, 1965).

Learned Negative Behaviors.   Some negative behaviors of children are not biological but learned. Temper tantrums, for example, can result from a chain of events in which children first demonstrate a behavior, parents react strongly to it, and children then develop a behavioral problem. For example, a child may be ill and parents are attentive; the child gets well and parents are less attentive; the child has an intense temper tantrum that upsets the parents and they resume being more attentive; finally, the child develops intense, coercive, aggressive habits. As Perry and Bussey (1984) have pointed out, children's behaviors and attributes, whether biological or learned, provoke reactions from adults and then shape their destinies still further. Children and the social environment influence each other.

Changes in Social Behavior With Age

The social behavior of children changes with age because their underlying thought structures change with age. Very young children tend to base judgments only on superficial variables they perceive as important (centration). They are likely to react to others more on the basis of their appearance, possessions, and observable effects on the environment than on the basis of their motives and other hidden factors. Children develop because moderately new experiences arouse curiosity motivating them to create new rules to account for events in their physical or social world.

During infancy young children have opportunities for learning important lessons about themselves and other people. These lessons influence the direction that children's development will take in later years. Through interaction with a sensitive and responsive caregiver, for example, infants are thought to develop a conception of themselves as effective, competent, and valued people, as well as a conception of others as reliable and trustworthy. During infancy children acquire habits of action, thought, and feeling that influence the ease with which they form satisfactory social relationships in later years.

Children are constantly trying to understand experiences that initially seem puzzling or a bit unusual to them. They are trying to assimilate these experiences to their existing schemas, that is, their mental representations of previous experiences. Smiling, crying, and exploring are all thought to begin with infants' attempts to fit incongruent events to existing schemas. Which of these three responses will result depends on how successfully the infant accomplishes his information-processing task.

Smiling indicates the infant has successfully assimilated a stimulus (Kagan, 1971). He has finally recognized as familiar something that at first seemed an odd blend of the familiar and the unfamiliar. For example, when infants are presented with a face they have seen several times before, they tend to spend several seconds scrutinizing the face and then they suddenly break into a smile, as if finally having found a familiar mental pigeonhole into which to place the face. A smile may mean a mental "Aha! I know what that is!" (Perry & Bussey, 1984).

Crying more likely represents a failure to assimilate. Kagan proposes that distress and crying occur when the infant experiences perceptual incongruity, but cannot find a suitable mental response to make. Distress is likely to occur if the stimulus is very intense. Partly this occurs because the infant may not know what kind of response is appropriate. If a total stranger suddenly looms toward the infant, for example, the infant may feel compelled to respond, but not knowing the person and his habits, may not be able to generate a response that will allow the infant confidently to control and pace the stranger's actions. An aroused infant becomes distressed if unable to find a response that makes incoming stimulation more predictable and controllable.

Exploratory responses allow the infant to cautiously but intently examine novel objects or people (see Figure 4–1). These responses may also be sparked by perceptual incongruity. The infant is fascinated by combinations of the familiar and unfamiliar and is trying to assimilate the new experience to see if it matches a mental representation of a similar experience. The infant will continue exploring so long as these conditions exist:

- The novel stimuli are not too arousing or threatening.
- The infant is not far from an attachment figure who can provide reassurance if needed.

FIGURE 4–1
Baby meets new people.

Exploration frequently leads to accommodation, or the formation of new schemas. For example, after extensive experience exploring a friendly stranger, the infant may form a mental image of the stranger's face, a small and significant act of creation. The next time the infant sees the stranger and recognizes him, the infant may smile, indicating an assimilation process (Perry & Bussey, 1984). Exploratory behaviors can result in assimilation and accommodation, the two main processes of cognitive growth.

Smiling is successful assimilation, crying is failed assimilation, and exploration is attempted assimilation turned accommodation.

Social Learning: The Role of Modeling

Imitation plays an important role in children's social development. Infants may be motivated to imitate because of their expectations that the people being imitated will imitate in return. Caregivers frequently imitate infants. Children delight in being the object of their caregivers' imitations, often smiling broadly and repeating the imitated response or trying something else to get the adult to imitate them again. Infants may enjoy being imitated because it leads to the understanding that "I have an influence" (McCall, Parke, & Kavanaugh, 1977). Infants work hard to get people to imitate them. A caregiver is most likely to imitate an infant if the infant has imitated something the caregiver has done (Papousek & Papousek, 1977). So infants may learn that it pays to imitate their caregivers first. Caregivers' playful imitation of their infants may help establish imitative tendencies in their infants.

McCall et al. (1977) found that infants cannot imitate novel responses, ones they have never made before, until late in the first year. Until their second birthday, children do not often imitate new actions in the model's absence (that is, long after having seen the model display the behavior). These various imitative capacities do not seem to unfold in a fixed sequence of stages but develop simultaneously, maturing at different ages (Parton, 1976).

Peer Relations

Most social development theorists emphasize very young children's social interactions with caregivers and other adults, but peer relations are also important. Cognitive developmental theorists (Kohlberg, 1969; Piaget, 1951) stress that peer contacts provide children with opportunities for developing their social-cognitive skills. Peer contact allows children to interact with people in increasingly sophisticated ways.

In social interactions with peers, children encounter differences of opinions. They cannot always turn to an adult to resolve differences. They must try to resolve the problem themselves. To do so they must perceive, acknowledge, and consider others' thoughts, feelings, and desires. Although infants cannot resolve differences through considering others' thoughts, feelings, and desires, peer interactions are important. Interactions with peers are likely to result in exploratory behaviors and eventually in smiling at a well-known peer. They can also result in distress when a peer confronts an infant by grabbing a favored toy or doing something else that is upsetting. Although the infant may cry, he will have begun the process of recognizing others' needs and wants. Infant social interaction with peers helps children's social development.

THE SOCIAL EXPLORATION MODEL

The social exploration model is used by adults to encourage children's exploratory behaviors. It centers on (a) enabling children to interact with an ever-widening range of adults and children and (b) encouraging children's exploration of new settings. The two steps in the model are open exploration and caregiver-guided exploration.

Open Exploration

In open exploration, three elements are important:

    1. Developing caregiver–child interaction
    2. Providing frequent opportunities for children to interact with other children and adults
    3. Providing opportunities for children to explore social interactions in new settings

Caregiver–Child Relationship. Children's primary relationship is with their caregiver(s). With infants the number of primary caregivers should be no more than two. Children should have the same caregiver(s) for as long as possible. The primary caregivers are usually parents, but others such as teachers, babysitters, siblings, and members of the extended family can also function as primary caregivers. This does not mean that children should not interact with others. Children should have the opportunity to interact with a wide range of people. However, they need a stable relationship with caregiver(s) whom they can come to depend on, knowing the caregiver will always be there when needed. In using the model, the caregiver interacts with children as much as possible. The interaction can begin with initiating or responding. The caregiver can initiate interaction with children by speaking to them, tickling them, and so on. The caregiver can also interact by responding to children's actions. This includes smiling back when a child smiles, repeating sounds a child has made, and picking the child up when he seems unhappy.

Meeting People. The caregiver seeks to extend children's social interactions to include a wide range of people, both older and younger, male and female, and representing many occupations. Children who have secure and satisfying relationships with their caregivers can have satisfying interactions with other people as well. These interactions can be intensive, such as playing a game of peekaboo with a neighbor. Or they can be limited, as might occur when an adult winks and smiles frequently at a child while standing in line behind him at the post office. When possible, the caregiver can withdraw from intensive-interaction situations if the child seems comfortable, allowing the child and the other person to interact without interference.

New Settings. Interactions can occur in familiar settings but should also include new settings. The more isolated the setting children are usually in, the greater the effort that should be made to introduce children to new settings and people. A child on a farm is likely to be isolated from other settings and people. A child living in a middle-class suburban apartment building is likely to be as isolated as the farm child, but in different ways. This second child may drive to banks and shopping centers with his parents but may actually interact with few people. At home he may be confined to the apartment, unable to wander down the hallways and lacking a place to play outside. A child in a day-care center may be surrounded by other children but may have little contact with settings outside the center and his home or with adults other than caregivers. Each of these children is isolated to some extent. Caregivers must make an effort to expand children's opportunities to experience new settings and new people.

Social Exploration.   In introducing children to new people and settings, the caregiver should keep in mind the diversity represented by the social world and incorporated into the social studies. The content of the social studies is often broken down into areas such as history and anthropology. Each area represents a facet of our social lives. An effort should be made to introduce the child to the complexity of the social world represented by the integration of all these facets of the social studies.

As children are introduced to new people and settings, the caregiver should approach the experience with a sense of openness and friendliness, welcoming children's and other people's attempts to make social contact. In open exploration, the caregiver helps children initiate new social contacts through placing children in a situation in which such contacts are possible. Then the caregiver encourages the child's efforts to initiate and respond to interactions with other people.

Caregiver-Guided Exploration

Part two of the model is caregiver-guided exploration. This part occurs after children have been initially placed in a situation in which social interaction can occur. In this phase, the caregiver extends his personal relationship with the child and can also build the child's initial relationship with others and with new social settings.

Caregiver–Child Interaction.   If social interaction is occurring solely between caregiver and child, the caregiver builds on former interactions and encourages the child to explore new activities. At first, the caregiver lets the child explore the situation and responds to the child's overtures. After exploration, social interaction is extended to forms that have not occurred before or previous activities that can be expanded. For example, the caregiver may use a new fingerplay, read a book, or dance to a record with a child.

The caregiver also may focus on body and sensory awareness because all experiences of the world begin with the human body. For very young children this involves, for example, learning the names and functions of various body parts, expressing themselves through movement, and using their senses to make contact with the environment.Emotional development follows because emotions are interpretations of body experiences. For very young children, the acquisition of a vocabulary relating to the emotions is emphasized. Caregivers use words such as "happy" and "angry" to describe children's emotions.

Interaction With New People.   When the child is near a new person, the caregiver allows the child time to observe the situation and to initiate interaction— open exploration. If no interaction occurs, the caregiver attempts to stimulate interaction. If interaction does occur and then lags, the caregiver attempts to expand the interaction.

Social interaction with new people may be encouraged by engaging the person in conversation about the child. For example, the caregiver may say, "This is my granddaughter, Aimee. She has just had her first birthday." It can also be encouraged through initiating a game such as peekaboo that the new person can also play. In the case of peers, toys can be provided that both children could use in play. Peers can also be introduced to each other and placed in proximity so they can examine each other.

New Settings.   After an initial period of open exploration in new settings, the caregiver points out special aspects of the setting to the child. An example of special aspects of a setting is the plastic shield between the child and a bank teller. The child is encouraged to touch, sit on, or otherwise explore special aspects of the new setting as is appropriate. The exploration should involve as many senses as possible. Manipulation of the special aspect through handling it, walking on it, and so on, should be encouraged so long as the behavior is safe and acceptable in the setting. The caregiver also introduces the child to people in the setting.

Children gradually become more conscious of the ways that social settings relate to their social obligations as well as to their expectations of others. Places begin to acquire meaning. For example, to a very young child, a church, a grocery store, and a living room all may be perceived as places for free exploration and play. However, as their perceptions begin to conflict with those of others, children discriminate between situations and make corresponding adjustments in their behavior. A church becomes a serious place, a grocery store becomes a place in which they must be careful, and a living room is a place in which they can act silly and be less inhibited. Every society expects children to learn how places are defined within that culture. Children make adjustments in behavior by becoming more aware of what they consider to be their obligations in various situations. They become more conscious of how others expect them to act.

In addition to trying to ascertain their obligations in a situation, children gradually begin to form expectations of how others are supposed to act. Watson and Fischer (1980) demonstrated that young children's awareness of social roles follows a developmental sequence. By 18 months old children are able to differentiate between reality and fantasy by engaging in pretend play. By 2 years of age they can make a doll do something as if it were acting on its own and most 3-year-olds can make a doll carry out several activities related to role, for example, a doctor or mommy.

Caregiver-guided exploration is the second and final phase of the model. The caregiver calls children's attention to special aspects of situations and to people within the situation. Should the child return to the situation, the caregiver calls his attention again to special people and/or aspects of the setting. Once the interaction is completed, the caregiver may talk about the experience and may model some part of the experience. For example, the caregiver may model a hairdresser blowing dry a customer's hair, or an attendant putting clothes into a washer at a laundromat. The child may imitate the modeling. The attempt to review the experience through talking about it or through modeling it is appropriate for children by the middle of the first year. It offers the child more opportunity to assimilate the experience and possibly to accommodate to it.

SUMMARY

Very young children in the sensorimotor stage of cognitive development are forming social schemas that enable them to organize and interact with their social world. The social exploration model encourages very young children to explore new interactions with caregivers and to establish social interaction with new people in new settings. The model follows a two-step approach: open exploration by children and caregiver-guided exploration. Caregivers, through following the model, provide an encouraging and secure social setting in which children can develop satisfying social relationships.

REFERENCES

CHESS, S., THOMAS, A., & BIRCH, H. (1965). *Your child is a person.* New York: Viking.

HAY, D. (1980). Multiple functions of proximity seeking in infancy. *Child Development, 51,* 636–645.

KAGAN, J. (1971). *Understanding children.* New York: Harcourt Brace Jovanovich.

KOHLBERG, L. (1969). Stage and sequence: The cognitive-developmental approach to socialization. In D.A. Goslin (Ed.), *Handbook of socialization theory and research,* 118–140. Chicago: Rand McNally.

MCCALL, R., PARKE, R., & KAVANAUGH, R. (1977). Imitation of live and televised models by children one to three years of age. *Monographs of the Society for Research in Child Development, 42* (Whole No. 173).

PAPOUSEK, H., & PAPOUSEK, M. (1977). Mothering and the cognitive head-start: Psychobiological considerations. In H. R. Schaffer (Ed.), *Studies in mother–infant interaction,* 63–85. London: Academic Press.

PARTON, D. (1976). Learning to imitate in infancy. *Child Development, 47,* 14–31.

PERRY, D., & BUSSEY, K. (1984). *Social development.* Englewood Cliffs, NJ: Prentice-Hall.

PIAGET, J. (1951). *Play, dreams and imitation in childhood.* New York: Norton.

WATSON, M., & FISCHER, K. (1980). Development of social roles in elicited and spontaneous behavior during the preschool years. *Developmental Psychology, 16,* 483–494.

5

THE EXPERIENTIAL
MODEL OF TEACHING

The primary aim of the experiential model is the development of children's process skills. A secondary aim is the acquisition of a body of knowledge, mostly in the form of facts but also including some concepts and generalizations. The experiential model of teaching is particularly appropriate for preoperational children but is also useful with concrete operational children when they are being introduced to a new area of study. It can be used with sensorimotor children in situations that are familiar and with which they already have some experience. Like all the teaching models, it focuses on accomplishing the major goals of the social studies. This model enables children to have firsthand, sensory experiences with the social studies during which they can practice their process skills (Renner, Abraham, & Birnie, 1988). In Piagetian terms, the primary goal of the model is to provide children with opportunities to exercise, expand, and change their cognitive structures (Kamii & DeVries, 1978). Through the processes of observation, inference, and classification, children adapt their cognitive structures to deal with information encountered in an activity.

The social studies are an attempt to find patterns in the social world. The teacher, in an experiential activity, brings a small part of the social world into the classroom and focuses children's attention on it. Through interacting with information, children learn (Gross, 1985; Renner, Abraham, & Birnie, 1988). They strengthen or modify the cognitive structures they already have; they assimilate. When activities provide information new to children, they may accommodate this information by building new cognitive structures. As children directly experience their environment and practice their process skills, they also have an opportunity to learn new content in the form of facts, concepts, and generalizations.

PARTS OF THE MODEL

The three basic steps in the experiential model are open exploration, teacher-guided exploration, and classification.

Step 1

The first step provides children with information and encourages them to explore it on their own (Eggen, Kauchak, & Harder, 1979). In this first step a teacher may introduce children to a large variety of bread such as white, rye, pumpernickel, and whole wheat. French, Italian, pita, and other forms of bread may also be included. Children will have the opportunity to examine whole breads and touch and taste smaller pieces of the various kinds of bread. During the first part of the activity children explore and experience the materials used in the activity. This step gives children time to familiarize themselves with the information and provides a bridge to the second step.

Step 2

After the children have explored the information individually, the teacher expands the process by asking questions. Initial questions ask for observations. For example, "George, tell us about one of the breads we have here." Children have a chance to share the information they have gathered and to acquaint themselves with one another's observations. For example, one child may have paid particular attention to the seeds in the rye bread while another may have noted that Italian bread loaves seem to be "fatter" than French bread loaves. Through sharing observations, children's attention is directed to aspects of the bread they may not have observed on their own.

The teacher can continue the discussion by asking for a variety of inferences. For example, "Why are some pieces of bread hard and some others soft?" or "Italian and pita bread are so different. Marcie said Italian bread was 'fat' and pita bread was 'skinny.' Why do we call them both 'bread' when they are so different?" Both these questions ask children for explanatory inferences. In discussing hard and soft bread the teacher might also encourage children to make a predictive inference—"Will this soft bread become hard?" The teacher could also encourage children to make generalizing inferences. The products of a generalizing inference are either concepts or generalizations (Taba, 1967). Content goals aren't the primary focus of experiential lessons. However, teachers may find opportunities to introduce concepts and generalizations during the course of the activity. After the children have an opportunity to make observations, share them with each other, and process some of them through making inferences, they are ready to move on to the final step.

Step 3

Classification.   In the final step of the model children are provided with opportunities to organize their observations and inferences as they practice their classification skills. In their study of bread, the children got together in groups of three. They took a pile of bread samples and devised a system for classifying them. Next, the teacher brought the small groups together into a large group. Each small group shared its classification system. Finally, the teacher asked each child to pick up a pile of 10 pieces of bread and to classify them in any way the child wished. These classification activities were an important part of this experiential lesson because the children were encouraged to understand that classification schemes are not absolute nor inflexible. By understanding that objects can be classified in more than one way, children learn that groupings can change and adapt to fit needs and circumstances.

Application.   The bread activity was continued by incorporating it into an art activity in which children glued magazine pictures of bread to a huge piece of paper shaped like a slice of commercial white bread, thus forming a large paper mosaic. Blending other areas of the curriculum with the social studies is to be encouraged although it is not a necessary part of the model. It provides opportunities for reinforcing learning through different areas of the curriculum. As the children worked on the art project, they continued to practice observing and classifying. They also had an opportunity to learn about concepts such as color, form, and design. The children were encouraged to discover relationships among different areas of the curriculum. The integration of the social studies with other areas demonstrates that learning is an integrated whole. A variety of experiences facilitates adaptation—the expanding and reorganizing of cognitive structures.

MAJOR CHARACTERISTICS OF THE EXPERIENTIAL MODEL

The three steps of the experiential model emphasize its three major characteristics:

1. A primary emphasis on process goals
2. Concrete and manipulative sensory experiences
3. No specific content objective

Concrete and *sensory* refer to items that children can experience with their senses. *Manipulative* indicates that children can handle objects they are working with. In the bread activity, the children had actual pieces of bread as opposed to pictures or verbal descriptions of them. They could touch, see, smell, and taste the bread. The reason for using concrete, sensory materials relates to the characteristics of the social studies. The social studies have been described as part of people's daily effort to find patterns in their social world. The idea of social studies as an integral part of our lives can be reinforced by providing children with objects and events that come from their own experience and by helping them find patterns in these experiences.

Processing unfamiliar information is a difficult task, particularly for children in the preoperational stage of development, approximately ages 2 through 7. Although children in this stage can classify and form concepts, they need concrete, tangible referents to aid them (Ginsburg & Opper, 1980). Sometimes concrete referents are impossible to use. When this happens the teacher can either (a) defer the topic until later, when children can more adequately deal with it in the absence of examples, or (b) use photographs, slides, or pictures. If pictures are used, they should be lifelike, realistic, and true in color.

Manipulative activities are also concrete, sensory experiences. As children actively interact with information, they involve their senses. Allowing children to see, touch, smell, hear, and (sometimes) taste the objects they're learning about is better than just having them passively look at them. Manipulative activities motivate children, who generally prefer doing something themselves to watching someone else do it. Encouraging children to play with the objects they're learning about provides a realistic experience of "doing" social studies.

TEACHING WITH THE MODEL

A major characteristic of experiential activities is their primary emphasis on process. Process and content are closely interrelated, so experiential activities are not and should not be content free. However, experiential activities are designed to teach children intellectual skills and processes, with the acquisition of knowledge a secondary goal.

Many different kinds of activities can emphasize process development. For example, when children bring in vegetables for soup making (perhaps after reading *Stone Soup*), a large number of observations can be made and compared. Then these can be grouped and labeled. A field trip to a bank can be followed by having children first recall, then classify, as many observations of the unique furnishings of the building as possible—tellers' booths, safe, safety deposit boxes, and so on. With each of these topics, inferential activities could follow. Experiential activities have no specific content objective. A teacher does not explicitly focus on certain concepts and generalizations. However, as opportunities to teach content occur during an activity, the teacher takes advantage of them. This model provides teachers with flexibility and allows them to adapt activities to the backgrounds, interests, and needs of the children.

Planning Experiential Activities

The planning phase of any teaching strategy involves everything a teacher must consider prior to actually doing the activity in the classroom. For experiential activities this involves:

- Considering the goals of the activity

- Obtaining the materials that will be used during the activity
- Setting up the grouping arrangement for the activity

Goals.   Planning begins with a consideration of the teacher's goals (McAshan, 1974). The goals for an experiential activity are simple; the teacher wants students to (a) develop their process skills and (b) gather an unspecified body of information. Two examples of goals are:

- Children will describe the unique character of the piece of material known as a "flag."
- Children will group a set of stamps on the basis of their appearance.

Each of these is an important and worthwhile goal for social studies teaching, but the two differ in their appropriateness for a particular teaching model. In the first goal, "flag" is a concept. It is a particular form of content. This goal could be reached in a concept attainment model activity. However, a set of miniature flags in the classroom could be available for children to observe and discuss in an experiential activity. The flags could serve as a source for observation of color and design. The goal of this activity might be, "Children will identify and classify characteristics of a set of miniature flags." This experiential activity could build a foundation of facts on which a concept attainment lesson could eventually be taught. Concepts such as "flag," which are typically not understood until children develop concrete operations, should be taught through the concept attainment model when children are ready for them.

The second goal, related to grouping stamps, is directed at developing children's ability to make observations and classify objects on the basis of these observations. Emphasis on the processes of observation and classification is a characteristic of the experiential model.

Considerable overlap exists among the processes used in each of the models so that the difference between them is primarily one of emphasis. In the first goal, children would be observing and inferring in order to develop the concept known as "flag." Although processes of thinking are important, the emphasis on them is reduced. Instead, the emphasis is on using processes to form concepts. In the second goal, the children are observing and inferring. These process abilities are the primary purpose of the activity. No specific concept is being built, although information is gathered. This is an experiential activity. During the course of the activity the teacher may think, "I am leading an experiential activity but the children are learning a concept." This is fine. The models are not mutually exclusive. The difference between them is the major focus of their goal. Goals aiming primarily at process skill development and fact gathering are experiential goals.

Providing Materials.   Because experiential activities have process skill development as their primary focus, the teacher must provide information that can be processed in the activity. Often this means the activity must be planned and materials made available for each child or pair of children. When the teacher cannot easily accumulate enough materials to satisfy adequately each child's need to experience the information the activity is based on, there are four alternatives.

1. Ask the children to bring in materials.
2. Set up a learning center when only a few materials are available.
3. When just one object is available, organize opportunities for each child to explore the object with the teacher and/or the person providing the object.
4. Use media when concrete materials are unavailable.

One way to accumulate materials is to have the children bring in their own. For example, in studying bread, each child could bring in a piece of bread. An abundance of information is desirable because it makes direct involvement by each child possible. Sometimes information is not available for use by the whole class, but the teacher still wants to involve the children in an experiential activity. A teacher who wants children to learn about different tools may bring a variety of tools into class and place them on a table for all to share. A practical way of giving children access to information when there is a limited amount of available items is to set up a social studies learning center. The teacher can encourage process development by asking questions such as the following:

What's happening here?
Which items go together?
Has anything changed here since yesterday?
How do these work?

These questions can be printed for children who are able to read. They may also be tape-recorded, or the teacher can visit the learning center with each child and discuss the questions individually. These questions should be discussed by the group later during the teacher-guided discussion phase of the activity.

An adult who brings a dulcimer into class could spend an hour helping children explore the instrument. Afterward she could encourage the whole group to sing along as the instrument is played for the class.

A fourth alternative for information gathering is to use media such as slides, magazine pictures, or cassette tape recordings, distributed either as a group activity or in the learning center. Although they are not concrete, media provide opportunities to bring parts of the world into the classroom that would otherwise be inaccessible to children.

Grouping.　The grouping arrangement of the children is, to an extent, determined by the availability of materials for children to work with. Experiential activities should allow children maximum opportunity to work with materials. This can occur in a variety of ways. Large-group, small-group, or learning center arrangements can be used equally well if careful planning occurs.

Implementation

The activity should be implemented after having considered the goals of the activity, gathered the materials, and decided on the appropriate grouping arrangement. The three steps of the implementation phase are open exploration, teacher-guided exploration, and classification.

Open Exploration.   Experiential activities begin with the process of observation occuring through open exploration. This is a logical starting point because all the information we receive about the world comes to us through our senses. When first introduced to the process of observation, children may approach it casually or may not understand what is being required of them. Most of them have not been encouraged to explore items and carefully observe their characteristics either in school or at home. Many children are allowed to explore but are not helped to develop their ability to observe. One way of teaching this skill is to provide each child with a common object like a paper clip. Children are often surprised when they learn that they can make many observations from just one object. This kind of activity needs to be repeated many times before children begin to develop and utilize the ability to make observations (Renner & Marek, 1988).

Teacher-Guided Exploration.   Besides the process of observation, experiential activities offer opportunities during teacher-guided exploration to practice making inferences (Eggen, Kauchak, & Harder, 1979). Teacher guidance can foster further development of observational and inferential skills. It can also help children add to their store of facts. Teacher guidance occurs after children have had ample opportunity to work with the information available. It occurs at a point when children have contributed nearly all they can and need help in order to go further.

Classification.   Classification generally occurs after open exploration by the children and after teacher-guided exploration (Renner & Marek, 1988). As a third phase it occurs when children have developed a wide base of information and are asked to organize that information. There are several kinds of classification. The particular form chosen should be based on logical and developmental considerations. Kofsky (1966) notes three levels of classification skills as they typically emerge:

- Consistent sorting
- Exhaustive sorting
- Hierarchical classification

Consistent sorting occurs when children adopt a particular classification strategy and use it without changing over to another system even though it means that not all items are sorted. For example, they may classify only round objects as "round" and ignore all others. Exhaustive sorting occurs when children use a classification system to sort all of a set of objects by some characteristic such as shape. Hierarchical classification is the process of creating groups within groups. For example, all the children in the room can be divided by hair color and then by the kind of shoes they are wearing. The particular classification system used is not important so long as it is based on observable characteristics and is applied logically and consistently. When first introducing the process of classification, the adult should not assume that all children automatically know how to classify. All children may not yet have achieved this understanding, even in the primary grades. One way to teach this skill is by modeling—performing the activity in front of the children while explaining what is happening and why. Modeling can be followed by individual or small-group activity to enable children to demonstrate their understanding of classification. By age 4 many children are able to understand consistent and exhaustive sorting, with appropriate experience. Hierarchical classification is much more difficult and requires lots of experience before it is developed. Most young children will not be able to classify in this way or they will be able to use hierarchies that have only two, or perhaps three, levels.

When introducing the process of classification, a good idea is initially to use small numbers of familiar objects. By making the classification easier, the learning task for children is simplified. After children feel comfortable with the sorting task and the groups they have formed, the adult can encourage them to regroup the objects. At first this may be difficult because some children tend to view the classes they have formed as the only ones possible. They may also feel that they have spent much time and effort building something, forming the original classes, and they don't want to destroy their systems and start over. To help them in this process, the adult should praise the groups that were formed, but encourage children to form new and different ones. The adult should model this process of forming groups and then reforming items into new groups.

Teacher Flexibility. Because learning in experiential activities occurs in a mainly unstructured manner, the adult must be flexible and responsive to the questions and answers of the children. This requires a skilled, sensitive, and insightful person who can respond to an opportunity to help children practice their thinking skills by using appropriate questions (see Figure 5–1). For example, it is strictly a function of the teacher's skill at the instant it takes place to ask the child to give a reason for a fact she observes. When children make observations about bread, for example, one child might state that some slices of bread have a notch on either side and a rounded top. A skilled teacher would immediately ask why she thinks the rounded top exists. After the child responds that bread puffs up before it is baked, the teacher would continue to probe. Leading questions would be "Why do you say that?" or "Does all bread puff up before it is baked?" This discussion could continue until the topic is exhausted or the children's interest has begun to wane. A less skilled teacher might miss the opportunity to probe altogether or might ask only the "why" question. The skilled teacher provides the children not only with some valuable practice in developing

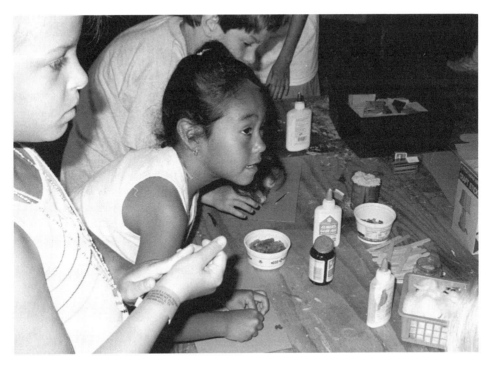

FIGURE 5–1
Other children do create some interesting things.

thinking skills but also with equally valuable practice in verbalizing their ideas, thereby developing language skills.

Evaluation

Because the primary focus of experiential activities is process skill acquisition, evaluation techniques in experiential activities focus on process development. Learning to perform a skill can be described as a three-stage hierarchical series of steps:

1. Begin with knowledge of the skill.
2. Progress to comprehension of its use in social studies activities.
3. Move to its application in other settings, whether in the classroom or in the world at large (Bloom, 1956).

At the first level of this hierarchy children can provide a definition of a process skill or can recognize a correct definition when they encounter one. Being able to state a definition does not ensure that the child understands the skill or could recognize its occurrence in a situation (Anderson, 1972). At the next level, comprehension, children are able to discriminate between instances and noninstances of the skill being performed. This level is a critical step in the mastery of skills, for without comprehension of the skill there is little chance that it can be applied in a systematic way in social studies activities. At the third level, application, the child is able to perform the skill in real life or in simulated settings.

This hierarchy is based on a view of skills as actions based on concepts, which are categories that are defined by their essential characteristics (Klausmeier, Ghatala, & Frayer, 1974). Among skill-related concepts are observing, inferring, and classifying. Each of these skills can be thought of as a category of behavior. Performance of the skill is dependent on an understanding of the concepts involved. For example, the process skill of classifying is based on children's understanding of what classifying is.

This hierarchical model of skill learning suggests a series of steps in teaching these skills. First, the learner must know and understand a skill before applying it. Related to this is the idea that failure to perform at one level may be traceable to a lower level (Gagne, 1977). A child's lack of comprehension of a skill may be the reason she cannot apply the skill. Comprehension is a lower level that must be developed before application occurs. Means by which to measure children's comprehension of different skills must be a component of evaluation strategies. Evaluating children's acquisition of process skills involves measuring their ability to do something. But, children's inability to perform a certain skill may arise from their lack of knowledge about that skill (Eggen, Kauchak, & Harder, 1979). For example, children who do not know what hierarchical classification is would be unable to take a set of objects and classify them hierarchically.

A hierarchical view of skill learning suggests a two-step method of evaluation in which the teacher measures children's understanding of a skill before asking children to apply the skill itself. Typical activities measuring understanding might be: "What do people do when they put things into groups (classify)?" or "Show me how you put these things into groups."

The second step, application of the skill, asks children to apply it in new situations. Application of a skill in a situation used before doesn't indicate whether children have learned the skill. It may indicate that they have memorized its use in a situation they have practiced. It does not demonstrate their ability to use it in another situation. Evaluation of the ability to apply process skills requires that children be placed in situations in which they can utilize these skills with selected items. Evaluation of process abilities, such as observation, can resemble the learning activities they are based on.

Criteria for determining success using the process skill of observation would be the number of observations and the extent to which the list was limited to observations. Measuring children's ability to make inferences requires placing them in situations in which inferential processes are called for, then evaluating their ability to perform. This measurement also requires the teacher to select and supply information to process. Criteria for success in classifying can include determining the child's ability to sort a given set of items using one of the levels of classification: consistent sorting, exhaustive sorting, or hierarchical classification. Then the child should be asked to resort the objects using a different system (such as shape rather than color), although the level of classification is likely to remain the same.

SUMMARY

The experiential model is complicated—materials preparation, a three-stage implementation process, evaluation. Yet it is not very different from what many teachers of young children do every day. Rather, it is an attempt to describe the structure of what is often done intuitively by teachers. The model is a description of a natural kind of teaching. It is natural because it is really appropriate for young children and is especially appropriate to the social studies.

REFERENCES

ANDERSON, R. (1972). How to construct achievement tests to assess comprehension. *Review of Educational Research, 42,* 145–170.

BLOOM, B. (Ed.). (1956). *Taxonomy of educational objectives. Handbook 1: Cognitive domain.* New York: David McKay.

EGGEN, P., KAUCHAK, D., & HARDER, R. (1979). *Strategies for teachers.* Englewood Cliffs, NJ: Prentice-Hall.

GAGNE, R. (1977). *The conditions of learning* (3rd ed.). New York: Holt, Rinehart & Winston.

GINSBURG, H., & OPPER, S. (1979). *Piaget's theory of intellectual development* (2nd ed.). Englewood Cliffs, NJ: Prentice-Hall.

GROSS, T. (1985). *Cognitive development.* Belmont, CA: Wadsworth.

KAMII, C., & DEVRIES, R. (1978). *Physical knowledge in preschool education: Implications of Piaget's theory.* Englewood Cliffs, NJ: Prentice-Hall.

KLAUSMEIER, H., GHATALA, E., & FRAYER, D. (1974). *Conceptual learning and development: A cognitive view.* New York: Academic Press.

KOFSKY, E. (1966). A scalagram study of classificatory development. *Child Development, 37,* 191–204.

MCASHAN, H. (1974). *The goals approach to performance objectives.* Philadelphia: Saunders.

RENNER, J., ABRAHAM, M., & BIRNIE, H. (1988). The necessity of each phase of the learning cycle in teaching high school physics. *Journal of Research in Science Teaching, 25,* 39–58.

RENNER, J., & MAREK, E., (1988). *The learning cycle and elementary school science teaching.* Portsmouth, NH: Heinemann.

TABA, H. (1967). *Teacher's handbook to elementary social studies.* Reading, MA: Addison-Wesley.

6

THE CONCEPT ATTAINMENT MODEL

The processes of observation and inference are used in the concept attainment model to teach social studies content through induction. The model focuses on forming concepts but also can be used to help children identify generalizations, describing the relationships between concepts (see chapter 2). Inductive activities provide children with information and ask them to find patterns in this information. The model is particularly appropriate for children who are concrete operational thinkers. It can be used with preoperational children when it utilizes information with which the children are very familiar.

The teacher's role involves (a) providing children with information to work with and (b) asking questions to help them focus on important aspects of the information. Although the teacher helps the students, a concept attainment activity is centered on an active exchange between children and their social environment. In a lecture-oriented lesson the teacher does most of the talking. Few questions are asked and these often require a specific answer. Concepts or generalizations are taught through being defined at the beginning of the lesson and then illustrated with examples. Activities following the concept attainment model use a reverse procedure, starting with examples and proceeding to the children's definition of a concept or generalization describing the information presented.

CONCEPT ATTAINMENT

The process through which children develop concepts has been the focus of much research. Two phases appear to be involved. Children initially develop a concept through understanding its critical attributes—the attributes that define this concept as different from other concepts. For example, a chair could be described as having the following attributes: a seat (something to sit on), a means of support (one or more legs), and elevation from the floor (the seat placing the sitter up off the floor). Recent research has explored what a best example of a concept might be and its effect on development of the concept (Tennyson & Park, 1983; Yoho, 1985). It appears that children are better able to develop a concept when they are presented with a best example of it to use as a guideline in evaluating whether something else is an example of the concept. Both learning the critical attributes of a concept and having a best example of the concept to use as a guideline help children in the second phase, forming a mental prototype of the concept (Park, 1984; Tennyson & Park, 1983). There is evidence that children eventually forget the specific critical attributes of a concept and utilize the mental prototype as their standard for judging whether something is an example of the concept (McKinney, Gilmore, Peddicord, & McCallum, 1987).

CONCEPT ATTAINMENT MODEL PROCEDURES

To help children develop their definition or description of a concept or generalization the teacher uses a set of seven strategies during the activity.

1. Information presentation
   The lesson begins with the presentation of small, easily considered units of information.
2. Making observations
   After the information is presented, the teacher asks the children to make observations related to the information.
3. Additional information presented
   The teacher provides further information, which can include both examples and nonexamples of the concept or generalization being taught.
4. Additional observations made
5. Generalizing inferences made
   The teacher encourages children to put their observations together into patterns.
6. Closure
   Children develop an abstraction defining or describing a concept or generalization.
7. Extension
   Children apply or extend the concept or generalization learned to another realistic situation (Kauchak & Eggen, 1980).

PLANNING FOR CONCEPT ATTAINMENT ACTIVITIES

Careful planning is a key to the success of a concept attainment activity. The teacher must (a) consider the goals of the activity, (b) select appropriate content, and (c) prepare information illustrating the content.

Goals of Concept Attainment Activities

Planning any activity must begin with a consideration of goals. Concept attainment activities have one major and two subordinate goals.

major goal
Teaching concepts and generalizations

subordinate goals
Teaching process skills
Helping students understand the nature of the social studies

Through working with information, analyzing it for patterns, and forming usable concepts and generalizations, children directly experience the activities of social scientists.

A concept attainment activity uses process to form specific concepts and generalizations. What differentiates experiential activities from concept attainment activities is relative emphasis. Experiential activities stress process development, whereas concept attainment activities use process to learn content.

Appropriate Content Selection

Content selected for use in a concept attainment lesson should be (a) developmentally appropriate and (b) consistent with the goals of the social studies. Concepts and generalizations to be taught can be selected from various sources, including state department of education social studies objectives, school textbooks, and texts used in introductory college courses in the social sciences (Schug & Beery, 1987). Later chapters in this book also describe appropriate social studies content.

Selection and Preparation of Information Used in the Activity

Once social studies content has been identified and a determination been made that it can be appropriately taught with the concept attainment model, the teacher moves to the planning step—selecting and preparing information. The teacher selects examples illustrating the concept or generalization that is the goal of the lesson. A teacher trying to teach the concept of "goods" could bring handcrafted and manufactured items into class for children to touch, smell, and see. As part of the preparation the teacher also decides on a best example of the concept. Nonexamples are also selected. A teacher wanting children to form the generalization, "Rules help us play together," could bring in the materials for several different games, have the children play each game, and have an observer record problems that develop and instances when the rules are consulted.

Concrete Items. Real items, such as a handcrafted toy or a checkers game, help young children understand the following:

1. Social studies activities in the classroom relate to the real social world outside the classroom.
2. As a result, knowledge and skills gained in the classroom are applicable in the social world outside the classroom.

The information used in a concept attainment activity is a piece of the social world. The more concrete the information and the more accurately reality is represented, the more fun the activity is likely to be for young children.

Manipulative Items. The teacher should provide children with the opportunity to interact with and explore the information in the activity as much as possible. If handcrafted toys are the source of information for the lesson, the teacher should pass them around so students can feel them, smell them, and look at them closely, familiarizing themselves with the information central to the activity. To internalize ideas about the world, children need to be actively involved in manipulating and interacting with it (see Figure 6–1). Providing opportunities to interact with information also helps children understand the nature of the social studies and the activities of social scientists.

    The more realistic the information, the more complete children's un-

FIGURE 6–1
The concept of "dough" is developed through manipulation.

derstanding of it will be. However, an 1850s military fort can't be brought into the classroom, and a field trip to visit it is not always possible. In such cases pictures will have to be used. The primary concern is to avoid teaching concepts and generalizations solely with words. When words alone are used, children tend to memorize them. Their understanding is limited to what they can recall from memory. Concepts and generalizations are reduced to the level of facts. As facts they are no longer able to summarize information and simplify the social world for children.

When information is limited, it might be better used in demonstrations or possibly in a learning center. Activities with expensive, rare, or delicate items might involve young children in watching rather than in manipulation or doing. Such activities should be held to a minimum because they limit active involvement.

Selecting Relevant Information. In selecting information to teach a concept or generalization, it is helpful to analyze its characteristics and those of related concepts or generalizations. Concepts are categories or sets of members. Membership is determined by the *characteristics*, or critical attributes, defining the category (Taba, 1967). For example, the concept "neighbor" has the major characteristic, nearby location. Using this characteristic children would determine whether the people living in a particular house or apartment building were neighbors of their school. The teacher would select examples that clearly show this characteristic. Some examples of neighbors would include people living in houses and in apartment buildings. Some would have a lot of property separating them from each other, some would be very close together. Neighbors of a variety of races and ages would be represented. Children could determine that race and age are not essential characteristics.

In learning concepts, children should be provided with nonexamples, so they can understand what the concept is not. For example, in teaching "neighbor" it is helpful to contrast positive examples with nonexamples. For example, two children in the group may be classmates but live miles apart and so they are not neighbors at home. While in class they sit at opposite ends of the room, so they are not neighbors in class either. However, when the teacher moves them so they sit next to each other, they become neighbors while in class. These examples help children to understand what the concept does not include, specifically membership in the same classroom. As a result, the concept formed by the children is clearer and more accurate. A variety of examples helps children understand that concepts refer to *categories*, or classes, of items rather than to specific items themselves.

Selection of information to teach generalizations is complex because generalizations involve the relationship between two or more concepts. The information used in the activity must demonstrate this relationship. The generalization, "Rules help us play together," should be taught with examples that show the interaction between rules and play. A nonexample might be the encouragement of a board game similar to checkers. The players could be told the object of the game is to capture the other player's pieces in any way they want—there are no rules. Soon the players would be in conflict, would be insisting that the other was playing unfairly, but would not be able to settle the conflict because no rules were in effect. A procedure using both nonexamples and positive examples enables children to become aware of the relationships in the generalization. It also reinforces the idea that the social studies describe the real social world.

Organizing Information.   The information has been selected; now it must be organized for presentation to the children. In organizing information for each activity the teacher weighs several factors:

- The amount of time available for the activity
- Children's ability level
- The relative importance of content and process goals
- The importance of communicating an accurate view of social studies

Depending on the priority each factor is given, the amount of structure imposed by the teacher will vary.

Overorganized information does not allow children to wrestle with the information or to make sense out of it. They are deprived of the opportunity to practice their skills of working information into some pattern.

IMPLEMENTING CONCEPT ATTAINMENT ACTIVITIES

Overview

In a concept attainment activity, children are presented with information, a piece of the social world, and asked to find patterns in it (see Figure 6–2 for a sample lesson plan). The patterns are the concepts or generalizations to be formed. The teacher provides children with information and helps them analyze it. Additional information is provided as needed. Children are active investigators, making observations and forming generalizing inferences. Once children have formed the concept or generalization, the teacher helps them clarify this concept and test its relevance in other situations.

Part 1: Information Presentation

The lesson begins with the teacher providing the children with some information related to a specific concept or generalization. Through the information, the teacher brings a small part of the social world into the classroom. Knowledge and skills gained in the classroom are, as a result, applicable to the world at large.

Information presentation also provides children with practice in developing process skills by enabling them to work with real and concrete examples.

Objective

Develop the concept of "neighbor," defining it in terms of proximity.

Procedure

1. *Information Presentation*
Gather children in a circle. Ask each child, "Who is sitting on either side of you?" Discuss. Focus children's attention on various items in the classroom and ask them what is on either side of the item. Distribute pictures of buildings and houses and ask children to look at the pictures and identify what is next to what in the pictures.

2. *Observation*
Ask children to show their pictures to the class, pick out one item, and discuss what it is close to. Write down comments.

3. *Additional Information*
Take the children outside the building. Have them look across the street, pick out something, and decide what it is close to. Return to the building. Point out the classroom farthest away from their classroom. "Is that classroom close to our classroom?" "What else in the hallway is close to our classroom?" "What is far away?" Return to the classroom.

4. *Additional Observations*
Ask children to think about what they saw outside and in the hallway. Discuss. Ask children, "Who lives closest to your house or apartment?" Talk about these people's age, race, and other characteristics. Pick out a child and ask who is sitting next to him. Then ask the children to widen the circle so the children are farther apart. Ask the same child who is sitting next to him. Widen the circle again and repeat the questioning. Then ask one of the child's neighbors to move to the other end of the classroom. Ask, "Who is sitting next to _____ ?"

5. *Inferences*
Summarize activity to this point by talking about what kinds of things the children have been working with—buildings, students in the class, people who live next door, items in the class, and so on. Is there anything that is the same about all these things? Discuss.

6. *Closure*
Verbalize the concept of "neighbor" and its definition. Write it down. Discuss.

7. *Extension*
Discuss the fish in the aquarium. Do they have neighbors? Are they all neighbors?

Evaluation

Ask children to draw themselves in on a dittoed map of the classroom. Then ask them to draw in three children who they think are often their neighbors in the classroom.

FIGURE 6–2
A concept attainment model lesson plan

Children become better observers and inference makers. They also begin to understand the role of these skills in the social studies.

Part 2: Observation of Information

In part 2 of a concept attainment activity children make and share observations of the information provided. Questions such as "What did you see? hear? smell? find? notice?" can be asked. In asking children to share their observations the teacher should be receptive to all observations and should regard them all as equal. When social scientists first investigate an area, they are not sure which observations are important. As many observations as possible are made and recorded. When the teacher accepts all the observations that children make he enables children to understand that social studies is not a set of situations in which all the answers are predetermined. Children are also less likely to feel a sense of failure. There can be no failure if each observation is equally acceptable. Even reluctant children may participate if all responses are equally welcome.

During this early part of the activity, the teacher can do several things to help children make accurate observations. First, all students can be provided with their own materials. If this is impossible and a demonstration is used, it could be repeated a number of times. For example, if a guest has come in to show the children a dulcimer, a number of songs can be played on it. Providing children with multiple opportunities to make observations when materials are limited helps them form abstractions related to those observations. Multiple opportunities to make observations ensure the observations are accurate and reliable (see Figure 6–3).

Teachers can also help children make accurate observations by drawing simple illustrations, tables, and charts on the board or overhead projector. The whole class can see clearly what is happening. Points can be clarified and essential aspects of the information emphasized.

After the children make observations, a number of things can occur. Teachers can present children with a best example of the concept to use as a standard to judge other possible examples of the concept. Children may form inferences on their own. If not, prompting and probing questions may be used to encourage children to make inferences. Or, it may be evident that the children need more information, and they need to make more observations in order to form inferences.

Part 3: Additional Information Presented

To help children develop and understand a concept or generalization, the teacher can present additional information. This option provides children with more opportunities to make observations and form concepts and generalizations on their own. The more such opportunities to make observations and inferences children are given, the more likely they are to form abstractions on their own.

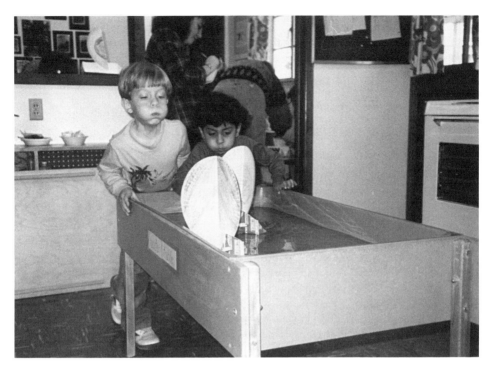

FIGURE 6–3
Appropriate materials can help us learn a new concept such as "sailboat."

A great deal of flexibility exists in a concept attainment activity. The additional information may sometimes be presented in the form of a nonexample. In developing the concept of "goods," for example, children might be presented with examples of "services" we pay directly for. Children might visit a barbershop and observe haircutting and people paying for the service. No physical product has been paid for. Although services are paid for, they are not goods.

Part 4: Additional Observations

After additional information is presented, the children should make further observations. They should be encouraged to be more selective in their observations. They might be guided to search for similarities and differences between these observations and previous ones. Questions such as "What belongs together?" and "Does this fit with that?" might be used. During this part of the activity children are encouraged to make observations directly related to identifying patterns. Children identify observations of aspects that are similar in all the examples. The teacher asks questions to focus children's attention on relevant aspects of the data.

Part 5: Inferences

Children are next asked whether they see any pattern in the new and previous observations they have made. Questions that might be used include:

> *What belongs under what?*
>
> *What would you call this group?*
>
> *What would you conclude?*
>
> *What does this mean?* (Taba, 1967)

They are being asked to make generalizing inferences. If children can't make spontaneous inferences, the teacher may have to provide additional information or refocus children's attention on earlier information.

As children link pieces of information to form a concept or generalization, the teacher should be supportive but questioning and noncommital. Questioning focuses the activity on children and their interaction with the information. Teachers remain supportive, but they respond to suggestions with questions such as, "Does all of the information agree with what you say?" This reminds children that the goal of concept attainment activities, and of the social studies, is to develop descriptions of the social world that accurately describe reality.

Part 6: Closure

After children have arrived at the concept or generalization, the activity moves to closure through accurate verbalization of the concept or generalization. Children can be asked to define the concept or describe the generalization in words that include the information at hand. They can also be asked to apply it to other instances not yet encountered. The statement can be in general rather than specific terms. It should be written out where all children can see it.

When the concept or generalization is written out, the children should examine it critically to ensure that it is each of the following:

- Complete
- Accurate
- Understood by everyone

The teacher should check to see whether individual children understand the abstraction. All children do not arrive at a concept or generalization simultaneously. If the abstraction is not written down, some children may feel uncertain about what they have learned.

Children can be encouraged to examine the adequacy of a concept definition by checking the characteristics in the definition against the examples provided. For example, in an activity on dulcimers, the teacher would want the children to decide whether the characteristics of "strings and a wooden body" apply to all dulcimers and whether a violin would satisfy a definition based only on these characteristics. As children practice applying those characteristics to the examples, they further refine the definition and produce a more complete and accurate concept.

Part 7: Extension

The last part of the activity involves extending or applying the abstraction in new situations. This helps children resolve any uncertainties that might exist. The extension part of the activity gives teacher and children an opportunity to evaluate how well the concept or generalization has been understood.

EVALUATION

Concept attainment activities teach two forms of content: (a) concepts and (b) the generalizations built when two or more concepts are interrelated. Both of these are abstractions people use to describe and understand the world. Abstractions are important because they can be used outside the immediate learning situation. Measurement items used to evaluate the learning of abstractions should focus on whether children have learned ideas that can be generalized outside the immediate learning situation. *Generalizable* means that ideas contained in abstractions can be extended or used in other situations with examples not previously encountered.

Levels of Learning

Measurement items may evaluate knowledge-level learning and higher levels of learning as described by Bloom (see Table 6–1). Knowledge-level learning usually

TABLE 6–1
Bloom's classification of levels of learning

Level 1	KNOWLEDGE Recall specific information, concepts, generalizations.
Level 2	COMPREHENSION Translate, interpret, explain, summarize, extend.
Level 3	APPLICATION Use concepts, generalizations, processes in a new situation.
Level 4	ANALYSIS Identify parts, elements, and their relationships.
Level 5	SYNTHESIS Put parts together, develop a plan, and communicate in a new way.
Level 6	EVALUATION Make a judgment using a specific set of criteria.

Source: Adapted from *Taxonomy of Educational Objectives. Handbook I: Cognitive Domain*, by B. Bloom (Ed.), 1956, New York: David McKay.

consists of recitation and reinforcement of appropriate responses. Examples of such learning are the memorization of the state capitals or of a list of presidents of the United States. When knowledge-level learning is measured, usually the learner is asked to reproduce the original content in basically the same form in which it was taught. In the case of a concept, this could involve recalling the definition for that concept as it was defined in class or in the text. For a generalization, the learner would need to be able to remember the generalization as stated in class or in the text.

Higher level learning involves the personal assimilation and interpretation of knowledge. The individual learns an idea so that it has meaning, which goes beyond being able to recite it. Higher level learning is evaluated in terms of whether the learner can relate it to the real world. Activities designed to teach at higher levels emphasize the importance of relating abstract ideas to concrete referents—the examples and information used in concept attainment activities.

Criterion for Success

A major criterion to be used in judging the success of concept attainment activities is whether the learner is able to use the new ideas to understand aspects of the social world not previously explored in the activity. Can children apply the ideas learned to new and original situations? For example, if children have developed the concept of "neighbor" through considering the location of people's residences, can they determine whether two trees are neighbors if they are given information on the trees' proximity?

Types of Measurement Items

Two types of measurement items, production and recognition, can be used. Production items ask children to do the following:

- Produce their own definition or examples of a concept
- Describe a generalization in their own words
- Provide an example of a generalization

For example, a production item used to measure children's understanding of the concept "neighbor" might ask: "List three examples of neighbors you know that we haven't talked about yet."

Recognition items provide children with a number of choices from which they recognize correct alternatives. The choices provided include options that were not previously discussed in class. A recognition item designed to measure the concept "goods" would be:

> *Which of the following are "goods"?*
> *five trumpets*
> *mail delivery by a mail carrier*
> *a blue 10-speed bicycle*
> *a shot given by a nurse*

Each type of item has advantages and disadvantages. Recognition items are often harder to prepare than production items, but they check each child on the same information. The teacher can make comparisons between children and across groups. Production items are easier to construct. They allow the teacher to see more clearly what is going on in the children's minds. Production items are generally harder for children to complete and may create anxiety in some children.

Measuring for Concept Attainment

Knowledge Level. Items that evaluate children's knowledge of a concept at the knowledge level will measure the ability to remember information previously presented in class:

- The definition of a concept
- Characteristics of a concept
- Examples of a concept

Children are thus evaluated on whether they remember the information in basically the form in which it was presented. This knowledge alone does not ensure that the children can generalize the abstraction.

Higher Levels. Measuring for concept attainment at higher levels requires children to work examples not previously discussed in the activity. Either production or recognition items can be used.

In using recognition items to measure children's understanding of a concept, the teacher should take care that the selection of examples measures the concept being taught, rather than some other type of content. If the examples used are unfamiliar, the item will measure children's knowledge of the examples rather than their understanding of the concept. For example, if a teacher trying to measure children's understanding of the concept "musical instrument" provides "ankelung" (a Thai musical instrument) as one alternative, the validity of the item would be in question unless it is likely that the children would have come in contact with the instrument. If children did not know what an ankelung is, then the item would be measuring this fact, rather than their understanding of the concept. This can be avoided by providing enough description in the examples to overcome any lack of previous learning.

Nonreaders' Concept Attainment. Measuring concept attainment can be difficult with young children because so many are nonreaders. For young children, measuring tools could include drawings and pictures. For example, an activity on the concept "musical instrument" could be followed by an art activity in which children are asked to draw a musical instrument different from the ones discussed in class but that contains an aspect discussed, such as strings or keys. Another option is showing the children pictures and then asking them to color or mark all the pictures that are positive examples of musical instruments.

Measuring for the Learning of Generalizations

Generalizations can be evaluated by the means used to evaluate concepts. They can be learned and evaluated at the knowledge level, but this is usually inappropriate. To evaluate for higher levels, teachers must design special items to measure higher level learning. Recognition, production, and a combination of both items can be used.

A recognition item could present children with a number of illustrations of the generalization and ask them to identify those to which the generalization applies. For example:

Which of the following stories shows that "rules help us play better"?

1. Marilyn and Tim both wanted to ride the tricycle. They started fighting over it. Then, Bob reminded them that there was a rule for riding the tricycle. They were to get the sand timer. When the timer was turned over, one of them could ride the tricycle until the sand ran out. Then the next child could turn over the timer and ride the tricycle until the sand ran out. Marilyn and Tim decided to use the sand timer.

2. Jimmy, Helen, and Coralee were playing hopscotch. Jimmy jumped along the areas they had marked out on the sidewalk. Then Helen and Coralee took their turns. Jimmy noticed that Coralee jumped in a different pattern from the way he and Helen had jumped, so he told her she was jumping wrong. Helen agreed with him. Coralee said her way was faster and better. Jimmy and Helen said they would play hopscotch together and Coralee could play her way with someone else. Coralee said she wouldn't play with them and left. Jimmy and Helen decided it wasn't fun to play with only two people so they stopped playing hopscotch.

This question requires children to consider several aspects of both situations and to carefully analyze the situations. In situation 1 the children initially fought. Then they were reminded of a rule that could solve the problem causing the fighting. They accepted the rule, used it, and played peacefully. In situation 2 the children started out playing together. They realized they were not all using the same patterns of movement in their game. They could not agree to establish a rule that would govern the movements in the game. The group playing hopscotch broke up. A production item to measure children's understanding of a generalization would ask them to provide examples of the generalization they had not previously discussed in class.

Application Problems.   Another means of testing understanding of a generalization is to ask children to solve a problem involving a situation they have not previously discussed. An example of an application problem is this:

Martin brought to school a board game, Chinese checkers. None of the children had played it before. Four children wanted to play. Martin said "OK" but added that he was going to play tetherball with some other children. Anne started reading the directions but it seemed to take too long to read them. So the four players started the game even though they didn't know what to do later in the game. It was fun until Anne told Carlotta she wasn't playing the right way. Carlotta said that she could do what she wanted because Anne didn't really know what was correct. Then Carlotta told Leonard he should play her way. Leonard and Hector decided they would play their own way. Soon, they were all arguing.

If another group wants to play Chinese checkers, what can they do to be sure they don't have the same problems the first group had?

Applying a generalization is the second step of a two-step process. In the first step, known as recognition, the child encounters the problem and recognizes it as being an example of the generalization. In the second step, known as production, the child reviews the information in the problem and applies the generalization to solve it.

Asking children to apply a generalization is an important evaluation strategy. A child who can apply a generalization remembers the generalization and recognizes situations in which it is applicable. Evaluation strategies involving application also are motivational. Children enjoy relating knowledge learned in the classroom to new situations.

SUMMARY

The concept attainment model teaches social studies content through induction. The formation of concepts is the focus of the model. Using inductive activities, children identify patterns in information provided through the activities. Teachers provide children with information and ask questions to help them focus on important aspects of the information. Children are helped to develop an abstraction defining or describing a concept. The last step in the model involves children in applying the concept in another situation.

REFERENCES

KAUCHAK, D., & EGGEN, P. (1980). *Exploring science in the elementary schools.* Dallas, TX: Houghton Mifflin.

MCKINNEY, C., GILMORE, A., PEDDICORD, H., & MCCALLUM, R. (1987). Effects of a best example and critical attributes on prototype formation in the acquisition of a concept. *Theory and Research in Social Education, 15,* 189–201.

PARK, O. (1984). Example comparison strategy versus attribute identification strategy in concept learning. *American Educational Research Journal, 21,* 145–162.

SCHUG, M., & BEERY, R. (1987). *Teaching social studies in the elementary school: Issues and practices.* Glenview, IL: Scott, Foresman.

TABA, H. (1967). *Teacher's handbook for elementary social studies.* Palo Alto, CA: Addison-Wesley.

TENNYSON, R., & PARK, O. (1980). The teaching of concepts: A review of instructional design research literature. *Review of Educational Research, 50,* 55–70.

YOHO, R. (1985). Effectiveness of four concept learning strategies on social studies concept acquisition and retention. Paper presented at the annual meeting of the American Educational Research Association, Chicago, IL.

7

PLANNING FOR TEACHING

Sandra Bradford DeCosta
West Virginia University

Teaching can be a demanding, frustrating, and laborious activity. It is also rewarding and fulfilling, spurring the teacher on to greater efforts and improved results. This is true whether it occurs in a classroom, a center, or the home. Some individuals are almost "natural" teachers; others struggle and strain with outlines, formats, examples, and rules. Regardless of these differences, any serious teaching effort begins with planning and organization.

BACKGROUND

Teaching automatically infers a curriculum or program around which activities, lessons, and goals are developed.

The term curriculum, unfortunately, is ambiguous, simultaneously meaning different things to different educators. Decker and Decker (1980) minimize the confusion by giving us a workable definition:

> The broadened scope of program planning is a problem to most administrators. Several years ago, programs were conceived as planned classroom experiences; the term curriculum was used to refer to these experiences. Today, programs still include classroom experiences, but have been extended to include planned home and community experiences; thus, the term program is used more frequently than curriculum to refer to this more comprehensive approach. (p. 26)

An additional concern must be addressed before planning can begin. Presentation of the social studies has often suffered from increased competition for teaching time. An emphasis on reading and math readiness has resulted in misunderstandings about or the minimizing of the social studies. As Fromberg (1977) has observed,

> many teachers of young children have been satisfied that social study
> has taken place when they have provided ritualized pagan calendar
> worship. Each week's unit adheres closely to the calendar that directs
> one holiday to end as another begins. (p. 273)

The social studies are not segmented lessons that honor a former president on his birthday or pleasantly contain and occupy children on rainy days. They must assist children in finding their own place in the larger society.

Enlightened teachers don't teach "a little citizenship" for a few minutes each day. They point out individuals who demonstrate proud citizenship skills. They introduce the heroes and heroines of both real life and fiction and tell about, even dramatize, their acts of humanity or patriotism. Committed instructors observe the actions of children for opportunities to encourage "good" or socially acceptable behavior.

Misunderstanding or misrepresentation of the social studies has not only bored children but has prevented them from an exciting entry into the study of their world. Committed teachers respond to the social studies as they really are—a natural part of all activities occurring at home, in the center, or in the neighborhood. They integrate the social studies into the overall curriculum or activities that children experience each day.

ORGANIZERS FOR PLANNING

All teachers face the problem of wondering how to begin. Perhaps the best way is to become familiar with the characteristics of young children, particularly as they relate to the social studies. Knowing what to expect of children—how they are likely to think and act and which skills they may be expected to possess— places the instructor in a much better position to engage in quality planning. Some modification of materials will always be necessary, but an informed beginning can ease the task of lesson development. Althouse (1981) provides an excellent set of general characteristics of children from approximately 3 to 6 years of age (see Table 7–1).

Interpreting the work of Piaget, Day (1983) writes that a good early childhood program must allow for exploration, experimentation, and inquiry, all within a structured yet creative environment. Therefore an appropriate Piagetian design for an early childhood program would be an open, creative learning approach. The following outline of assumptions supports this approach:

1. Children grow and develop at unique rates that are often unrelated to chronological age. In an effort to meet the needs of all children, learning activities at various challenge levels should be provided. Even within the range of preoperational learning, many levels exist.

2. Children's natural curiosity and eagerness to learn are enhanced if they are free to follow many of their natural interests. Piaget has said that children learn best through direct, immediate involvement with the environment. They learn through sensory input of observation, manipulation, and testing.

3. Learning is what children do; it is *not* something done to them. The child must be directly involved in doing the learning. Teaching by telling the child may result in empty verbalizations.

4. Play is the child's way of working and learning. Children acquire many skills through play. They try new roles, solve problems, learn how to make sense of the environment, and practice social skills.

5. Children learn many things from each other, including respect for themselves and others, ways of learning how to learn, and a sense of responsibility and achievement. They also learn basic attitudes toward the center, the school, and the teacher.

6. A stimulating learning environment, equipped with concrete and sensory learning materials, is essential in helping children to learn. Ideally, this exists both at home and at school but, in many cases, it is constructed by the teacher. The child's environment must somewhere provide the materials the child needs for exploration and learning.

With a clearer understanding of the likely capabilities of most young children, the instructor is now ready to ask the questions that precede lesson planning:

- What do I want to teach?
- Who decides?
- How are these decisions made?
- How can I make a conscious effort to identify the needs and interests of the children, their parents, and the community?
- How can I teach most effectively? In other words, how can I use my skills and talents and feed my own creative energies, while assuring that each student is provided opportunities for the highest levels of achievement?

Any response to these questions must be based on what is already known. This encompasses theories of learning, teaching effectiveness research, the characteristics of the social studies, knowledge of child development, community and parental values, the number of children in the group and its ethnic/gender composition, instructional dollars available, personnel, and evaluation. All play their separate roles and guide the development of any quality program.

In some settings, for example, texts are provided and instructors are asked to follow the sequence presented in the text. In other instances, instructors may be expected to conform to a list of themes that have been developed by others

TABLE 7–1

Representative characteristics of young children related to social studies

From About 3 Years of Age	To About 6 Years of Age
1. Is self-centered—sees things from own point of view	1. Begins to consider viewpoints other than own—may not reach until seven or eight years
2. Parallel and associative play prevail	2. Cooperative play prevails
3. Perception dominates reasoning—seeing is believing	3. Perception continues to dominate thinking
4. Is unable to construct knowledge from abstract materials	4. Source of knowledge and meaning is largely confined to concrete materials
5. Shows anger and frustration through physical aggression	5. Verbal aggression gradually replaces physical aggression
6. Is anxious to win the approval of adults	6. Is still anxious for adult approval; peer approval is becoming important
7. Play groups are small, two to three children	7. Play groups are larger, five to seven or more children
8. Finds sharing difficult—believes possessions are symbols of self	8. Is more willing to share; understands that possessions and self are separate entities
9. Finds difficulty in learning rules—becomes confused when some aspects of a new situation are the same and others are different	9. Finds rules easier to understand—is beginning to recognize similarities in situations in spite of differences
10. Has difficulty in thinking of self as a member of a group	10. Thinks of self as a separate entity at the same time as a member of a group
11. Identifies own sex and that of others	11. Is aware of own sex and differences in sex roles

or are the product of earlier work by the school or center staff. Perhaps a commercially developed social studies program has been purchased and is already in place. In that case, texts, materials, and teaching manuals would likely be available. In still other settings, the instructor may be expected to proceed independently by assuming the roles of both teacher and planner. This means reviewing and selecting texts, identifying an appropriate program, or researching the literature for typical teaching themes and then creating all the materials. Teachers may expect variations on any or all of these.

The instructor who is expected personally to develop all the teaching materials may wish to consult two excellent sources. Day (1983) has written a learning activities book that describes and illustrates many lessons for young children. All the content areas are included and many activities are designed as

TABLE 7–1
Representative characteristics of young children related to social studies *(continued)*

From About 3 Years of Age	To About 6 Years of Age
12. Is conscious of racial prejudice	12. Racial prejudices may develop depending on the environment
13. Judges people by acts, not intentions	13. Begins to consider motives that prompted actions
14. Understands the here and now	14. Understands today, yesterday, and tomorrow
15. Believes in artificialism—that human beings create natural phenomena	15. Artificialism is still present; begins to seek logical explanations for natural phenomena
16. Believes in animism—that inanimate objects are alive and have human characteristics	16. Animism is still present; begins to differentiate between animate and inanimate objects
17. Does not conserve length and distance	17. Does not conserve; a few may conserve length and distance
18. Sorts objects according to likenesses—simple form of classification	18. Uses multiple classification; a few may understand class inclusion
19. Begins to understand topological relationships—proximity, enclosure, order, and separation	19. Understands most topological relationships; begins to view objects as rigid in shape (Euclidean geometry)
20. Views positions of objects from own point of view independent of perspective	20. Begins to view objects in relationship to other objects
21. Cannot use an imaginary or concrete set of axes as reference systems to position objects	21. Cannot establish a reference system to compare distances and positions simultaneously

Reprinted by permission of the publisher from Althouse, Rosemary, *The young child: Learning with understanding.* (New York: Teachers College Press, © 1981 by Teachers College, Columbia University. All rights reserved.) table on p. 85.

integrated, multisubject lessons. Hess and Croft (1980) have produced a similar book but written in lesson-plan format. Both books have done much of the preliminary organization and planning for the user and both contain excellent resource lists.

IDENTIFYING A THEME

The theme motif seems to be increasing in popularity, particularly as finances for texts and other teaching materials grow scarce. Although commercially produced theme books are available from which copies can be made, the teacher must expect to assume major responsibility for materials development. The theme type of program is often developed as an annual plan for teaching. Each month, teaching in each of the content areas is focused on a different topic or topics. The teacher collects and constructs all the materials necessary to teach the theme. Of course, the teacher must also develop the specific lesson or unit plans. This requires a tremendous amount of work the first year but somewhat less labor in succeeding years, when adaptation or modification to meet new student needs constitutes the major preparation. This approach does have the advantage of allowing a teacher to utilize her own skills and talents and to plan with a specific group of children in mind.

An example of an annual social studies theme plan follows. Note that a theme and possible content are suggested. Lessons or units of study would be developed around the theme but with a primary focus on the topic of the moment.

SUGGESTED ANNUAL THEME PLAN

Month	Topics
September	Theme: Socialization Getting Acquainted Being a Friend Learning to Share Learning to Cooperate
October	Theme: Change Fall Is a Time of Changes People Change Too My Many Moods
November	Theme: Preparation for a New Season Insulating Homes Dressing for Warmth Learning to Knit
December	Theme: My Family—Customs and Traditions Holiday Traditions Family Celebrations The Joy of Sharing
January	Theme: Self-Improvement Making a Resolution How to Be a Family Helper Some Ways to Be a Friend What I Like (and Don't Like) About Me
February	Theme: Traditions Why We Have Valentine's Day Whether Others Celebrate Around the World
March	Theme: My Family Members and Responsibilities Definitions of Family Human and Animal Families

April	Theme: Beyond Home and School
	My Neighborhood
	My Community
	Who Helps
	Some Essential Community Jobs
May	Theme: The Environment
	Improving the Park
	Antilitter Campaign
	Recycling and What It Means
	Making a Safe and Clean Environment

Using appropriate themes, teachers need to write specific objectives that identify what it is they want the children to learn about each theme. This leads to the identification of procedures and essential materials to create a lesson or series of lessons, known as the unit.

To see how it works, let's brainstorm from the October theme and see the numbers and kinds of early childhood lessons that readily emerge. We can begin with something obvious—visual changes in nature during the fall season:

- Leaves—colors, dropping, crunchy, piled into nests
- Trees—stripped, sleeping, looking naked or dead, squirrel nests and old bird nests, caterpillars wearing heavy coats and moving slowly, bugs and spiders gone
- Ice on a pond
- Icicles forming around the house
- Heavier fur coats on cats, dogs, cows, and horses

As we think about fall in this way, a number of ideas for possible lessons come to mind. Imagine what would happen if three or four of us were sitting around creating and listing images of fall.

Let's play with the topic a bit more until the ideas really flow and we are comfortable with the task. A more challenging list to create might involve changes we see and feel and smell in fall:

- Wind making a fierce sound
- Cold, frosty mornings and evenings, too
- Visible breath
- Windowpane frost
- Car-window scrapers
- More darkness in the morning and late afternoon
- Numb fingers and toes
- Eyes squinting from the cold air
- The strange smell of leaves when they burn
- Everyone in heavy, bulky clothes
- Heads down most of the time
- Bodies bending when it's windy
- Nostrils "stuck" together

CHOOSING THE RIGHT TOPICS

In the identification of topics, common sense should serve as a guide. One instructor might select topics that seem appropriate for a particular group of young children at a given time. Another might base the selection in part on a personal interest or a suggestion from a parent. The children often mention topics and, in fact, listening and responding to student interests may assure an attentive audience. Topics can be developed around the ethnic composition of the group. On other occasions, contemporary events may dictate topics. Helping children better understand distance and time, while expanding their horizons, is sufficient justification in choosing a topic to be covered.

Selection of topics may be a team effort, with all of the school or center instructors choosing a series of social studies topics for the year. Instructors may identify topics to be commonly, simultaneously addressed. If a long-term program is designed, students are assured that the same general topics are presented again, when they are developmentally more able to handle them.

Topic selection may involve an instructor's unquestioning adherence to a list provided by a center director. A series of topics could even be drawn from the table of contents in a basic text. In any case, perhaps the most critical requirement in topic selection is that the teacher comprehend both the characteristics of the social studies and the developmental characteristics of young children.

Historically, a limited number of shopworn topics have been used for early childhood social studies programs. For the most part, they dealt with the home and family, thought to be the only themes appropriate for this age. Some eventual branching out into the neighborhood allowed community workers to be included. An effort was made to include some aspects of the communication and transportation topics.

Increased understanding of the capabilities of children has influenced change, but this has created new problems. As the world has grown smaller, global teaching has found its way into childhood education. Some text and curriculum developers have expanded the early childhood social studies topics to include comparative family study. Children are asked to try to understand their own social structures and then compare them to those of families far away or even living abroad. Spodek (1978) warned against this approach, unless quality audiovisuals, books, artifacts, and other materials are used and are sufficiently concrete to assure that the children can comprehend these distant and unknown families and their environments. Althouse (1981) issued a similar caution in reporting about a social studies unit covering Hawaii. Some young children indicated that "Hawaii is right up the street" and one said, "Everyone in Hawaii wears sarongs and dances all day" (p. 107).

To avoid creating confusion, the teacher might consider an approach through literature. We know that children respond well to stories about faraway places. They eagerly listen to the stories of "Grandma as a little girl in the old country," another faraway place. "The world" encompassed in these activities is one that young children can comprehend because reference points are everyday people and things. The point is that teachers' selection of social studies topics for young children and identification of their scope and sequence must be a thoughtful, cautious, intellectual process.

CREATING THE LESSON

When the topic has been selected, the instructor must begin to break the planning into small, manageable parts. It's a kind of task analysis with a listing of questions and concerns. From this list will come the basic organizers for teaching. The activity is exciting because it starts with only an idea and quickly develops into a lesson or teaching unit.

The kind of self-questioning that occurs at this point in the planning is suggested by these questions:

- Should this be a single lesson or a longer unit of study?
- What do I already know about this topic?
- What information do I have on hand?
- Where can I get more information?
- What kind of additional information do I actually need?
- Does the center have any helpful materials?
- Can any of my colleagues give assistance?
- Do I know an "expert" who can help me?
- Do the family profiles I collected at the beginning of the year indicate that I have an expert among my parents?
- Who is a likely community resource?
- How much information should I cover with young children?
- How can I meet majority needs and remember to personalize this teaching for children with special needs?
- What kinds of activities can I plan or construct to motivate the children and still provide diversity and maintain interest?
- How can I plan to be sure that all children enjoy some measure of success?
- How can I integrate this topic into the other content areas to provide increased meaning and greater understanding?
- What are my overall goals in teaching this topic?
- How do I determine objectives?
- How do I evaluate the children's learning?
- How do I evaluate my own planning and teaching?

Many of the questions provide their own answers as the process of writing the lesson plan unfolds. The lesson plan serves as a kind of recipe or road map for the instructor. It is an organized set of steps that will be undertaken to reach a particular objective. The strength of the lesson itself depends on the thorough development of the plan and the quality of delivery. The lesson plan is comprised

of several sections. Each has specific information requirements. Most plans follow
the basic outline that follows.

LESSON PLAN COMPONENTS

Goals   These are the objectives for the lesson, stated in broad and general,
nonspecific terms.

Prerequisite Skills   Before they attempt this lesson, what skills or knowledge
must children possess?

Objectives   These are the behavioral or performance terms that describe children's behavior or identify a change that is expected because of the lesson—
that is, the kind of learning that is likely to occur. These should demonstrate
changes that can be observed or measured in some way. Objectives are written
for the children and identify what they are to achieve.

Materials   These are the books, equipment, charts, maps, and all materials
necessary for teaching and participating in this lesson. Often two sets are
needed: materials used for and with the children and resources or references
used in preparation by the instructor.

Procedures   The lesson introduction should be motivating to students. The
procedures should include a brief description of the strategies, steps, and activities to be used to develop learning. These may include films, pictures,
games, speakers, and even field trips.

  The procedures are written for the instructor and are the guide to the
actual teaching. Each of the procedures should be timed to provide an esti-
mate for the entire lesson.

  The lesson itself ends with a summary and an activity that brings closure.

Evaluation   The evaluation consists of descriptions of (a) any procedures, formal or informal, that will be used to assess children's attainment or achievement of the objective(s) and (b) the teacher's assessment of success in motivating children, planning, implementing, and in determining the appropriateness
of the lesson. Teacher evaluation should include strengths and weaknesses of
the lesson.

  Provision should be made for reteaching the lesson or organizing the
information in a new way for those students who failed to achieve the objectives. For example, the lesson may have been too abstract for several students,
who may need a set of different experiences built on more concrete materials.

A lesson is ordinarily written for a group of children, but some modification may be necessary for individuals who are operating at different developmental levels and cannot progress with the lesson provided. Although this may require only limited restructuring of the lesson objective(s), it will certainly require different procedures. The following lesson, suitable for young children and designed for group presentation, includes opportunities for lesson adjustment to meet special needs.

LESSON PLAN: TEACHING ABOUT SIZE DIFFERENCES

Goals   Children will recognize that they and adults are different sizes.

Prerequisite Skills   Children need attending skills and some basic cutting and tracing capabilities.

Objectives   Children will identify size differences among children and adults by engaging in measuring and comparing activities.

Materials   Construction paper, felt markers, scissors, tape, and chart paper are needed.

Procedures   Children will trace a foot on a piece of construction paper. Each shape will be cut out and labeled with the child's name. Teacher and aide will also trace and cut foot shapes. All foot shapes will be displayed on the carpet. Children will be asked to classify the feet by size. Children will be asked to order by size (largest to smallest or smallest to largest). Children will be asked to make inferences about the shapes. ("Mindy has the smallest foot of all!") Children will be encouraged to make conclusions about the foot shapes.

Evaluation   From the children's conclusions, we will make a graph that reflects their findings. Footprints and body size will be compared to assess individual learning and progress. The information will be further tested by making familiar comparisons, such as the estimated foot sizes of various family members. Children will be encouraged to generalize their findings to other items in the center or home. For example: "Babies are little so they have little beds" or "My feet are small so my boots are smaller than my Mom's" or "My big brother wears a bigger shirt than I do." A checklist is kept of all the objectives each of the students has met. Children who have experienced difficulty will have the lesson presented again but with procedures that are matched to meet specific needs.

Personalizing and Individualizing

Personalizing every lesson to meet the needs of every child in the group is a formidable task. The committed teacher need not go to such dramatic ends. Each lesson can be altered or modified slightly to address a variety of student needs. Modification might simply be the addition of a procedure, the assignment of an independent activity, the use of more or different examples, or even the inclusion of a few more concrete objects. The following profiles of three children provide an opportunity to identify existing skills as well as specific needs and to relate them to the lesson on measuring and comparing.

PROFILE I

Marcie, aged 4 years and 7 months, is the oldest of three children. Her mother completed 10th grade and is 23 years old. The father is not present in the home. He left home a year ago to seek work and hasn't been seen or heard from since. The mother is very interested in her children but is overwhelmed by her personal problems and her many responsibilities. She has never worked at any job and doesn't feel that she has the skills to work at anything that will pay well enough to cover sitter or day-care costs. Marcie is an easy child to be near. She seems eager to learn. She is interested in everything that is presented and plants herself in the front row. Marcie is very verbal and has well-developed language skills. She has good recall skills about her work at the center and all the events that occur at home. She is "mothering" to everyone in the group— even me! Marcie can count to 10. Sometimes she ventures higher but never with certainty. She recognizes the basic colors and names them in several contexts. She knows the names of many wild and domestic animals because her mother reads to her from a book called *Animals Everywhere*. Marcie touches everything within reach. She always uses a gentle touch but seems to have to feel to confirm. Her listening skills are good. She can sit quietly and listen to directions. She demonstrates understanding of what I say because she follows through immediately. She is content to play alone but is a cooperative and accepted child in the peer group. She is a perpetual questioner and seems to be an explorer, too. She wants to find out whatever she can. Marcie has made tremendous gains in a few short months. In the measuring lesson, Marcie wanted to make lots of feet by herself. She cut them out and seriated smallest to largest. She watched me graphing the information and proceeded to make her own graph with another piece of paper. It was apparent this lesson was too simple for her and I need to devise a continuation lesson.

PROFILE II

Toby is 4 years and 5 months old and is one of two boys. His brother is age 8. His mother has a high-school diploma and works the night shift at a local truck stop. Toby's father has a drinking problem. He worked at a gas station off and on but the manager had to let him go when he began arriving at work drunk. This family is struggling to make it but Toby's mother is really too busy to be able to help him much at home. Toby is very overweight, a restless and lethargic child. He often seems sleepy but manages to participate in most of the activities. He doesn't seem particularly excited to be at the center but he doesn't complain either. Toby knows three colors: red, blue, and yellow. He calls all other colors by one of these three names. He can count to 10 aloud but does not recognize the numbers, or his name, or any letter of the alphabet. He never asks questions. He seems to lack curiosity and I have not yet found an activity that really excites him. He seems to go passively along with whatever is asked. I have not been able to identify any progress in the past 3 months. He seems to be the same child he was when he arrived. I am very worried about Toby. On the measuring lesson, Toby cut the tracing of his foot into dozens of tiny pieces, and before I knew it, he cut up his sock, too! He didn't participate in the ordering but did commend a friend for the good job he did. Toby spent most of the lesson just sitting, occasionally watching, always smiling when he caught someone's eye. I think the lesson was completely over his head. I need to reteach but at a level more suitable for his unique and limited capabilities.

PROFILE III

Mindy is 7 years old. She is an only child. She is bright, alert, questioning, and has had excellent school experiences up to this time. Both her parents are college educated and are employed. A live-in sitter cares for the home and this child while the parents are at work. Her parents travel in the summer, taking her with them, so she has seen much of the country. Mindy has been read to and was a reader herself from age 5.

Her language is developed well beyond her years. Her school work reflects her interest in learning. She hasn't a favorite subject but neither does she indicate a dislike for any aspect of school. She is a healthy, comfortable, and confident little student. She is eager to please her parents and teachers. Mindy is a kind child in her interactions with others. She extends friendship to the other children in the group. She often helps them with their work and is eager to loan a crayon or pencil. Her peers respond well to her and have awarded her a leadership position. Mindy has one problem area. She overreacts to her occasional errors because she expects perfection. These moments may end in tears or a minor temper tantrum. Aside from that, she is a normal child in every way. This lesson was far too easy for Mindy. I am thinking that it should be extended to do two things: encourage her to work on these concepts independently and allow personal exploration at greater depth. I should also provide her an opportunity to be a peer tutor to others who need review. Some minor adjustments should make both possible.

The lesson can be more appropriate and meaningful to all three children.

To experience the "feel" of matching a lesson to a child, identify the individual needs of each child by rereading the profile carefully. Assess the child's capabilities and needs. Use the lesson as the teaching foundation from which to alter the objectives, add or subtract some, shift the sequence of events, or simply reteach on a one-to-one basis (see Figure 7–1). Structure each of the procedures to fit the most appropriate strategy, based upon the needs of the child, the content of the lesson, and the desired outcome. Recall that the social exploration model is the natural starting point for young learners; the experiential model emphasizes the development of process skills in children; and the discovery approach assumes that learners are more experienced and can engage in acquiring more concepts.

COMMERCIAL LESSONS AND UNITS

Commercially prepared lessons and units are readily available, but they require careful use and a personalizing touch. For example, these materials often consist mostly of pencil-and-paper tasks. This signals the need for some modification. Pencil-and-paper tasks presume quiet sitting for long periods of time. The learning activities may rely primarily on reading of pictures or print, then coloring, filling in the blanks, or matching. These are not the best methods for teaching young children. Therefore, use of "canned" materials must be carefully balanced with

FIGURE 7–1
Organized lessons can include many materials and creative activity.

the selection of more active and varied forms of learning. Further, commercial materials are designed with the "average" child in mind. This means that the lessons must be adjusted to meet the individual needs of the children. The materials are often designed with tear-out sheets that make them consumable and costly.

Regardless of the materials chosen, teaching effectively requires a conscientious teacher who is willing and able to personalize for the interests, capabilities, and needs of all the students.

THE LEARNING STATION

The lesson plan can be delivered by the teacher overtly engaged in the teaching process; that is, the teacher is one who develops, presents, guides, questions, prompts, encourages, and assesses the lesson with active responsibilities from start to finish. However, the teacher can carefully construct the lesson in such a way that the students are asked to be more responsible for their learning. The learning station is simply the lesson plan developed for presentation and use in a different way. It still requires planning, organization, and monitoring by the teacher. But the actual implementation is the responsibility of each participating student.

Following the same elements of a lesson, the teacher must organize all materials essential to the lesson. They must be assembled in a prominent place in the classroom or center as a "study game." The station must be visually appealing so that it invites children to participate. Posters or pictures should accompany the station. Perhaps an interactive bulletin board will be a component. Certainly the reasons for participating (the objectives) must be evident. The directions for use must be clearly stated in rebus form, in print, or on cassette tape. The activities should be numbered to assure accurate and independent progression through the procedures to the achievement of the objectives.

A child can be trained to serve as a peer tutor, or helper, for each station. This form of teaching encourages independence while it frees the teacher to conduct other lessons that do require active teacher involvement. To test whether the station has been successfully designed, the teacher can ask herself these questions:

- Do the children select this center out of interest?
- Have I provided several different independent activities?
- Can the children proceed independently or at least with the help of the peer tutor?
- Are the directions simple and clear enough for the majority of students to follow?
- Have I built a hierarchical sequence into the activities?
- Is there an easy way to keep track of children who have used the station?
- Have I accounted for the children's learning?

- Could I make the station more durable or more appealing?
- Do I need to revise or extend any of the activities?

THE TEACHING UNIT

In many instances, the lesson that was so carefully designed has become too long for completion in one session. Occasionally lessons will extend to 2 or 3 days before a comfortable point of closure is reached. However, the teaching unit extends even beyond this. The unit is designed from the start with the expectation that it will be a series of lessons, taught over time, and developed around a particular theme. It will be broader, deeper, and more diverse than a single lesson can be. It will provide many more opportunities for integration into the total curriculum. Lessons are likely to encompass art, music, physical education, the language arts, and all the possible subject areas. This is done to involve and sustain more children through their areas of personal interest and individual skills. A unit might be likened to a chapter in a textbook because the goals are often global in nature. Several concepts will be taught, a variety of activities are planned, and the extended time is essential because of objectives built on one another.

The ideas for a unit are all around us. Current events of a national nature (the space shuttle disaster) or a regional or local happening (a devastating flood or the state fair) may prompt the development of a unit. Special skills or interests of the teacher or the group itself (such as the teacher's recent trip to southern Italy or the presence of several Asian children in the classroom) may provide motivation for developing a unit. The simple decision by the teacher that a text does not or cannot approach a topic in a way that will meet student needs may be adequate reason to write a unit.

Once the topic has been selected, the preparation period begins. The teacher cannot know all there is to know about a given subject and must engage in research. That process often leads to the collection of too much information, and so a careful sifting and sorting must occur. The essential information is extracted and the process of writing a unit begins. This might involve one teacher or a team. A brainstorming session could surely include children asked to share ideas and questions to be answered by the unit. At this point, a simple outline might prove helpful to keep the task from appearing too burdensome:

The Teaching Unit Outline
Title _____
  I. Topic
  II. Overview (what is to be taught and rationale statement)
  III. Objectives
  IV. Content (material to be covered and questions to be answered)
  V. Activities and Procedures
  VI. Evaluation (teacher and students)
  VII. Materials and Resources (for teacher and students)

This simplified unit outline will assure that the teacher can easily organize a series of lessons into a meaningful whole.

SUMMARY

Effective teaching cannot occur without training, knowledge, commitment, and a desire to improve the lives of children, but none of this makes any difference if there isn't a system for the organization of information. Teaching and learning programs—whether designed for the year, the month, each day, or even for the moment—must be organized into a usable framework to meet the needs of children at their various developmental levels. This chapter has provided a variety of ways in which teaching can be organized in manageable ways to achieve meaningful results.

REFERENCES

ALTHOUSE, R. (1981). *The young child: Learning with understanding.* New York: Teachers College Press.

DAY, B. (1983). *Early childhood education: Creative learning activities* (2nd ed.). New York: Macmillan.

DECKER, C. A., & DECKER, J. R. (1980). *Planning and administering early childhood programs* (2nd ed.). Columbus, OH: Merrill.

FROMBERG, D. P. (1977). *Early childhood education: A perceptual models curriculum.* New York: Wiley.

HESS, D. J., & CROFT, R. (1980). *An activities handbook for teachers of young children* (3rd ed.). Boston: Houghton Mifflin.

SPODEK, B. (1978). *Teaching in the early years* (2nd ed.). Englewood Cliffs, NJ: Prentice-Hall.

8

EVALUATING AND
MEETING CHILDREN'S
NEEDS

When students hear the word "evaluation," what do they usually think of? Probably "grades," "passing or failing," and "tests" come to mind, carrying with them connotations of fear, nervousness, and threat. Learning and evaluation are closely tied together. Unfortunately, many people see this tie as a negative one. Evaluation should be positive. Its goal is to help adults meet children's needs—a most positive role. In this book evaluation is defined as the process of making value judgments based on behavioral information about the effectiveness of a program in meeting the needs of children enrolled (Cook, Tessier, & Armbruster, 1987). The evaluation process should tell us:

- What children's needs are
- How well we have met children's needs
- What we can change so that we will be better able to meet their needs

Evaluation should help adults create a nurturing environment, fostering children's self-concept and sense of understanding of the social world. The evaluation process in the social studies should do the following:

- Have a specific purpose
- Measure what it intends to measure (have validity)
- Be appropriate to unit or course objectives
- Match children's characteristics
- Be continuous as children work toward mastering objectives

As the evaluation process is carried out, it can have two general purposes. First, it can be formative in nature. Formative evaluation is ongoing and checks on how well students are doing while an activity or a unit is in progress. As a result of formative evaluation, a teacher may find that a need exists for more application activities or for review. Alternatively, the teacher may find that children are comfortable with the activity and will not need additional time or activities. Second, it can be summative. In summative evaluation children's progress is examined at the end of an activity, a unit, or some other portion of the program to determine the level at which children have learned processes and/or content they have worked with. The summative evaluation determines whether they should progress to the next portion of the program.

The evaluation process is accomplished through assessment. Assessment is either a test or an observation that determines a child's strengths or weaknesses in a particular area (Cook et al., 1987).

TYPES OF ASSESSMENT FOR EVALUATING WHETHER OBJECTIVES HAVE BEEN ACHIEVED

Both formal and informal means can be used to evaluate. Formal means include teacher-made and standardized tests. These tests can include multiple-choice items, matching items, true/false items, fill-in-the-blank items, or short essays. With young children formal tests are difficult to construct and are not heavily used. Informal evaluation includes observation, interviews, the collection of work samples, group discussion, and performance testing. The various kinds of formal and informal evaluation can be considered in regard to whether they will measure objectives related to (a) content, (b) motor or simple skills, and (c) the affective area (see Table 8–1).

Evaluating Children's Abilities

Before teaching begins, adults should have a clear understanding of what children's abilities are. This does not mean the content children know but rather their ability to utilize various thinking processes. Chapter 3 describes the use of different models of teaching, based first on children's cognitive developmental level and then on their familiarity with the content under study. Teachers must determine the level of development present among their students and the children's familiarity with an area when they structure their objectives and select a teaching model. The evaluation process helps teachers to make this decision. In determining a child's cognitive level of development, Ginsburg and Opper (1979), Levin (1983), and Flavell (1977) should be helpful. These authors identify specific tasks developed originally by Jean Piaget that children may be given as a means of identifying their cognitive developmental level. This is a type of performance testing. Among the areas that Piagetian cognitive developmental tasks could be used to assess are these:

- Perspective
- Multiple classification

TABLE 8–1
Types of assessment that can be used to evaluate objectives

	Types of Objectives		
Types of Test Items	**Content**	**Motor or Simple Skill**	**Affective**
Formal:			
Multiple choice	X		
Matching	X		
True/false	X		
Fill in blanks	X		
Short essay		X	X
Informal:			
Observation			
Anecdotal records		X	X
Checklists	X	X	X
Interviews	X	X	X
Work samples	X	X	X
Group discussion	X		X
Performance testing	X	X	X

Note. X indicates types of objectives in social studies that can be evaluated using various forms of assessment.

- Moral reasoning
- Class inclusion
- Conservation of substance
- One-to-one correspondence
- Successive states versus transformations
- Conservation of weight
- Perception of liquid level
- Seriation

Other areas can be examined to fill out the portrait of each child's development. Later chapters in this book relating to specific social studies areas delineate strategies through which children's development in a particular area can be ascertained. Among them are chapter 10 (social and moral development), chapter 11 (development of a sense of time), and chapter 12 (spatial development).

The following example of a Piagetian task relates to multiple classification:

Place ten shapes (circle, triangle, rectangle, square, oval) of two colors, red and blue, in front of a child. Ask the child to put all the shapes that go together in one pile and all the others in another. How does the child group the shapes (usually by color)? Talk with the child about how the groups were formed. Then ask the child to mix up the shapes and group them again but in a different way. The second grouping is likely to be by shape. Some children may start to group one way then in the middle of doing this will change their approach. They are confused about the criteria they are using. This task requires children to realize there is more than one way to group things—multiple classification ability. Typically four- and five-year-old children are able to do this fairly well. (Sund, 1976, p. 122)

Levin (1983) and Flavell (1977) describe difficulties inherent in the traditional cognitive development evaluation tasks, like the one just given, that have been identified by researchers such as Donaldson (1978). Although difficulties exist in using the traditional tasks, as Levin (1983, pp. 185–186) suggests, Piaget's view "of an active mind, built to move ahead as long as opportunities to interact with the environment are present," is evidently widely accepted. Teachers need to identify the abilities and limitations of this mind.

This discussion has focused on children's cognitive developmental abilities. Other abilities, particularly social abilities, are also important. These abilities may best be evaluated by relatively informal means as described in the next section and in chapter 10, although standardized tests are available to determine children's development in areas such as self-concept. Two such tests are the Children's Self-Social Constructs Test (CSSCT) for ages 3 to 8, produced by Virginia Research Associates, Ltd. in Charlottesville, Virginia, and the Self-Concept and Motivation Inventory, with preschool and primary grades forms available from Person-O-Metrics in Dearborn Heights, Michigan. Goodwin and Driscoll (1980) is a good resource for identifying cognitive, psychomotor, and affective measurement instruments for use in early childhood programs.

Informal Evaluation

Informal evaluation occurs when adults collect information in a structured manner that does not involve direct testing of children. The form of the evaluation is well-organized and thought out beforehand, but the evaluation situation is tailored to the individual child and the progress of the situation is generally not highly structured nor easily predictable (see Figure 8–1, p. 96).

Observation.   Teacher observation of children is probably the most frequently used form of evaluation. Teachers closely observe children throughout the day, often for very short time periods. This spontaneous observation typically is not recorded. It gives the teacher information regarding how an activity is going and how a particular child is responding to it.

More structured observation is frequently used. A teacher may observe specific children at repeated intervals. This usually happens when a teacher has a concern about a child's social abilities or attention span. The teacher systematically observing a child should keep a record. With the constant interruptions and complexity of classroom activities, a teacher should not rely on memory; too often a single incident is remembered because it is outstanding in some way even though it is not typical of a child's behavior. The *anecdotal record* is frequently used for recording a child's behavior. This record is simple, listing the child's name, the date, and the time of day a behavior occurred. The teacher describes the behavior as objectively as possible without drawing any conclusions. This is an example:

RECORD 1

Name:
Marisa

Date:
11/13   Time: *2:15*

Event:
Marisa entered the block area where Jaime and Ellen were building a block tower. She did not speak to them. She slowly walked over to them, sat down on the floor next to Ellen, silently picked up a block, and offered it to Ellen. Ellen did not take the block. Marisa picked up another block and offered it to Ellen. Ellen did not take the block but kept on adding others to the tower. After 2 or 3 minutes Marisa hit Ellen with the second block she had offered her.

RECORD 2

Date:
11/15   Time: *1:30*

Event:
Marisa entered the block area where Jaime and Ellen were building a block building. She said, "Hello, I want to play with you." She sat down next to Ellen. Marisa said, "I want to play with you." Ellen said, "OK." Ellen handed Marisa a block and said, "You can play with this block, the rest are mine." Marisa said "OK" and played with that block. After about 5 minutes she got up and left the block area, dropping her block in Ellen's lap.

FIGURE 8-1
Informal assessment: "Can you identify an item by touch?"

The teacher has recorded two of Marisa's attempts to play with Jaime and Ellen in the block center. The records are objective and do not make inferences regarding the behaviors of any of the children involved. The teacher has mentioned important facts, such as: who was involved, what the setting was, the time interval during which the event occurred, and what happened. If the teacher keeps recording Marisa's efforts to enter into block play with Ellen and Jaime, she should acquire enough information to make appropriate inferences regarding the children's interactions. These inferences, based on objective information, should enable the teacher to determine whether a problem does exist, whether the children are working it out, whether the teacher should interfere, and if so, what form the interference should take.

Checklists are often used to guide observation. These are lists of significant, important behaviors. Checklists structure the observation because the teacher acquires specific pieces of information and is not recording other items. Checklists allow the teacher to observe more children because observation is generally shorter and less intensive. An example of a checklist is given in Table 8-2.

TABLE 8–2
Globe study checklist

Feature Identified	Name		
	Ann	Tomas	Jim
1. Colors on globe	x	x	x
2. Ball shape of globe	x	x	x
3. Globe as a model of earth	x	x	x
4. Water and land	x	x	x
5. Differences in size of land masses	x	x	
6. Circle symbol as a city	x		

This checklist enables the teacher to record information as the children work through activities. It narrows the information to a specific area. The teacher is able to record a lot of information for several children quickly. However, the information recorded does not reflect the range or depth that can be recorded using an anecdotal record. Each method of collecting information has positive attributes and limitations. The method should be chosen to fit evaluation needs. Is a lot of detailed information needed on a child? Or is specific information needed for several children? Richarz (1980) and Beaty (1986) are helpful guides to observation methods and the use of instruments such as checklists.

Interviews.   Interviews are structured evaluation forms that have some similarity to anecdotal records but that are affected by the adult's conversation with the child. A useful interview is one on one, that is, one child talking with one adult. The adult should have a list of prepared questions or topics to guide the interview. Every effort should be made to follow the list; otherwise, the interview may wander and needed information will not be collected. An example follows of an interview list using a picture of an adult calling out to two children, who are both pulling at a toy:

1. What do you think is happening in this picture?
2. What do you think is going to happen next?
3. How will it end?
4. How does the adult feel?
5. How do the girl and boy feel?
6. Do you think they are learning anything? (if yes) What do you think they are learning?

The adult should not make comments or offer information unless it is necessary to restate or otherwise clarify a question that has been asked. The adult's role is that of a good listener. When the child's comments wander, the role becomes that of a pleasant guide. Information regarding the child's comments can be written down, tape-recorded, or checked off on a checklist. More accurate information is recorded if it is done immediately after the child has responded rather than after the interview is over. The recording method should be chosen to match the children's experience and to be nonthreatening. A tape-recorded interview might be played back to the child at intervals during the interview or at the end of the interview. Children often enjoy listening to these tapes. Interviews with young children should be informal, pleasant, and relaxed. If a child does not feel like talking, it's best to stop and try again another day. Some topics might best be described by drawing a response, by dancing it out, or by acting it out. Interviews often provide lots of information. The adult should review notes of the interview and summarize them soon afterward. Otherwise, the volume of information builds up and becomes overwhelming.

Work Samples. Children's work should be collected on a regular basis. Teachers often keep work samples in a folder. These samples include artwork, worksheets, language experience stories, and other items produced by children. These should be collected to reflect various areas of children's work. If possible, at least one sample should be collected weekly. Young children will often balk at letting the teacher keep the work sample. They will want to take it home with them. One strategy that can be used is "borrowing"—telling the child you will borrow the work for just a day and then return it to him. A photocopy of the work can be made to keep. Or a child may allow the teacher to borrow the work eventually for longer and longer periods. Another strategy is putting the work together in a special book that will be presented to the child's parents at the end of the school year. The work will be "a special present we are making" that the child will help to assemble each time a piece of work is kept. After a while the teacher can examine the work and look for changes in the amount and kind of detail expressed, attitudes expressed, vocabulary, expression of concepts, and general ability to express ideas. Because work samples offer much varied information, the teacher should list specific items to be identified. This list will focus the examination of the work samples.

Group Discussion. Much time is spent in group discussion during social studies activities. All three models of teaching have a focus on interaction between people. Group discussion is one form of such interaction, offering opportunities for evaluating learning activities and social behaviors. Extensive notes of children's responses are not taken by the teacher. Charting of responses may occur, for example, when children vote on their choice for a field trip site. Group discussion often occurs in early childhood classrooms during "circle time." Children can evaluate work periods, work groups, field trips, study skills, and information-gathering activities. As children evaluate changes in practice, work groups or other factors can be proposed and plans can be made to experiment with these changes. The teacher must encourage the children to summarize and, as appropriate, review planned strategies for carrying out work to be done.

Performance Testing. Earlier chapters (5 and 6) described performance testing in conjunction with the experiential and concept attainment models of teaching.

In performance testing, children are asked to perform a skill they have learned or to apply a concept in a new situation. Performance testing is often concrete and manipulative. An example of a performance test might occur when children draw a map of their classroom and identify main paths of movement through the room, then draw a second map after the room has been rearranged, and successfully identify the new paths of movement resulting from the room's rearrangement.

Formal Evaluation

Teacher-Made Tests. Earlier chapters (5 and 6) described evaluation using teacher-made tests for the experiential and concept attainment models. The tests used production and/or recognition items. Teacher-made tests can be performance assessment tests that are either manipulative or paper and pencil. When paper-and-pencil tests are constructed, multiple-choice, matching, true/false, fill-in-the-blanks, or short essay items can be used. With very young children, short essay tests are best given through asking the children to dictate language experience stories related to social studies activities the children have been engaging in. Many primary-grades children can write and illustrate short essays related to social studies activities. The other types of items must be carefully constructed and can focus on either production or recognition. Good resources for information on constructing test items are Gronlund (1982); Bloom, Madaus, and Hastings (1981); and TenBrink (1982). All tests developed should be criterion referenced; that is, they should measure the child's performance against himself. Has the child met the objective of the activity or unit? Criterion-referenced tests do not measure the child against other children but against his own performance prior to the activity or unit.

Standardized Tests. Standardized tests are not commonly used in early childhood social studies. However, many general achievement tests do have social studies items. Among these tests are the Iowa Every-Pupil Test of Basic Skills (Houghton Mifflin), Metropolitan Achievement Tests (Harcourt Brace Jovanovich), Tests of Basic Experiences—Social Studies (McGraw-Hill), and SRA Achievement Series (Science Research Associates). Standardized tests enable teachers to compare a child's performance with the performance of other children who are the same age. This is called norm-referenced testing, in contrast to the criterion-referenced testing mentioned earlier. Some states also test children using tests they have developed that match statewide objectives or learning outcomes for social studies. Standardized tests usually are given late in the school year as a form of summative evaluation. They summarize a child's achievement and are often used in planning the child's placement during the following school year. Often these tests are also used to evaluate how well a school has taught social studies in comparison to other schools in the school system or state. Goodwin and Driscoll (1980) discuss sources for information on standardized tests, including Buros' *Mental Measurements Yearbooks* and *Tests in Print*, both of which are usually available in college and university libraries as well as some large public libraries.

Both informal and formal testing can be used to evaluate the abilities and needs of children, to evaluate social studies instruction, and to evaluate the social studies curriculum (see Figure 8–2).

EVALUATING CHILDREN WITH SPECIAL NEEDS

Children in Crisis

Children who have experienced serious illness, a death in their family, a divorce, emotional stress, or abuse may respond best to informal evaluation methods. Formal testing may place additional stress on them, particularly in the case of standardized tests, which usually have time limits and ask questions in an unfamiliar manner. These children often are most in need of continuous evaluation in order to adapt the program to their needs. Informal evaluation methods place little additional stress on the child. They are useful with both the child who has withdrawn and the one who is aggressive as a result of the crisis experienced. Other children demonstrate few effects of a crisis but may need to be evaluated

FIGURE 8–2
Records of children's progress can be kept in many ways.

to make sure they are coping well with their situation. These children may regress in behavior and in abilities. They may demonstrate immature responses in social and academic situations. Often, if every effort is made to relieve their stress, they will return to age-appropriate responses after an adjustment period of weeks or months. Continuous, nonintrusive evaluation should be maintained so that support is provided to the child when it is needed.

Multicultural Factors

In evaluating children, developing an understanding of their cultural background is important. Some cultures are less concerned than is mainstream North American culture with being the "best." Some cultures are more concerned with children's social development than with their academic development. Some prefer children to be quiet and unquestioning in contrast to being talkative and curious. Some encourage children to be assertive and boastful. Some place high value on seatwork and little value on group discussion of a problem.

Because of the many cultural backgrounds among North Americans, all the variations just described are found along with many others. Each teacher has his own version of what is appropriate social behavior and of what responses children can be expected to make. These personal versions differ between teachers, and between teacher and parent, and bias our evaluation of children. Children bring their culture to school with them. Teachers must avoid evaluating the culture instead of the child. Many tests, both standardized and teacher-made, reflect mainstream North American culture. These tests will not correctly evaluate children who come from a different cultural background. Informal testing may be more accurate. However, informal evaluation can reflect the teacher's own biases, because it is less rigorously constructed.

Teachers must make a strong effort to learn about their students' cultural backgrounds. This understanding will help them to evaluate children, instructional methods, and curriculum appropriately. Chapter 9 discusses multicultural factors extensively.

Children With Handicaps

Children with many different types of handicaps participate in the social studies program. These handicaps can include mental retardation, visual impairment, hearing impairment, speech problems, language development delay, behavior disorders, physical disability, and learning disabilities. Cook, Tessier, and Armbruster (1987) provide an excellent discussion of handicapped young children and of adapting curriculum and evaluation procedures for them. Herlihy and Herlihy (1980) have described mainstreaming children with handicaps in the social studies. Public Law 94–142 requires that all children have access to a free and appropriate education in the least restrictive environment. The least restrictive environment for many children with handicapping conditions is the regular public school classroom. Today many of these special-needs children are found in the regular classroom.

Many handicapped children do well in school and need relatively minor changes in the evaluation program. A visually impaired child usually can respond to a teacher-made test if the test is audiotaped and the child's response is also taped. A hearing-impaired child or one with a speech problem may be able to draw or write out responses. Many children with handicaps must work hard to focus their attention on the task at hand. Hearing-impaired children work very hard to watch a speaker's mouth and hands. The effort handicapped children must put in to compensate for their handicapping condition is tiring. As a result, they are worn out much more quickly than are other children. Their attention span is generally shorter because of fatigue. When they are tired, they may not respond or may exhibit nervous, highly active behavior. Evaluation methods need to take the fatigue factor into account. Informal evaluation methods are often able to account for handicapped children's special needs and their quicker fatigue. Formal evaluation methods will have to be adapted to their needs and broken into smaller sections that do not tire children.

The regular teacher needs to work closely with special education personnel. Their advice and help will be needed in evaluating children and in adapting curricula and evaluation procedures to their needs. All children who are receiving special education services will have an IEP, an Individualized Educational Program, as required by public law 94–142. The IEP includes:

1. An evaluation of the child's present level of achievement
2. Long- and short-range goals for the child
3. Specific services that will be provided for the child
4. The child's level of participation in the regular school program
5. When the child's progress will be reevaluated

IEPs do not always specifically address social studies goals for the child. If not, the child's social studies program must consider the goals set forth in the IEP, and objectives must be developed that work toward those goals. Children's evaluation must be in terms of social studies objectives congruent with IEP goals. When children are evaluated, and the objectives and curricula of the social studies program developed, the effects of handicapping conditions must be considered. Reference texts such as those cited earlier should be used.

As a beginning point in evaluation and planning, an overview of the types of handicapping conditions follows.

Mental Retardation.   Children with mental retardation tend to exhibit immature behaviors; lag behind in development (the age at which they first crawled, said their first word, and so on); have a shorter attention span than their peers; become frustrated with a task more quickly than their peers; have poorer language skills; and often have difficulty in getting along socially with their peers. These children need short, concrete, manipulative tasks utilizing as many of their senses as possible. They need lots of opportunities to practice skills and to talk about what they are doing or the way they did something. Evaluation should not rely on their verbal, reading, and writing skills. Performance-based testing is often appropriate. Reinforcement and praise and patience should be part of teaching and evaluation.

Visual Impairment.   Children with major visual impairment are usually identified before a teacher receives them in the classroom. Children with minor impairments may not be identified; this is often the child who needs eyeglasses but the problem hasn't yet been identified. Some of these children will show no interest in a beautiful fall maple tree changing color across the street from the school because they see only a blur that far away. Or they may squint a lot, rub their eyes, tilt their head to one side, complain of headaches or nausea after close work, or have poor eye–hand coordination. These children should be referred for testing. Visually impaired children whose sight cannot be corrected to approximately normal vision with eyeglasses need some special considerations in learning activities and evaluation, although typically they are normal in every way except for their visual impairment. The classroom should be arranged so they can move freely without bumping into things. They should have verbal instruction and evaluation as much as possible. Maps and globes with raised contours and other learning aids that can be "felt" should be used. They should work in teams with other children and often be placed in a leadership position to encourage their participation. Praise and reinforcement are important. Finally, adults must not overprotect the visually impaired child; independence must be fostered and reasonable demands made.

Hearing Impairment.   Just as with visually impaired children, hearing-impaired children are usually normal in all respects except for hearing and sometimes language development. Hearing impairment is often less well-identified than is visual impairment. Hearing impairment may be mistaken for mental retardation if the child shows poor language development. Because the child does not hear language normally, he does not speak normally nor does he develop language at a normal rate. As with visual impairment, major problems are more likely to have been identified than minor problems. Hearing impairment should be suspected if a child has poor speech abilities; speaks very loudly or very softly; is reluctant to speak; doesn't respond when spoken to or says "what?" or turns his head toward the speaker; looks intently at the speaker's face; has a short attention span when spoken to but works well at visual and tactile tasks; or has earaches or pain in the head around the ear or down the neck. In teaching and evaluation activities, the teacher should seat the child so he can see others' faces, use visuals such as overhead transparencies, use sign language if the child uses it, and speak clearly in a normal voice. Key words and phrases in activities should be identified and written on the chalkboard or overhead projector if the child is a reader. The child should work in teams with a partner and should be encouraged to lead. Concrete, manipulative activities are important because they often present opportunities for the child to learn new vocabulary and to interact verbally with others.

Physical Handicaps. A wide range of physical handicaps are found among children. Generally, some impairment of motor skills is involved. This child will usually require learning aids prescribed by medical and special education personnel that overcome some of the child's motor limitations. Evaluation and teaching tasks should be structured to deemphasize the need for motor skills. When such skills are involved, tasks should be sequenced in short steps. Working with partners should occur. Reward and reinforcement are important. Independence should be encouraged.

Speech Problems/Language Development Delay. These handicaps can be associated with hearing and other handicaps, or they may occur alone. Children with speech and language problems are usually identified at an early age and benefit from working with speech/language therapists. The therapist will recommend procedures the teacher should use. With all children who have speech/language problems, the teacher should use normal, clear speech and should listen attentively when the child speaks. Evaluation procedures should deemphasize the need for speech.

Behavior Disorders. Children with behavior disorders are usually either overly aggressive or overly withdrawn in comparison to their peers. The cause of the disorder may be physical; for example, nervousness induced by allergies. Or it may be psychological; for example, a reaction to a family crisis. The child's behavior should be evaluated in comparison to that of his peers, because some neighborhoods or cultures may promote assertiveness, passivity, or other characteristics that to the teacher seem extreme. If the child is very different from the peer group, perhaps a behavior disorder does exist. Special education personnel will have to help in evaluating the child, determining the cause of the disorder, and planning procedures to help the child. In evaluating and teaching the child, the teacher will likely have to expect a short attention span, a low threshold of frustration, and a need for reinforcement and reward. The child will require emotional support and patience.

Learning Disabilities. These children have a wide range of learning problems. Special education personnel will have to identify the best learning and evaluation procedures to use. As a general rule, these children will need reinforcement, rewards, and a patient approach. Providing emotional support is important, because the children often are frustrated by their disability. Because many young children will mature out of their disability, they should not be pressured but helped to develop self-assuredness and self-respect.

Gifted Children

Gifted children are usually curious and creative. They will often provide creative responses to assessment procedures. On standardized tests and some teacher-made tests, these creative responses are marked wrong. In interviews these children often deviate from questions with creative responses, or they may delve much more deeply than do other children. Informal evaluation procedures should indicate gifted children's level of development and pace of growth. These children need to be encouraged, but their curiosity and creativity can be exhausting to teachers. Assessment procedures should encourage gifted children and be wary of rejecting novel responses.

FOCUSING ON CHILDREN'S SIMILARITIES RATHER THAN THEIR DIFFERENCES

Despite their differences, special children—the gifted, those with handicaps, and those whose family is in crisis—are more like other children than they are different. They should be viewed and evaluated as normal children who have special needs. All children, including those who are considered normal, need special consideration at times. Children with handicaps and gifted children need just a bit more special consideration than do others. But their needs for special consideration should not override their need to be treated first as a child and only then as a special child.

SUMMARY

Evaluation is a positive process helping teachers structure the learning environment to meet children's needs and develop their abilities. The first step in evaluation is to determine children's abilities as well as their limitations. Understanding of the children we work with makes it possible to plan an effective social studies program. Informal and formal methods can be used to evaluate the program, determining whether its objectives have been met. As children are evaluated, they must be approached in terms of their similarity to other children even when they have special needs that must be considered.

REFERENCES

BEATY, J. (1986). *Observing development of the young child.* Columbus, OH: Merrill.

BLOOM, B., MADAUS, G., & HASTINGS, J. (1981). *Evaluation to improve learning.* New York: McGraw-Hill.

COOK, R., TESSIER, A., & ARMBRUSTER, V. (1987). *Adapting early childhood curricula for children with special needs.* Columbus, OH: Merrill.

DONALDSON, M. (1978). *Children's minds.* London: Croom Helm.

FLAVELL, J. (1977). *Cognitive development.* Englewood Cliffs, NJ: Prentice-Hall.

GINSBURG, H., & OPPER, S. (1978). *Piaget's theory of intellectual development* (2nd ed.). Englewood Cliffs, NJ: Prentice-Hall.

GOODWIN, W., & DRISCOLL, L. (1980). *Handbook for measurement and evaluation in early childhood education.* San Francisco: Jossey-Bass.

GRONLUND, N. (1982). *Constructing achievement tests.* Englewood Cliffs, NJ: Prentice-Hall.

HERLIHY, J., & HERLIHY, M. (Eds.). (1980). *Mainstreaming in the social studies.* Washington, DC: National Council for the Social Studies.

LEVIN, G. (1983). *Child psychology.* Monterey, CA: Brooks/Cole.

RICHARZ, A. (1980). *Understanding children through observation.* St. Paul, MN: West.

SUND, R. (1976). *Piaget for educators.* Columbus, OH: Merrill.

TENBRINK, T. (1982). Evaluation. In J. Cooper (Ed.) *Teaching classroom skills* (2nd ed.) (pp. 363–403). Lexington, MA: Heath.

9

THE MULTICULTURAL LIFE OF THE CHILD

Theresa McCormick
Iowa State University

The young child's world is full of wonder and exploration. The child is learning not only about her body and environment but also about the similarities and differences among and between people. The child is forming attitudes toward people that will be influential throughout life. Thus, the question for early childhood educators is, How can we develop in children an appreciation and respect for *all* people, including themselves and their own families?

Starting with an understanding and appreciation of oneself is the basis for accepting others. The early childhood teacher starts where the child is—with her language, customs, traditions, and values—and builds on the growth of self-understanding and acceptance to promote respect and appreciation of others. Development of a positive self-concept is a necessary condition for the child to grow as a learner and to establish positive feelings about other people.

> By sharing cultural backgrounds such as: family customs, languages, foods, music, values, family relationships, lifestyles, cultural celebrations, and ethnic heritages—children develop a healthy acceptance to themselves and a positive awareness of others ("Bringing Our Worlds Together," 1986, p. 20).

LANGUAGE DIFFERENCES

A primary means of enhancing the development of children's self-concept is through respecting and being aware of their home language or dialect and using this knowledge in teaching. Goodman has noted that, in the United States, bilingualism in children is often thought of as handicapping and undesirable (1970,

p. 21). Because of this attitude, Goodman believes that bilingual children are at a disadvantage in our schools.

The teacher must understand that language is at the very heart of cultural identity; that the bilingual child may have intellectual advantages and greater conceptual flexibility than the monolingual child (Ramirez & Castaneda, 1974). However, the teacher should also be aware that a bilingual child may have differing levels of competence in the two languages and thus "may be able to do different things with each language," but may not have developed either one to the degree that a same-aged monolingual child has (Gingras, 1983, p. 71). Research indicates that, in general, a child will be more likely to attain native-like fluency in a second language when exposure to it occurs early. However, current research isn't conclusive in regard to whether very early bilingualism is desirable. Evidence indicates that children should begin learning a second language before puberty but is unclear about how early this should be (Gingras, 1983, p. 73).

Although a teacher may be saying the "right" words to a child, her nonverbal cues (gestures, facial expressions, intonation, and so on) may convey a totally different message. Especially with limited or non-English-speaking children, the teacher must be aware of the importance of nonverbal nuances, for these are children's main way of absorbing meaning from an otherwise unintelligible jumble of words. When the school atmosphere is nonthreatening and relaxed, both non-English-speaking children and the teacher will function best (Neugebauer, 1987, p. 50).

CULTURAL DIFFERENCES

Cultural difference as well as language difference may place a child at a disadvantage in school. Native American children, taught at home to be more cooperative than competitive, may refrain from participating in classroom games in which there is a winner and a loser. Williams and Williams (1979) reveal, in their study of childrearing practices in three minority subcultures (Mexican-American, Native American, and African-American), that cultural values instilled in the home often are in direct opposition to Anglo values promoted in most public schools. For example, classroom conflicts may result from different orientations to time when a Mexican-American child has a present-time orientation, and the teacher is future oriented.

Concerning cultural value differences between African-American homes and Anglo-dominant schools, Gay (1975) says many black children's problems in school stem not so much from limited cognitive abilities as from conflicting orientations as to the conditions and attitudes most appropriate for learning, as well as the difficulties in making the transition from the frames of reference and ways of behaving of the home to those of the school (p. 30). Gay (1975) suggests that black children may find schools prefer values that are different from those that are promoted by the home. For example, African-American culture may emphasize spontaneity more than do schools. Hale has considered the different cultures children bring with them to school and notes that early childhood educators commonly accept that preschool environments should be as homelike as possible and therefore they try to create a learning environment that complements the culture of the child's home (1982, p. 159).

PHYSICAL DIFFERENCE

Another difference that is often a stigma and a barrier to achievement and personal growth for some children is race. James A. Banks (1981) notes that we need to develop educational programs and policies that are designed to make students more accepting of cultural differences and also deal seriously with problems caused by racial differences. Otherwise, we will not solve our most basic intergroup problems (p. 185).

> Carol observed thoughtfully: "See how colored my hands are." Herman commented, "My mother's brown skinned." Stefan said: "My mother's *that* white." ...Thomas studied the children around him and said: "There are two white children here and all the rest are colored." (Goodman, 1970, p. 27)

These comments, recorded by Goodman in racially integrated New England nursery schools, illustrate that children are very aware of racial attributes in themselves and in others at an early age. Goodman found that young children not only make racial classifications of such things as degree of lightness or darkness in skin color and hair form, but also evaluate these differences. One little black girl in Goodman's study (1952) said, "Black people—I hate 'em!" And as she picked up a brown doll, the girl said, "This one, I'm holding, it just gets on my nerves." Goodman concluded, "The social definition of the child's racial identity is more important than his *actual* color or racial features" (p. 176).

"The more things change, the more they stay the same" seems to epitomize the situation in which schools did very little over 35 years ago in Goodman's research to stimulate racial awareness and learning in children, and they do very little now. Goodman (1952) observed the following:

> Racial identity is deliberately and consistently ignored; racial differences are dealt with by behaving as though they did not exist. This is the official policy, and departures are rare, private (as in conversations between teachers), or instigated by the parents or the children themselves ... it is believed to be sound pedagogy to ignore sex talk, "cuss words," and other four-year-old provocations, so why not race talk too....
>
> So the racial hush-hush hovering over the nursery school works both to create a repressive atmosphere and to allow the prolongation of incidents which might otherwise be "nipped in the bud." The repressive atmosphere reduces the possibilities for racial learning at school while the other half of the policy works to increase the possibilities. (pp. 134–135)

The teacher or parent who has clear and honest "pictures" about race in her own mind can more easily find ways of spontaneously and simply providing effective guidance for the young child. Such efforts should be attuned to children's interests, personalities, and experiences. The adult might handle Andrea or Steve's question "Why are those people black?" in a manner similar to this:

Why are they black? Can you think of anyone who is *really* black as this piece of construction paper? Let's look again. No? You're right, the people you were wondering about are not really black. But, what color are they then? Brown? Yes, but there are lots of browns, aren't there? Some people are dark brown like daddy's shoes or lighter brown like the chocolate milk shake you had yesterday. Some are very light brown, as light as mommy's coffee when she puts more cream in it. Look, you and I aren't exactly the same color, are we? Right! See the differences? People just grow naturally with different colors of skin. Some have lots of brown and some have very little. There are people like the Wongs down the street, who have a little pink and yellow mixed in with the brown. All these different shades of brown, pink, and yellow aren't so important except that they make people more interesting than if they all were the same as this tan wall. Now, let's look at each other again. We are all colored a bit differently but we are also alike in lots of ways. What are some of the ways in which we are alike? That's right, we all have two eyes. What else? Yes, we all have socks on. What else? Yes, everybody in class seems pretty happy today. And so on.

The value in these kinds of informal discussions is that Andrea and Steve are getting the idea that skin color is a topic that can be talked about openly and rationally instead of being hushed up. However, the discussion should also lead into similarities. Similarities should be stressed as more critical in human relationships than differences (see Figure 9–1). If possible, children should be encouraged to consider similarities in feelings as well as in physical aspects.

LEARNING STYLE

Educators must be aware of differences in cognitive or learning style in order to effectively meet the needs of children from diverse backgrounds. Learning style refers to the child's characteristic pattern or strategy for acquiring and processing information. According to the National Task Force on Learning Style and Brain Behavior, learning style "is the composite of characteristic cognitive, affective, and physiological behaviors that serve as relatively stable indicators of how a learner perceives, interacts with, and responds to the learning environment" (Keefe & Languis, 1983, p. 1). Some children demonstrate an analytic orientation toward information processing that is related to the notion of field independence. Others demonstrate a relational (or global) approach that is linked to field dependence (Kagan, Moss, & Sigel, 1963).

Field independence–dependence is one of the most thoroughly researched dimensions of learning style. Rooted in the psychological research of the late 1940s on distinctive perceptual characteristics of people, field independent–dependent concepts are widely recognized for their significance in educational settings (Witkin, Moore, Goodenough, & Cox, 1977). The fact that

FIGURE 9–1
We all like a party.

individuals vary greatly in their abilities to differentiate objects from their backgrounds led Witkin and his associates to investigate the extent to which a person's perception of an item was influenced by the context (field) in which it appeared (Guild & Garger, 1985, p. 28). Bennett (1986) explains that field independence–dependence is now ascertained through the use of a simple embedded-figures test. Bennett suggests that we visualize people along a continuum from extreme field dependence to extreme field independence. People at the field-dependent end are unable to locate simple figures embedded in the complex pattern. Field independent people can quickly separate the simple figure from the background. (p. 98)

Learning styles are independent of intelligence or ability to learn but they are important in determining instructional strategies that will help, rather than hinder, students' ability to learn (Gollnick & Chinn, 1986, p. 95; Witkin et al., 1977). Field-independent children tend to be more comfortable with impersonal abstractions and independent activities, whereas field-dependent students are more responsive to close personal interactions and group work.

Knowing the cultural background of students should help the educator determine how to structure the classroom in order to provide the most effective instruction. Learning styles may be correlated with the student's assimilation into the dominant society. Students from nonwhite minority groups are more likely to be field-sensitive (dependent) than most white students. Most instruction in the past has been provided in a field-independent mode, favoring the non-minority students (Gollnick & Chinn, 1986, p. 264).

Spencer Kagan's research (1974) pinpoints differential child-rearing practices (in a study between rural Mexican and urban American parents) as one of the most probable causes of difference in cognitive style orientation. Werner (1979) and other researchers identify differences in achievement motivation of mothers, restrictiveness and stress on conformity, obedience training, adherence to authority, and type of discipline and punishment as causal factors of difference in cognitive style. In sum, a large body of research indicates that cognitive styles are formed, stimulated, and reinforced by social interaction in family and close friendship groups.

In addition to connections between learning style and family or primary group, another closely related area of influence of which the teacher must be aware is that of ethnicity and ethnic group. Longstreet (1978) has done considerable study of *intellectual modes* and ethnicity. She says that children's externalization of their thoughts can be linked to their ethnic group. Children's behaviors are modeled after others in their ethnic group at such an early age that soon they are used completely and unconsciously by preschool children. They become a structural part of the way the children externalize their thoughts about things—the way they approach a problem, the things they give their full attention, the details they are most likely to recall, or the questions they are likely to use while learning. (p. 107)

The insights of Longstreet and other researchers are particularly significant for the educator concerned about the growth and development of children with heritages different from a white, Anglo-Saxon, Protestant background and also with differences among subgroups within the white, Anglo-Saxon, Protestant group. The research indicates that a link is likely to exist between learning style, the sociocultural context, and the ethnicity of children's families.

Cohen (1968, p. 201) studied the requirements for school success and found them to be "derivatives of the analytic conceptual style" (field independent). The work of Longstreet (1978), Kogan (1973), and others also indicates that success in schools is linked to the analytic model. However, both Kogan and Cohen suggest that, in light of the adaptive social requirements for future life circumstances (for example, increasing interdependence), field dependence may be more socially relevant than field independence. For example, strengths of field dependence exist in the area of interpersonal relations and in situations in which compromise and consensus are essential (Kogan, 1973).

Currently, problems arise for young children when there is culture conflict between the school and the home. Culture conflict surfaces when children bring to school conceptual skills that differ from and/or conflict with those required by the school (Neugebauer, 1987; Trueba, 1987). Another dimension of culture conflict comes from negative value judgments of culturally different children made by teachers on the basis of the sociobehavioral correlates of different conceptual styles and not the conflicting learning skills themselves (Cohen, 1968, p. 208).

The classifications "disadvantaged" or "deficient" are no longer appropriate to use for culturally different children whose behavior does not meet the expectations of the middle-class teacher. Rather, their cultural/ethnic difference is the more appropriate dimension to be considered. Children must be perceived according to their particular learning style, with their achievement being measured on more than one continuum. The general consensus of the research is that there are different, not deficient or deviant, learning styles; that there is no one way of knowing and processing information; that differences reflect diverse sociocultural antecedents; and that there are strengths and weaknesses in different styles of thinking and behaving.

Accommodation of different learning styles in the early childhood years is of particular importance because children's attitudes toward self, success/failure, and others are critical and still malleable during this time. Acceptance and appreciation of all groups of children with their diverse backgrounds and learning requirements is basic to multicultural early childhood teaching. The question is, How can early childhood teachers modify or change their classroom climates, teaching strategies, and materials so that they are more compatible with and complementary to the learning styles and cultures of all children? Some help in answering this question and others will be explored.

CONCEPTS, ATTITUDES, AND VALUES IN THE CHILDREN'S HOMES

The family and home are vital determinants of young children's self-concept and learning style. In addition, and equally important, the family is the primary influence on children's formation of concepts, attitudes, and values. Thus, an understanding of multicultural education and the social studies for young children begins in the home.

Mr. Gabor showed his inquisitive preschoolers a large, colorful picture of a slender woman in an apron serving breakfast to Bobby and Sally and at the same time waving good-bye to her husband, who stood at the open door, briefcase in hand. Mr. Gabor said to the children, "Let's talk about this picture. Roberto, do you see anything in the picture that you think is interesting?" Roberto scratched his head, wiggled uncomfortably, and finally mumbled, "Naw, looks kinda funny to me." "Well, Alisha, what about you?" "M-m, that mommy looks like a maid I saw on TV once. Do some mommies really do that in the mornings? My mommy sleeps late 'cause she works the night shift, so daddy puts the cereal out for Robby and me. Then he takes us to school. Sometimes we're nearly late when he forgets his lunch pail." Miranda looked troubled and barely whispered, "My daddy was carrying something big—big like a suitcase, when he left last year. He just hollered something at Mommy and left." Mr. Gabor commented understandingly, that all families do not have a mommy and daddy nowadays. Then Arnie interrupted, "Yeah, but my Uncle Ed says he loves me just like daddy did—he even took Billy and me to the show. Then he came over last night and asked, 'You kids OK? How's about a hug for me? I've got a big surprise for the first one who can touch his nose to his toes.'"

Smiling, Mr. Gabor said, "That reminds me of the time my granddad surprised us kids with a 'magic toy'—it was a wooden thing that he had carved which looked like a chain. He could twist it 'just so' and then it would fall apart." Gilberto, who had been very still and uninvolved until now, burst out, "My pap'pa does magic shadows with his hands, all the time. See, he stays with us in a little room all his own. So every night he says, 'Who wants to guess the magic shadow? Sometimes, the shadow looks like a rabbit or a monkey. Most times, I get it right, 'cause he does the same ones over and over." Bonita shrugged and said importantly, "Well, my grandma and grandpa play games with me all the time. Well, see, I live with them most of the time. Sometimes I see mommy on weekends, but it's more fun with them 'cause they tell me stories about 'long time ago.'" Then Betty excitedly told about her grandmother who used to make quilts for the family. "Now, she just quilts for fun." Mr. Gabor joined in, "Betty, do you think your grandmother might like to show us some of her quilts?" Betty said, "I think so, 'cause she's always showing them to someone. I'll ask her. OK? She might even show us how to quilt." Mr. Gabor said, "That's great. I hope she will."

In his discussion with the children, stemming from the picture of a "typical model," white nuclear family, Mr. Gabor's goal was to help the children understand that having a different kind of family is acceptable and that traditional sex roles are changing. As they drew from their own family stories, it became clear that, even among a small group of children, many different kinds of family arrangements and sex roles exist. No one model American family fulfills the American dream (Fantini & Cardinas, 1980). Yet many children's picture books and storybooks would have youngsters believe this myth.

By showing interest in the children's grandparents and encouraging their participation at school, Mr. Gabor was helping the children to appreciate their own heritage and to bridge the gap between the aged and the young. Mr. Gabor knows that children need to have social interaction with people of all ages in order to see other points of view and to understand how other people feel and live.

In the models of teaching that have been discussed, involvement of parents is basic. Involvement of grandparents, although desirable, is not always possible. When the teacher is able to involve the family in the classroom, children get the message: "My family and background are OK and I'm OK too." By showing respect and appreciation for children's family, the teacher is demonstrating real caring for them. One more bridge has been crossed in closing the gap between home and school and one more child's self-concept has been bolstered.

Involvement of parents and grandparents in the classroom gives the teacher an opportunity to learn more about the child's learning style, language, and cultural heritage. These insights can be incorporated into the teacher's daily planning for individual children and into general curriculum planning for the social studies.

MULTICULTURAL EDUCATION GOALS AND THE TEACHER

The goals and values of multicultural education, early childhood education, and the social studies are compatible and overlapping. All find common ground in the goal to develop concepts, attitudes, skills, and values in young children. The teacher's ability to fulfill the goals and values of multicultural education depends upon her concept of the field as well as her own attitudes, beliefs, and values.

According to the American Association of Colleges for Teacher Education (AACTE), multicultural education is

> education which values cultural pluralism. Multicultural education rejects the view that schools should melt away cultural differences or the view that schools should merely tolerate cultural pluralism. Instead, multicultural education affirms that schools should be oriented toward the cultural enrichment of all children and youth through programs rooted to the preservation and extension of cultural alternatives. Multicultural education recognizes cultural diversity as a fact of life in American society, and it affirms that this cultural diversity is a valuable resource that should be preserved and extended. (1973, p. 264)

With this understanding of the goals and values of multicultural education, the teacher can examine her own philosophy of education as well as personal attitudes, beliefs, and values concerning others. Parker (1977) provides a good checklist that an early childhood teacher committed to multicultural education may use for self-examination. He says such a teacher has the following qualities:

1. The teacher prizes the uniqueness of the individual and has pride in herself and her own heritage.
2. The teacher recognizes that people are different and the same, and supports the right to be different.
3. The teacher has empathy for others' cultural backgrounds. Empathy is based on knowledge; therefore, the teacher also needs to study various subcultures of the national society.
4. The teacher has skills in human relations and intergroup relations, with the ability to function effectively with people individually and collectively. (p. 26)

MULTICULTURAL APPROACHES FOR EARLY CHILDHOOD TEACHERS

The most fundamental approach to multicultural education for a young child is appreciation, respect, and involvement accorded to her family; what are some other considerations the teacher should be aware of?

Piaget's work tells us that children's mental development is influenced by four interrelated factors: maturation, experience, social interaction, and equilibration (Charles, 1974). Through our observation as teachers we know that children's experience and social interaction in the home can have both positive and negative effects on their development. The teacher must be aware of the factors in children's sociocultural world that have the potential of impeding or enhancing their full development. Having this knowledge enables the teacher to create and implement a responsive multicultural learning environment for all young children.

What can a teacher do when faced with a multiplicity of cultures and personality-need-dispositions of children in a school setting that possibly has a differing set of social norms? Holloman (1977) says there are no foolproof techniques for dealing with conflicts between cultural values, school social norms, and the personality-need-dispositions of children. The teacher neither defends nor offends particular social norms or cultural values. The teacher facilitates, stimulates, and evokes discussion of differences and similarities in points of view. (p. 7)

Differences and Similarities

Young children can understand the concepts that "people are different" and "people are the same." The teacher of young children should explore differences and similarities from the child's-eye view. Earlier in this chapter, a teacher–child vignette portrayed a discussion of skin color. Other discussions from children's point of view could center on such questions as these: "Is Tommy as tall as Mary?" "Does Sam have the same color (or texture) of hair as Ramone?" "Who has freckles in the room?" "Does anyone have a dimple?" "What other physical differences can you see?" "Yes, Mary I'm a lot taller than you are." "Do these differences mean one person is better than another?" Such a good–bad value question about being different can have significant impact on young children when associated initially with physical differences, according to Parker (1977). In addition, he says, differences in people as well as ethnic groups can be assessed from the viewpoint of uniqueness—what is special and important about the person or group (p. 13).

After discussing physical differences between people, the teacher can lead children to explore cultural differences, emphasizing the reasons for these differences in terms the children can understand. For example, Kim, a Japanese 4-year-old, in addition to having some physical and language differences, may also have some cultural characteristics that give the teacher an opportunity to expand the children's awareness of the unique cultural contributions of different groups. Kim may have a doll collection to share that has been passed down to her from her great grandmother. Or her mother may be willing to come to school and prepare a tempura for deep frying shrimp and vegetables that the children can taste. Seeing and touching the traditional clothing of the Japanese family is also a way for the children to concretely emphathize with Kim and her culture.

Just as young children need concrete, "close to home" experiences to understand physical and cultural differences, they can also learn about similarities between people through examples drawn from their own school group.

"Raise your hand if you have black hair. Oh, I see that five of you have black hair. But how many have curly black hair? That's right, three. Who has blond hair like mine? Mary, Sam, Nedra, Francine, and Arnie. Five of you have blonde hair." The teacher can expand this discussion to include comparison of similarities with another group of children, such as Ms. Simoni's next-door class of 3-year-olds. "How is our class like Ms. Simoni's? Yes, most of the children are 3 years old, too. Good Tony, both of our classes have boys and girls, and both classes get to have orange juice and crackers at snack time."

Similarities between cultural groups can be explored through topics that are common to the lives of all children, such as family units/homes and celebrations/holidays. Although varying from culture to culture, holidays contain some commonalities. By sharing information about one another's special days, young children learn that most people have gift-giving occasions and that often games are tied to these celebrations. Other areas of commonality between cultural groups that young children can understand and enjoy are folk toys, crafts and art, music, folk tales and heroes, dress, foods, games, and dances. Such commonalities transcend time and produce a sense of community among people of all ages. These topics and activities help make social studies come alive for young children.

Seefeldt (1977) emphasizes the urgency of establishing the basics for global understanding during a child's early years:

> Young children, through activities involving relationships with others, cooperative groups experiences, and many forms of firsthand experiences, can develop awareness of: (1) the interdependency of humans on one another, (2) the cultures of our world, and (3) the similarities between people everywhere (p. 153).

Parker (1977) suggests that another way in which young children can experience the concepts of similarities and differences between people is a visit to another center where the children come from different economic or cultural backgrounds (p. 13). He notes that careful preparation must be made by both teachers for such exchange visits. Playing games, doing art projects, and having snacks together provide opportunities for social interaction between the two groups. After the visit, the teacher should talk about the experience, eliciting the children's concerns, feelings, or questions. Follow-up visits or a joint picnic may be a good idea. Observing the children's comments for weeks after these exchanges will enable the teacher to gain some insight into their internalization of the concepts of differences and similarities.

Another excellent means for young children to grow in understanding of similarities and differences between individuals and groups of people is to invite community helpers or *cultural carriers* to the classroom. Cultural carriers are people who remember and/or continue to practice the unique ways of their cultural heritage. Of course, parents or the extended family of the youngsters are a natural source of cultural carriers, but they may also be community members, friends, and neighbors. When a teacher seriously initiates this search and opens the door to them, it becomes clear that cultural carriers literally encompass the school. People in the community, and especially older retired folks, find being a part of young children's lives very rewarding.

Avoiding Stereotypes

A word of caution is in order for teachers who involve cultural carriers in their classrooms, especially classrooms in which the children are from homogeneous backgrounds. The teacher should avoid reinforcing any old stereotypes or creating new ones about groups of people. If, for example, a Native American visits the classroom to do a dance in costume and to show cultural artifacts, such as drums or jewelry, help the children understand the traditional nature of the dance and how it relates to the lives of Native Americans now. "All Native Americans do not wear this kind of costume, but some do on special days." Help the children understand the time frame ("a long time ago" or "nowadays") of any cultural event and the purpose of a particular event or artifact. "Native Americans wove beautiful blankets to keep warm a long time ago and now they still make them to use, but they also make them to sell to people who like their beautiful colors and patterns."

Just as with cultural carriers, the sensitively aware teacher will use caution in avoiding old and new stereotypes in any kind of classroom activity, presentation, film, picture, storybook, or unit that deals with a cultural or ethnic group. Part of the perpetuation of harmful stereotypes about cultural and ethnic groups lies in the language we use. The teacher herself may have said, "Now sit in our circle like an Indian" or "You kids are acting like a bunch of wild Indians." Classroom comments may reflect a negative, dirty, or "bad" imagery of African-Americans. These racist and similar sexist stereotypes are not only part of our everyday language, but they are built into our formal language. Our dictionaries are witness to this.

Classroom Climate

The classroom climate and environment are critical determinants of young children's ability to reach their maximum potential. Young children need a setting in which they can be actively involved in exploration. Charles (1974) says that a classroom consistent with Piaget's ideas should be arranged and equipped to enhance an activity-oriented curriculum. Quantities of materials should be provided in convenient work areas. Some spaces should be set aside for individual activities, others for small group activities (p. 28). The necessity for flexibility in an early childhood classroom arrangement is also the key to an effective multicultural plan. Children with different needs and backgrounds must have options for movement and use of space.

Just as important as the physical arrangement of the classroom is the psychological climate. Psychological climate is largely created by the teacher.

Piaget's work suggests that the optimum climate for child growth and development is free and spontaneous. The teacher provides guidance and materials, suggests activities, and works with and helps the children (Charles, 1974).

The psychological climate for multicultural education is enhanced by a multisensory approach to teaching. In this approach, children are active learners involved in problem solving through inquiry and discovery. All the child's learning domains are activated: cognitive, affective, and psychomotor. In addition, the teacher must ensure that opportunities for social interaction are woven into the children's daily activities.

Another aspect of classroom climate concerns the "fit" of the interaction and communication styles of the teacher and the children. Most schools are incompatible with the styles of minority group children because of the schools' individualistic, formal climate; their competitiveness; their emphasis on rationality and the written tradition in communication; and in their lack of interactional and communication patterns that integrate the cognitive, affective, and psychomotor domains.

Concerning accommodation of the classroom climate to the needs of African-American children, Gay (1977) suggests placing emphasis on experiences and assessment techniques that use aural and performance inclinations, employ more informal classroom climates, and focus on consensus-based, cooperative, group-centered learning activities (p. 55). In short, a psychological climate conducive to multicultural education of young children is open, informal, spontaneous, and accepting of diverse interaction, learning, and communication styles (see Figure 9–2).

INTEGRATION OF MULTICULTURAL CONCEPTS INTO THE CURRICULUM

Unless a concept, topic, or subject is scheduled into the structure of a curriculum, it may not be given adequate attention even by well-meaning teachers. A hit-or-miss approach—with fragmented bits of information, an occasional visit by a cultural carrier, a focus on African-Americans during February, or a unit on Native Americans during November—is doomed to failure. It pays only lip service to multicultural education for young children. Neither can an additive approach be successful. Here, multicultural concepts or activities are tacked onto a curriculum that stays basically the same.

Multiculturalism must be a regular part of the daily curriculum, woven into all of the child's activities: the social studies, language arts, dramatic play with manipulative materials, the creative arts, math, science, nature, and health studies. For example, the housekeeping area should have men's and women's clothes and multiracial dolls. Dramatic play activities should encourage girls to act out nontraditional career roles and boys to play nurturing, care-giving roles. Manipulative materials, such as puzzles, should show children and adults of different races, girls engaged in active play, and women in varied occupations.

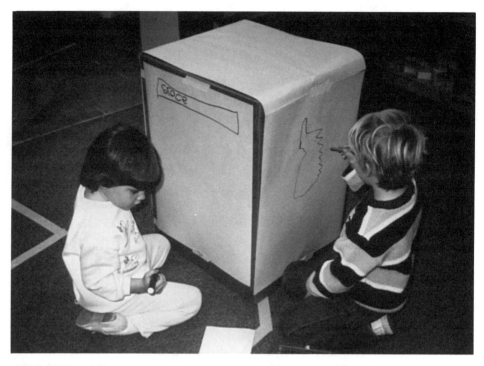

FIGURE 9–2
The classroom climate can foster working together.

In the social studies, children should discuss, dramatize, and hear stories about the differences and similarities between and among people. Puppets, flannel-board figures, and posters should be multiracial. Pictures and stories used in the social studies should honestly portray different lifestyles (for example, diverse family styles and sex roles); show children and adults of different cultures and races working and playing together; portray men sharing homemaking and child-care activities; present girls actively participating rather than passively watching boys do things; and in general, convey that alternatives exist for boys and girls and men and women of all cultural and racial groups. Kendall (1983, pp. 58–75) gives more detailed suggestions for integrating multicultural concepts into the curriculum for young children.

All materials in an early childhood education program should be culturally fair and unbiased. Accuracy is of utmost importance (see chapter 16 for literature suggestions). Teacher-made materials may be necessary if the ones available are biased or inaccurate; however, a critical examination of the "old" ones by the teacher and children may provide a valuable learning experience. With the help of adults, children may create their own books using a language experience approach.

An integrative and experiential approach to multicultural and social studies education helps young children internalize the relationships between the many parts of their environment and gives meaning to the diverse elements in their day. It seeks to educate the whole child as a unique human being and to provide the opportunity for each child to reach her maximum potential.

EXPERIENTIAL MULTICULTURAL ACTIVITIES

Multicultural activities for young children, which help them understand the concepts of similarities and differences between people, can be integrated into social studies by using some of the following ideas. The ideas can be used as "starters" and then expanded according to the children's interest. The activities are presented with brief background information for the teacher's use.

Folk Toys

Folk toys are passed from one generation to the next with few changes in the design over the years. The makers of folk toys were creative and resourceful in the use of local or "found" materials. The toys' "trickiness" reveals the humor of the folk toy creator, an aspect that is appealing to young children (Schnacke, 1974).

Folk toys are a good means of communication between generations and a way for children to interact with others positively. Young children will be attracted to making toys using inexpensive, "found" materials such as spools. Invite cultural carriers, parents, or grandparents to work with the children in making these toys.

SPOOL TOYS

1. Collect an assortment of spools: wooden, styrofoam, plastic, and so on.
2. For very young children, help them thread the spools onto heavy yarn to make a pull toy or a "rattle" necklace.
3. Encourage children to use their imagination in creating spool people and animals:
   - Stack spools in different combinations to make the head, body, and legs.
   - When pleased with the arrangement, stick it onto an old stubby pencil. The creation can be taken apart and rearranged if the child desires.
   - For a permanent toy, glue the spools together; add paper feet and accessories and pipe-cleaner arms; and make the face with small marker pens.

Crafts

Crafts activities provide a way for children to explore their own cultural heritage and understand that making beautiful and useful things is a similarity that all cultures share. Creating crafts by hand is as ancient as people's first efforts to make crude tools. Multicultural crafts activities can be integrated into the social studies in a number of ways. One way is by choosing an ethnic or cultural group and focusing on its crafts. Another way is to focus on the materials used in craftmaking: paints, yarn, fabric, natural materials, "found" objects, synthetic materials, metals, paper, and so on.

Following is an example of an activity using the ethnic or cultural group approach. The teacher and children can expand with more ideas and explore other cultures and other materials.

KACHINA DOLLS

Make kachina dolls, not as a novel craft activity, but as a means of building appreciation for the Native American cultural heritage. Perhaps involvement with this project will lead to exploring other forms of Native American crafts: weaving, sandpainting, bead-making, jewelry, woodcarving, pottery, or totem poles. Discussing the integral part that crafts played in their lives will help dispel the stereotype of Native Americans as "wild savages."

Kachina dolls made by Native Americans were a manifestation of over 300 kachina spirits. Thus, there were many variations and interpretations. Experts point out that the Hopi and Zuni motifs were not limited to those sanctioned by tradition. Therefore, with the children's creations, it is legitimate from the traditional viewpoint to encourage individual interpretations.

1. Help young children make a kachina doll by using a cardboard tube for the body.
2. Wad a piece of newspaper for the head.
3. Cover it and attach it to the body with strips of paper toweling dipped in wheat paste.
4. Make rolled paper arms and attach to the body with strips of paper toweling dipped in wheat paste.
5. Let the doll dry; then paint and decorate it.

Music

The lungs, mouth, tongue, vocal cords, throat, chest, and body of people were the first natural musical instruments. Singing is a good way for children to experience the ways people express their happy or sad feelings and ideas related to the life forces of birth, death, religion, marriage, and other culturally important events.

Cultural characteristics are kept alive through music. People tell stories through music and thus preserve their heritage and traditions. Music, then, is truly a universal language that reflects the life experience of people: their culture, traditions, voices, instruments, ideas, dreams, and feelings. Young children can fit right into this pattern, make their own music, and be a part of an ongoing tradition.

VOCAL FOLK MUSIC

Because folk songs reflect so many cultures, they are a good source to use with children. Some folk songs came to the United States from other cultures with little change, whereas others were changed in the process. Still others were created here. These songs reflect the everyday life experiences of people and thus they appeal to children's emotions and imaginations. Folk songs are appealing because they are not "completed." Ready to grow like children, folk songs are always changing and adapting. Folk songs can be demonstrated in schools by local folk musicians, who generally are eager to share their talent and love of music with youngsters. They can involve the children in singing games, patting-and-clapping songs, work songs, call-response songs, and some listening, story-type songs. Children will begin their own motions of clapping, skipping, or dancing to folk songs if the classroom climate is open and encourages responsiveness.

1. If some children refuse to sing, begin by letting them just listen and pat a rhythm while others sing. Usually class involvement in a play-party song or a dancing game will draw out the shy children (see Chase, 1967). Good songs to start with are "The Paw Paw Patch," "Shoo Fly," or "Old Joe Clark."
2. Let the children act out these songs or dance freely. "Old Joe Clark" is a square-dance tune with a refrain that encourages rhythmic play: "Round and round, old Joe Clark; round and round, I say; round and round, old Joe Clark; I ain't got long to stay." The children will enjoy turning round and round until they are "dizzy" and fall down.
3. Learn some folk songs from other cultures. If there are children from other cultures in the school or in the classroom, ask them and their parents to share songs with the group. Listen to recordings, such as Hap Palmer's "Folk Song Carnival" (1970).

INSTRUMENTAL MUSIC

Children will be fascinated to learn that "musical instruments have existed since the first man [sic] blew into a shell, through a blade of grass or through gaps in his teeth, jangled tiny bones, rattled dry seeds in a pod, clapped pieces of wood together to scare birds, banged stones or rasped sticks" (Willson, 1966, p. 7).

In the beginning, start with simple instruments that the children are familiar with, whether rhythm-band instruments (such as tambourine or maraca), an African mbira (thumb piano), or a Native American drum (Faulhaber & Underhill, 1974; Hunter & Judson, 1977). Gear activities to the children's developmental level, incorporating any musical talents and skills the children or their parents possess and emphasizing the ethnic music that is part of their lives.

Clothing

Clothing as a topic will capture children's interest and motivate them to (a) learn why people dress differently; (b) understand the effects of climate and availability of materials on the way people dress; and (c) think about the reasons for clothing: protection against the extremes of different climates, protection for certain kinds of play and work, and adornment. They can touch real samples of basic materials from which clothing is made: animal products (wool, silk, fur, skin, hair); plant fibers (leaves, grass, bark, cotton, flax); or synthetic cloth, which is plant fibers mixed with chemicals.

In Africa, as well as other parts of the world, people wear beautifully printed and embroidered fabrics made by local craftspeople. They also wear jewelry and head attire for the sake of beauty and sometimes to denote their rank. Some African men wear a dashiki, a ceremonial shirt with beautiful patterns. Now, dashikis are worn in the United States and in other countries.

People who live in hot countries (located near the equator) often wear white clothing. A white costume is cooler than a dark one because white does not absorb heat as quickly. People wear clothing appropriate to the climate.

DRESS UP

1. Talk about clothing that is appropriate for hot climates and for cold climates, using pictures and real clothing to demonstrate the ideas.
2. Have a dress-up box of scarves, beads, hats, shoes, jackets, dresses, pants, and large rectangles of fabric available for the children to select from.

3. Let the children pick a "hot" or "cold" type of costume to create, choosing materials from the dress-up box that would be most appropriate for the climate and culture chosen.
4. Let the children make a show-and-tell presentation (to another class) of their costumes with appropriate hair ornaments, headdresses, and face decorations or makeup.
5. Help the children make a dashiki (de-she-ke). Fold a piece of an old sheet (12 by 36 inches) and cut a hole large enough for the child's head. Leave the sides open. The child can decorate the dashiki with marking pens. Use of a sash is optional.

Games

Games provide another common bond between children of differing cultures. Similar games are known by different names throughout the world. The game known as hopscotch in the United States is called *tua-ma-tua* in Ghana. An African version of "It," a game found in different forms in many cultures, is called "I'm Looking for a Friend" (Ely, 1963). Jump-rope jingles and rhymes are enjoyed by children of all cultures; whether the words are Spanish, English, or Swahili, common elements of rhythm and repetition exist. Games of chance are also common in different cultures. Children will enjoy playing the Jewish dreidle game of chance.

DREIDLE GAME OF CHANCE

The dreidle is a small four-sided top with a different Hebrew letter on each side (*gimel, nun, hey,* and *shin*). A small prize such as coins, candies, nuts, or beans is placed in the center of the table. The dreidle is spun and the outcome of the game depends upon which letter of the dreidle is facing the child. If *gimel* lands up, the player takes all; if *nun* lands up, the player gets nothing; if *hey* lands up, the player gets half the prize; and if *shin* lands up, the player takes all but puts one back in the "pot."

Foods

Children have a keen interest in foods; thus, making and tasting foods from different cultures is a good way for them to learn that there are various ways for people to satisfy nutritional needs. For example, they can be told that bread and cereal used around the world are made from corn, rice, wheat, macaroni products, and oatmeal. All people need some kind of protein, whether in the form of meat, chicken, fish, nuts, lentils, eggs, or peanut butter.

PEANUT BUTTER

Peanut butter is a good source of protein and is used as a meat substitute. Children will enjoy learning about George Washington Carver along with this activity. A man who began life as a slave, he became a well-known scientist through hard work and study. Dedicating his life to agricultural research, Carver developed over 200 products from the peanut, including a milk substitute, ink, flour, and bleach. This activity could be introduced by reading to the children the story of Carver's life (Brandenburg, 1965).

RECIPE

Ingredients
1 cup salted peanuts
1 tablespoon oil
Place peanuts and oil in blender. Blend and then stir with a rubber spatula (with motor off). Add more oil as needed.

Blend until a smooth consistency is reached. Let the children help as much as possible (for example, by measuring the peanuts) when making the peanut butter and let them spread it on crackers to taste.

Special Days

Around the world, people celebrate special days. Although they vary from culture to culture, these holidays and festivals have some similarities. For instance, July 4 is our Independence Day; Ghana's Independence Day is March 6. Harvest festivals ("yam" festivals) are celebrated in Ghana (Africa for the elementary grades, 1968, p. 93), whereas in the United States we have Thanksgiving Day. A culture's customs, traditions, values, and beliefs are handed down from one generation to the next through such special celebrations. By sharing information about holidays—which often include gift exchanges, food, games, and dancing—we teach children that they have much in common with others of different cultural backgrounds.

The tradition of making piñatas is a part of Mexican fiestas, Christmas, and birthday celebrations. Originally ("a long time ago"), blindfolded children tried to break a ceramic jar filled with candy, nuts, and toys, using a stick. When the jar was broken, all the children rushed to pick up the treats. Now, piñatas are made of paper and may still be filled with candy, but often they are used as decorative hangings for celebrations. Piñatas may be large or small and come in many shapes. Now, Mexican piñatas are displayed in restaurants and sold in the United States (Fiarotto & Fiarotto, 1976).

PIÑATA

Materials: One large balloon, newspaper, wheat paste, string, two-inch strips of tissue paper, white glue, candy, gum, etc.

Directions:
1. Blow up and tie balloon.
2. Cover balloon with quarter-sized pieces of newspaper dipped in wheat paste.
3. Let dry and cover a second time with newspaper pieces, leaving an opening at the top to insert the goodies. Characters such as birds, animals, or clowns can be created by adding cardboard and wadded paper features and then painting them.
4. Dry the piñata thoroughly and decorate it by gluing on strips of fringed tissue paper.
5. Fill with goodies.
6. Cover the hole with fringed tissue paper.
7. Attach a string to hang the piñata.
8. Invite parents and grandparents to come and enjoy the piñata celebration!

SUMMARY

Multicultural awareness activities woven throughout the early childhood social studies curriculum provide a sound way for teachers to lay the foundation for intergroup and international understanding. The teacher must start where the children are—with concrete experiences—in order to lay this groundwork for expansion of their understanding and acceptance of others. Providing children with the necessary skills, knowledge, and understanding to live productively and cooperatively in our rapidly changing, complex, and interdependent world is central to early childhood education.

REFERENCES

AACTE Commission on Multicultural Education. (1973). No one model American—A statement on multicultural education. *Journal of Teacher Education, 24,* 264–265.

Africa for the elementary grades. (1968, October). *Grade Teacher,* pp. 48–93.

BANKS, J. A. (1981). *Multiethnic education—Theory and practice.* Boston: Allyn & Bacon.

BENNETT, C. I. (1986). *Comprehensive multicultural education—Theory and practice.* Boston: Allyn & Bacon.

BRANDENBURG, A. (1965). *A weed is a flower: The life of George Washington Carver.* Englewood Cliffs, NJ: Prentice-Hall.

Bringing our worlds together—A multicultural approach to teaching. (1986, November–December). *Scholastic Pre-K Today,* pp. 19–23.

CHARLES, C. (1974). *Teacher's petite Piaget.* Belmont, CA: Fearon.

CHASE, R. (1967). *Singing games and playparty games.* New York: Dover.

COHEN, R. (1968). The relation between socio-conceptual styles and orientation to school requirements. *Sociology of Education, 41,* 201–220.

ELY, M. (1963). *Reading roundtable series: who is it?* New York: American Book Co.

FANTINI, M. D., & CARDINAS, R. (1980). *Parenting in a multicultural society.* New York: Longman.

FAULHABER, M., & UNDERHILL, J. (1974). *Music: invent your own.* Chicago: Albert Whitman.

FIAROTTA, P., & FIAROTTA, N. (1976). *The you and me heritage tree.* New York: Workman.

GAY, G. (1975, October). Cultural differences important in education of black children. *Momentum,* pp. 30–33.

GAY, G. (1977). The black Americans. In M. Gold, C. Grant, & H. Rivlin (Eds.), *In praise of diversity* (pp. 34–56). Washington, DC: Teacher Corps/ATE.

GINGRAS, R. C. (1983). Early childhood bilingualism: Some considerations from second-language acquisition research. In O. Saracho & B. Spodek (Eds.), *Understanding the multicultural experience in early childhood education* (pp. 67–74). Washington, DC: National Association for the Education of Young Children.

GOLLNICK, D., & CHINN, P. (1986). *Multicultural education in a pluralistic society.* Columbus, OH: Merrill.

GOODMAN, M. E. (1952). *Race awareness in young children.* Cambridge, MA: Addison-Wesley.

GOODMAN, M. E. (1970). *The culture of childhood—Child's-eye view of society and culture.* New York: Teachers College Press.

GUILD, P., & GARGER, S. (1985). *Marching to different drummers.* Alexandria, VA: Association for Supervision and Curriculum Development.

HALE, J. E. (1982). *Black children—Their roots, culture, and learning styles.* Provo, UT: Brigham Young University Press.

HOLLOMAN, J. W. (1977). Some straight talk on the subject of the multicultural classroom. *Dimensions—A Journal of the Southern Association for Children Under Six, 6,* 5–8.

HUNTER, I., & JUDSON, M. (1977). *Simple folk instruments to make and play.* New York: Simon & Schuster.

KAGAN, J., MOSS, H. A., & SIGEL, I. E. (1963). Psychological significance of styles of conceptualization. In J. C. Wright & J. Kagan (Eds.), *Basic cognitive processes in children* (pp. 73–112). Monographs of the Society for Research in Child Development, *28* (2, Serial No. 86).

KAGAN, S. (1974). Field dependence and conformity of rural Mexican and urban Anglo-American children. *Child Development, 45,* 765–771.

KEEFE, J. W., & LANGUIS, M. (1983, Summer). *Learning styles network newsletter,* p. 1.

KENDALL, F. E. (1983). *Diversity in the classroom—A multicultural approach to the education of young children.* New York: Teachers College Press.

KOGAN, N. (1973). Creativity and cognitive style: A life-span perspective. In P. B. Baltes and K. W. Schaie (Eds.), *Life-span developmental psychology—personality and socialization* (pp. 145–178). New York: Academic Press.

LONGSTREET, W. S. (1978). *Aspects of ethnicity—Understanding differences in pluralistic classrooms.* New York: Teachers College Press.

NEUGEBAUER, B. (Ed.). (1987). *Alike and different: Exploring our humanity with young children.* Redmond, WA: Exchange Press.

PALMER, H. (1970). Folk song carnival. 33⅓ recording, AR524. Freeport, NY: Educational Activities.

PARKER, J. A. (1977). Multicultural education in preschool classrooms. *Dimensions—A Journal of the Southern Association for Children Under Six, 6*(13), 26.

RAMIREZ, M., & CASTANEDA, A. (1974). *Cultural democracy, cognitive development and education.* New York: Academic Press.

SCHNACKE, D. (1974). *American folk toys and how to make them.* Baltimore: Penguin Books.

SEEFELDT, C. (1977). *Social studies for the preschool–primary child.* Columbus, OH: Merrill.

TRUEBA, H. T. (Ed.). (1987). *Success or failure—Learning and the language minority student.* Cambridge, MA: Newberry House.

WERNER, E. E. (1979). *Cross-cultural child development.* Monterey, CA: Brooks/Cole.

WILLIAMS, H. B., & WILLIAMS, E. (1979). Some aspects of childrearing practices in three minority subcultures in the United States. *Journal of Negro Education, 48,* 408–418.

WILLSON, R. B. (1966). *Musical instruments.* Henry Z. Walck.

WITKIN, H. A., MOORE, C. A., GOODENOUGH, D. R., & COX, P. W. (1977, Winter). Field-dependent and field-independent cognitive styles and their educational implications. *Review of Educational Research, 47,* 1–64.

10

PSYCHOLOGY AND VALUES IN YOUNG CHILDREN

Psychology, as one of the social studies for young children, primarily focuses on four areas:

1. Development of a positive self-image
2. Development of self-confidence
3. Beginning to accept others
4. Beginning to relate to others

The first two, accepting and understanding oneself, are the foundation for the second two, which are a foundation for living with others as a social being (Pagano, 1978). These four areas work toward a goal—encouraging children to feel good about themselves and to accept their individuality. This goal is supported by the development of values, an integral part of each child's psychology.

THE SOCIAL AND PHYSICAL ENVIRONMENT

Respect for Others as a Key Characteristic

Adults have responsibility for setting up the environment so that it promotes children's development of positive feelings about themselves and acceptance of their own individuality. The key characteristic of that environment is respect. Adults demonstrating respect for each other are modeling behaviors desired among children. Ultimately the adult who shows respect for others also has self-respect.

Self-respect is demonstrated through self-confidence. Confidence engenders trust in children, which in turn results in a greater willingness on children's part to accept limitations the adult has. This trust, and acceptance of limitations, allows children to develop respect for adults (Maxim, 1989). The respect is enhanced when children see the adult make mistakes, acknowledge them, and then proceed with the activity at hand. An adult who is able to learn from mistakes is one who can be respected.

Classroom Physical Environment

The classroom environment, through its physical layout, can encourage discussion of situations among children and with adults. More fundamentally, the classroom environment can demonstrate respect for children through planning for their needs. The physical layout should provide a home base for children, a spot that is theirs. This can be a particular seat at a table or a cubbyhole with the child's name taped on it and a hook for clothes and personal items. Once children have a home base, they feel more comfortable with making forays away from it. Next, children need places where they can congregate in groups and also places where they can get away from others for a while. Other aspects of physical arrangements of classroom space also indicate a respect for the users of that space. These include aspects frequently found in early childhood settings, such as child-sized furniture, storage areas within easy reach of children, a rug for comfortable floor sitting, and lots of small areas where congenial groups can work together or near each other.

CURRICULUM

Involving Parents

Acceptance of, and respect for, children is also communicated through the curriculum. The involvement of parents in the classroom will support the curriculum used by the teacher. It is unlikely that the teacher can provide all the material upon which a rich experience base can be built. Parents are involved in a wide variety of activities in many schools (Sunal, 1986). They can directly become part of the curriculum. For example:

When Mr. Drennon's class became interested in cloth, parents contributed hundreds of scraps which could be examined. Mira's mother invited the children to her home to watch, and try out, weaving on her loom. On another day she came into the room with a drop spindle, demonstrated it and worked with the children in using it. She arranged for them to use the drop spindle to spin yarn from the hair of mohair rabbits. The children then were assisted by Becky's mother in the construction of a simple loom of cardboard with notches which held the yarn. With this they constructed several small woven hangings.

Mr. Drennon hadn't known mohair rabbits existed nor could he use a drop spindle or weave on a cardboard frame when the children's cloth investigations had begun, but he did know about these things when they were finished. Both children and teacher had a lot of experiences, few of which would have occurred if parents had not been involved in curriculum design. Parent involvement enriched the curriculum and communicated the teacher's respect for the knowledge and abilities of the parents. Respect for what parents can bring to the classroom indicates acceptance of them and respect for their children.

Recognizing Children's Culture and Prejudices

Involvement of parents in curriculum building should lead to incorporation of children's culture into the curriculum. Each culture provides an alternative means of solving social problems, of thinking about life, and of extending human experiences. (See chapter 9 for further discussion of incorporating children's culture into the curriculum.) Making the children's cultures part of the curriculum helps children overcome their prejudices (see also chapter 9). Prejudices are attitudes that prevent cultural understanding. Evidence suggests that prejudices begin forming early (Allport, 1958) and can be seen in young children to some extent.

Prejudices are most likely to appear and to be supported in an authoritarian environment (Goodman, 1964). In such an environment, there is only one acceptable way of doing things. Other ways are suspect. Children also adopt prejudices because parents, peers, and teachers share them and are willing to listen to the child denigrating a member of the group against which the prejudice is held.

Young children know when they are rejected and are very hurt by such rejection. Adults should deal with children's experience of rejection by first admitting that prejudice occurs and encouraging children to talk about their experience with it (Ramos, 1975). After the initial recognition of prejudice, experience with one another's cultures helps. This can be extended by continual efforts to build each child's self-concept and to talk about prejudices (Grant, 1977).

Enhancing Children's Positive Self-Concept

Building children's positive self-concept is a basic means of demonstrating respect for them. This can begin through assisting children in the identification of positive personal attributes. The following is an example of how one teacher incorporated the highlighting of children's positive attributes into daily activities.

Every day Mr. Drennon identifies a positive physical attribute of each child. On Monday he talked with Alex about what a good thumb wrestler he was—a rarity in four-year-olds. On Tuesday he mentioned Alex's large eyes. On Wednesday Alex's biceps were mentioned. Thursday brought comments on Alex's skill at ball throwing. Friday was the day that Alex's clear singing voice was mentioned. Alex was certainly overweight, moved slowly, was short and generally rumpled-looking. Yet, when he began to observe Alex to find one mentionable positive physical attribute, Mr. Drennon found quite a few. All it took was a willingness to really observe Alex with a view to finding positive traits while ignoring negative ones.

Mr. Drennon repeated the positive traits for several weeks. By the fourth week the children were used to thinking of themselves as possessing the positive traits named and began to show interest in the traits expressed for other children. At this point, Mr. Drennon began announcing each person's trait of the day at "circle time." After several weeks the children could identify many of the traits every other child possessed. They also began announcing unidentified characteristics such as Shannon's ability to jump long distances or Jerry's long eyelashes.

Mr. Drennon eventually added a helpful or supportive trait of the day. Alex never fooled around in the bathroom, he always made sure that nobody had to wait a long time for him. Mr. Drennon used the same procedure for acknowledging positive personal behaviors that he had for acknowledging positive physical traits. Later in the year, Mr. Drennon talked with the children about helpful and supportive traits. The children eagerly described these traits in their peers and added several more to the ones Mr. Drennon had identified.

A positive appreciation had been built, as had respect. Mr. Drennon had respected his children and now they respected one another.

AREAS OF SPECIAL CONCERN

Children's self-image is affected by their ability to develop a sense of independence, cope with feelings of jealousy, cope with fear, cope with aggressive feelings, develop the ability to play with others, develop friendships, and regulate the role of fantasy in their life.

Independence

Young children can and do act independently, but they also act dependently. Bursts of strong independence and dependence often quickly follow each other (Sears, 1963). The general trend is toward increasing independence. It is accelerated by physical maturation, enabling children to move about freely, control toileting functions, and eat and dress without help. Cognitive development allows children to plan solutions to problems and to understand the environment better. As children become much more capable, they are able to do many things independently.

Children often enjoy independence and pursue opportunities to act independently. Some of these independent actions are unsafe or disruptive. Generally, adults exert effort to control, limit, or eliminate undesirable behavior. Attempts at independence viewed as positive, however, are generally rewarded.

Young children must gradually increase the scope of their independent activity; they must continue to work at growing up. Yet, they also need to continue to depend on adults and older children for some things (Maccoby and Masters, 1970). When children try to do something by themselves and find they cannot, they will fall back on adults and expect their help. This help should be freely given, but only after the child has been able to make a genuine attempt at the task. Help that is given too quickly enforces dependency. Enforced dependency results in learning that develops much later than it should have. It also results in frustration, which can be expressed aggressively in a tantrum or through withdrawal into a strong unwillingness to attempt something new. For example, buttoning a shirt is difficult for young children. When they have made a real effort and have been unable to accomplish it, they will turn to someone else and ask for help unless they are tired or hungry, with little emotional control. If they are used to being made dependent by an adult, however, they will immediately become very angry or will withdraw. These symptoms of little emotional control result from too much emphasis on dependency by important adults in their lives.

Children become independent when they are expected to be responsible (Quilty, 1975). Putting toys away after finishing with them, cleaning up after snack, keeping one's things in one's own cubbyhole are all responsible actions. Expectations of responsibility should be accompanied by reasons. "Your boots are in your cubbyhole, because you put them there. Aren't they easy to find? They will always be easy to find if you put them in your cubbyhole." Responsibility is not built by fault finding or by threats. It is best built by a calm expectation that something will be done expressed in clear terms, telling children that when they have done what they are expected to do they will be able to do something else. An example is "When you finish putting those blocks away, your snack will be ready for you." Young children are responsible but do not work as directly on a task as do adults. They may be working away responsibly at a task, but they take longer and do it in a more circuitous manner than would an adult. Efforts at responsibility should be recognized and rewarded. Independence and responsibility depend upon one another. A child who is not expected to be responsible isn't likely to be thought of as capable of independent behaviors. Expecting and encouraging responsibility and independent behavior show respect for children as individuals who are in the process of "growing up " (see Figure 10–1).

Jealousy

For young children to feel jealousy is natural. Feelings of jealousy partly result from children's egocentrism. Children believe that others have the same viewpoint (Ginsburg & Opper, 1979). To find that someone else is the center of attention is hard for children, even if the other person is a newborn baby whose needs must be looked after. Young children may know, as a fact, that the baby cannot feed himself but will not understand the ramifications of it. Egocentrism results in a lack of understanding that ushers in feelings of jealousy.

As children mature their egocentrism wanes, understanding grows, and jealousy as a poorly controlled reaction lessens. Even though jealousy is normal in young children and to be expected because of their egocentrism, it is a threat to their self-respect. A person who feels jealous is unsure of the affection of another person in the presence of a third party. Being unsure of a place in the affection of another lessens self-respect.

FIGURE 10–1
Independence is developed by learning skills.

Expressing Jealousy. Children express jealousy in several ways. It is often seen in physical attacks on the child they are jealous of. Another common reaction is the display of immature behaviors.

Another form of expression of jealousy is the boasting commonly seen among young children. Boasting indicates jealous feelings, but generally need not cause much worry. Only when a child is boasting much more than is common among his peers is there cause for concern. Using children's peers for comparison is important, because boasting is more common among some groups of people than among others.

Avoiding Activities That Can Stimulate Jealousy. Contests between children in which some will be winners and some losers should be avoided (French, Brownell, Graziano, & Hartup, 1977). An emphasis on each child's doing as well as possible is important. Contests or decisions about who is best promote jealous feelings in children and limit self-respect. A related problem is identifying one child as a model and stating that the others should emulate this model.

Adults who work with young children are not perfect. They do and say things they should not do and say. However, if an adult is aware of the negative results, it is less likely to happen again.

Fears

Most people don't like going alone into a dark basement at night. Part of this fear is reasonable because a person is at risk going down into a dark, lonely basement, if only because he may fall and injure himself. Walking alone late at night into a large, poorly lit parking garage in the center of a city is likely to be much more dangerous than going down into the basement of one's house. Some fear accompanied by increased alertness is healthy in the center city parking garage, because it may save the person from being mugged or otherwise endangered.

Understanding Children's Fears. Infants show some fear. Their earliest reflexes respond to a sensation of falling. A sudden loud noise may frighten them. But the fear is not long-lasting nor does it worry them in advance. Fear in social situations begins developing and manifests itself frequently between ages 2 through 5. Young children often develop fears that seem unreasonable to adults but that seem justifiable to children. For example, Jane, at age 3, woke up saying she had dreamed about "Daddy going down the shower". She was impressed by the noise the shower made and also by the fact that the water didn't stay in the shower stall, as it did in the bathtub, but instead rushed down the drain. This force and power seemed to be great enough to carry someone away down the drain. Because her Dad used the shower more than anyone else in the family, she feared he would be swept down the drain. Maxim (1989) suggests that such a fear occurs in a young child because the child doesn't understand size relationships. An older child may be startled by the noise a particularly loud shower makes but wouldn't worry about anyone being washed down it, because a person is too big to fit into the drain. The young child doesn't understand that this fear is absurd because he doesn't understand the size relationships involved and is overwhelmed by the perceptual dominance of the loud, rushing sound of the water. Immature thinking abilities keep the child from tempering the interpretation of observations with some conceptual understanding. As the ability to make mature interpretations of observations develops, fears subside and, where still found, are more realistic.

Helping Children Cope With Fears. All efforts to help children cope with their fears require patience. Three points concerning patience are important:

1. To the child, the fear is a real one, directed at a real possibility.
2. The child cannot objectively evaluate the fear because of immature thinking processes.
3. The child will mature and will probably grow out of the fear. Most of us do.

To test point 3, and therefore points 1 and 2, think of a fear you had and gradually overcame or of a nightmare that repeatedly scared you but that you grew out of. A particularly strong fear takes a long time to work out of. For all fears, the process is a gradual one.

Every young child develops some fears. An adult can rarely guess what sort of fear will develop. It is important not to promote any fear consciously. One detrimental activity is to use a threat to enforce discipline, such as "Eat your food or the scarecrow will come out of the garden and yell at you." Such comments build fears. These fears will seem reasonable to the child because of his belief in the person who warned him about the danger.

Teachers must not pass their own fears on to children. This is difficult to avoid because children are quite sensitive to adult emotions. A real effort to withstand fear will lessen the chance of the child's acquiring it. If the child senses that an adult is making a valiant effort to combat the fear, the child is more likely to be impressed by the effort rather than by the fear. Adults also sometimes induce fears when they are making a well-intentioned effort to gloss over something that is distressing. An example of this is saying that "the angels are bowling in heaven" during a thunderstorm. The child who has been to a bowling alley knows that the sound of a ball hitting the pins is loud. But, compared to thunder, it is a whisper. If angels can make such a loud noise bowling, can you imagine how big and strong they must be? What if a pin falls down from heaven on you? In view of the misinterpretations children can make, and of the fears they can develop, sticking to the truth is best.

Fear is often expressed so strongly that the adult can't help but be aware of it. The best approach is to listen to the child, discuss the fear, and show sympathy for the child's feelings (Maxim, 1989). The fear is not likely to be quickly talked away. But at least its effects won't be compounded by apathy, rejection, or ridicule from an adult. The child will know his fear has been recognized as real and upsetting. An understanding adult who is not affected by the same fear provides a sense of security for the child in the face of that fear. Large-scale events, such as thunderstorms, are enjoyed by some children for their awe-inspiring qualities and produce fear in others for those same qualities. Seeing worms on the sidewalk after a rain, napping in a very dark room, and watching a jumping spider are kinds of events that can cause fear in some children while others don't mind at all. Adults who anticipate such reactions can reduce them by diverting children's attention or by attracting attention to the event. Strategies that seek to divert children include introducing a game, story, or snack. Attracting attention to an event can occur, for example, when the teacher has children watch lightning flashes and count until the sounds of the crack of the lightning come to them.

Children's fears are real to them, are to be expected, and should be recognized. The child who seems to have no fears may be the unusual child. Likewise, the child who has many fears should cause concern in adults. As always, a child's peers are a good index of what is to be expected, because culture influences the number and kinds of fears children have.

Aggressive Feelings

Aggression can be considered partly a personality trait because some children are consistently more or less aggressive than the average child. But aggression is also influenced by the situation a child is in. It has been found that some people become aggressive when frustrated. They usually have not been strongly reinforced for reacting to frustration by sharing, cooperating, talking, and other prosocial behavior. Patterson (1976) found that aggression often was a way of turning off family members' irritating and annoying behaviors, humiliation, and lack of attention.

Aggressive children often come from homes in which parents use erratic physical punishment. The children are aggressive as a personal style and to avoid the parents. These children believe the only reason not to be aggressive is to avoid getting caught and punished. They become hardened to punishment and take it as a cue to further aggression. These children don't know how to share and cooperate, and they seek out peers who share their aggressive patterns of behavior (Perry & Bussey, 1984).

Aggressive models in real life and in the media teach children aggressive behaviors and elicit aggressive responses. Children learn that aggression under some circumstances is more justified than under other circumstances. They learn to be guilty when they aggress inappropriately. Children who learn to feel negative about themselves for aggressing tend to avoid aggression (Perry & Bussey, 1984).

Several strategies can control aggression. These include eliminating stimuli that provoke aggression, such as frustration and viewing aggressive television programs; teaching children that aggression does not pay (for example, using time-out procedures); teaching children about prosocial modes of interacting and resolving conflicts; and instructing children how to monitor and control their own behavior. Overall, the goal should be to teach children that mature, prosocial behavior leads to attention, affection, and approval (Perry & Bussey, 1984).

Playing Together

Young children notice other children. Babies just a couple of months old seem to have a special response to a child and to each other. Children do seem to want to be near other children even as infants (Ross & Goldman, 1977). But, because they are egocentric, children do not quite actively seek out other children until around age 4.

Solitary Play. Children's level of friendliness is tied closely to their ability to play with another child. Children primarily engage in solitary play during their first few years. Although they do like to play alongside another child, they wish to do their own thing rather than actually to play with the child.

Associative Play. Around age 3 to 4 children begin to demonstrate the ability and desire to engage in associative play (Garvey & Hogan, 1973). At this age children will play with others to the extent that they are all sharing an activity. For example, several children may all be playing with a set of toy cars, driving them around a sandbox. They probably won't share in the construction of a road for their cars; instead, each is likely to build a separate road. Sometimes, though, they may work together. They also become more likely to have some special friends.

Cooperative Play.   Associative play takes a long time to appear, but it usually takes much less time to fade in favor of cooperative play (Ginsburg & Opper, 1979). This involves cooperation with others, such as when building a sand castle or playing tag. Cooperation requires sharing and the discussion of plans and problems—actual interaction with one another. The amount of disagreement and strong conflict will be greater because interaction is required. Interaction creates conflict as well as cooperation. The actual amount of time children can play cooperatively is small at first but increases with maturity and experience. As children experience clashes, the desire to resolve them exerts itself because children really do want to play cooperatively. This desire is combined with the practice the child is gaining in finishing conflicts. A conflict can be finished in many ways: by stalking off, sulking, hitting the other child, throwing something, yelling at the other child, or talking until a solution is arrived at. Gradually children erupt into fewer and shorter lived negative reactions, because they find that such reactions hinder the playing they really like to do. As negative reactions are fewer and shorter, more opportunity exists for positive effort to work out the disagreement. Lots of experience and a lessening of egocentrism are needed before a disagreement can be worked out in a cooperative manner. Children need to find ways to reduce the build-up of frustration, develop patience, be less egocentric, and develop strategies for working out a disagreement. Each child will develop a personal repertoire of strategies that work. The more opportunities that occur to play cooperatively, the more chance there is for conflict, but also the more chance for developing strategies that reduce and resolve conflict.

Adult Roles in Fostering Cooperation.   Adults need to encourage cooperative play and to realize it won't always stay cooperative for very long. To encourage cooperative play it is necessary to encourage an easygoing environment in which children can encounter and attempt to play with each other. Enough space should be available so that several groups can form and play without interfering with one another. Space should be sufficient so that a child can get angry, walk off, and settle down without bumping into someone else. Enough material should be available so that a small group of two to four children will have ample opportunity to play. Children need to learn to take turns and share scarce materials, but a constant scarcity of lots of materials makes sharing and taking turns difficult to learn. Constant scarcity may encourage aggressive behavior and hoarding of what is available. In summary, cooperative play behaviors can be encouraged by providing the following:

1. An easygoing environment
2. Ample space for play, disagreement, and "cooling off"
3. An ample supply of simple play materials

Finally, an adult must be prepared to help children resolve conflict situations. A few logical rules can be enforced to limit conflicts. These can involve taking out materials and replacing them when finished. Other rules can deal with other areas that may cause conflict. When a conflict does arise, the adult should be sympathetic to all children involved. Choosing sides will only introduce feelings of rejection in some children. It often helps to move out the children involved so they are away from the scene of the conflict and can settle down in a place that doesn't remind them of it. Discussion should be used to help children settle down. Some children would rather settle down by themselves and talk about it later. Their needs should be respected. No matter how full of conflict the day may be, children really do want to play cooperatively (see Figure 10–2).

Friendship

Children continuously enlarge their circle of acquaintances. They also gradually develop special friendships—mutually satisfying relationships with a peer. Listing the characteristics of a friend is difficult, because children of different ages expect somewhat different things from friends.

FIGURE 10–2
Cooking activities foster cooperation.

Making Friends.   Children usually make friends with children who are similar to themselves in age, race, sex, interests, degree of sociability, and values (Singleton & Asher, 1979). Children's expectations of friendship change with age. The first stage lasts through the early elementary school years. Children prefer a friend who is easily accessible, has nice toys, and plays easily. Although there is an emphasis on someone who quickly rewards attempts at friendliness, even pre-school children do form reciprocal, mutually satisfying relationships in which both parties frequently reward and are rewarded by each other (Perry & Bussey, 1984). During the middle of the elementary school years children enter a stage in which shared values and rules become important. Mutual acceptance, ad-miration, and loyalty are important to friendships. Friends are supposed to help each other and to be satisfied by the amount of help they receive (Perry & Bussey, 1984).

Socially competent children who can make and keep friends are skilled in at least three areas: at initiating interactions with their peers, at maintaining ongoing interactions, and at resolving interpersonal conflicts. Children best make friends by greeting another child directly ("Hi! What's your name?"); asking ap-propriate questions ("What's your favorite game?"); giving information ("I like to play tether ball"); and trying to include the new friend in their activities ("Do you want to play tether ball at recess?"). Socially competent children keep trying to make friends even when rejected. They have the necessary self-confidence to keep trying.

Keeping Friends.   Once a friendship has begun, competent children continue it through prosocial rewarding of their friend. They smile at, imitate, approve of, pay attention to, comply with and share their toys often with their friend (Hartup, Glazer, & Charlesworth, 1967). They also communicate well and are good listeners. Their speech is unambiguous and gives information needed by the listener. They also accurately judge their own and others' social status in their peer group. Finally, they have a more sophisticated understanding of morality. They judge less on whether an action brings reward and punishment and more on whether an action has violated respect for others' rights and welfare (Perry & Bussey, 1984).

Socially competent children are better able to solve disputes. Preschoolers tend to argue over possession of a toy or other item; older children argue over what activity to engage in, which children to be with, and who is to blame for some negative event. Competent children tend to disagree less but when they do they tend to cite a general rule for their disagreement and to provide an acceptable alternative (Putallaz & Gottman, 1981).

Social skills coaching has been shown to be an effective means of teaching children social competence. This involves telling or showing children how to enact a specific social skill, providing children with opportunities to practice the skill, and giving children feedback with suggestions for improving their use of the skill. Among the skills which have been taught are asking questions, learning to give positive reinforcements to peers such as smiles, making good eye contact, speaking clearly, and taking turns (Perry & Bussey, 1984).

Fantasy

Fantasy is a part of play for young children. Children can easily cross over into a fantasy world. A child who has decided that he would like to live on a farm may tell the neighbors about the farm his mother just bought. He may even tell them he will be moving to the farm soon and that they will be moving in a U-Haul. After the neighbors talk with the mother and find out she hasn't bought a farm, they will either listen indulgently to the child or scold him for lying. Both of these are typical adult reactions.

Because fantasy is easy for a young child to slip into, the best reaction is the indulgent one. The child knows there is a real world with which he is familiar (Piaget, 1954). But, he is likely to be attracted by pleasant aspects of a life different from the one he now leads. Aware of his lack of knowledge of many things, the child can easily think, "Who knows what is possible? If I say my Mom has bought a farm, maybe it will happen because I say it." The line between reality and fantasy is an indistinct one in young children. A child who sees a live porpoise jumping up out of a tank of water is seeing something very different from what occurs in his everyday life. So it may be hard for the child to judge how real this porpoise is. The child who has a wide range of experiences has a greater basis for judgment of what is reality and what is fantasy.

Dreams (Piaget, 1951) and television characters both seem real. Young children are likely to be confused about the reality of each of them. Dreams are a part of our sleeping life, which is mysterious in itself to children. Television characters often are present during many of our waking hours. They are always simply there; who is to say they are less real than the child's uncle whom he sees only every six months or so? Today's children, because of the pervasiveness of television, may have more difficulty in separating the real from fantasy than did children in pretelevision generations.

Children make an effort to live in the real world but can easily move across into the world of fantasy. Adults can often discover children's needs and desires from fantasy life. This fantasy life should be viewed indulgently by adults because, as children mature, much of it will slip away. Some will remain in daydreams, in poetry written as a grownup, in sculpture, or in the creative solution to a difficult problem. What remains will enhance the life of most adults. Although fantasy should not be discouraged in young children, an awareness of reality should be encouraged. Children need help in understanding what is real. For example, death is real; it isn't just a long sleep. A favorite blanket is a real blanket; we can talk to it but it won't hear us, although it can give us needed comfort and security through its softness.

Evidence suggests that culture has a strong influence on fantasy and on play involving it (Smilansky, 1968). A culture can strongly discourage fantasy and imaginary play so that children rarely demonstrate either one. Or it can be encouraged. Such encouragement is preferable because fantasy and imaginary play contribute to creative thinking. Encouragement is provided through an environment that is indulgent with children's fantasy and at the same time tries to help children to determine what is real. In such an environment, adults themselves get involved in imaginary play, easily become a participant in children's sociodramatic play, and enjoy beginning imaginary play situations that children can continue. This environment doesn't enforce stereotypes on children; a boy can pretend to be a mother or a girl can be a football player. Materials will be available for children to use in their play. These materials should not be expensive but should be plentiful. A box can be used as a car, a bus driven by the child bus driver, a cave out of which pops a bear, and so on. When the box falls apart, it can be replaced. An expensive item, however, is not so easily replaced and often results in a reprimand for the child who has damaged it, which certainly doesn't foster imaginative play. The best environment is one that is willing to let both child and adult have some fun.

VALUES

Values are a part of human psychology. Our values identify us to our peers. They are a part of our self-image. Values are decisions about the worth of something based on a standard we have set. When we value something, we believe it is worthwhile or that it has worth. Our morals serve as standards—judgments of rightness and wrongness determining our values. Young children are in the earliest stages of moral development and of setting personal values. In the early years of their lives children are learning which values those around them hold. They don't really understand why those values are held, but they recognize them (see Figure 10–3).

Moral Development Theories

Theories regarding children's moral development have been postulated most effectively by Jean Piaget and Lawrence Kohlberg. Some disagreement exists about how accurately their theories predict moral development, but much of what is suggested by the theories has accuracy. Piaget studied children and found that moral development seemed to occur in stages. His first work concerned children's conception of rules (Ginsburg & Opper, 1979).

1. In the *egocentric* stage children do not knowingly follow rules. They do not understand right and wrong. They decide what is wrong and what is right on the basis of what adults permit or forbid them to do.
2. The second stage, that of *incipient cooperation*, involves children's understanding that rules are made to help solve interpersonal conflicts. Children are more social and cooperative.

FIGURE 10–3
We value our efforts when we have pride in them.

3. The last stage, that of *real cooperation*, occurs when children can develop appropriate rules and understand why rules are needed.

Kohlberg (1969) enlarged on Piaget's work. Testing individuals from a variety of cultures and economic levels, he found similarities in development. Kohlberg outlined his ideas as follows:

1. Cognitive development is the major factor in social behavior. Children's ability to understand morally appropriate behavior is limited by their cognitive development. As cognitive development occurs, understanding of morally appropriate behavior and the reasons for that behavior also occurs.
2. Cognitive development, and hence social development, occurs in stages, each of which is qualitatively different from the others. Each new stage represents a different quality of development rather than a quantity.

3. Each new stage is dependent on the achievement of the preceding stages. One cannot jump a stage.
4. Maturational factors and the continuing restructuring of behavior through experience and maturation result in the requirement that no advanced stage may be attained unless all
preceding ones have been attained.

Kohlberg's Stages.   Kohlberg developed a moral Judgment Scale to determine
which of six stages a person was in (see Figure 10–4). Stage 1 was a premoral
stage. People in this stage obeyed because they did not want to be punished for
not obeying. They might suggest, for example, that you should not steal something
because you will get caught and go to jail. Stage 4 represents the middle of the
scale of stages. In this middle stage people believe in maintaining authority. They
believe in the standards set by society and in conforming to accepted law and
order. A stage-4 individual might say that, no matter how good the result and no
matter what the reason, if you steal you have violated what the Bible says regarding
taking someone else's property. A stage-6 person is in the stage of highest moral
development. This person has individual principles of conscience. These principles are always acted upon regardless of the popular norm of behavior. This
person would believe that stealing is usually wrong, but when the life of someone
requires a food or drug that is obtainable only by stealing, then stealing is right,
and a person is wrong who does not value life highly enough to steal what is
needed to maintain it. In between these three stages are other, intermediate ones.

A Dilemma.   Kohlberg's scale determines the stage a person is in by presenting
him with a dilemma. In the dilemma a problem is presented that has many
solutions, each reflecting the moral basis upon which a person decided the
answer given. An example of one of Kohlberg's dilemmas is this:

> In Europe, a woman was near death from cancer. One drug might
> save her, a form of radium that a druggist in the same town had re-
> cently discovered. The druggist was charging $2,000, which was 10
> times what the drug cost him to make. The sick woman's husband,
> Heinz, went to everyone he knew to borrow the money, but he could
> only get together about half of what the drug cost. He told the drug-
> gist that his wife was dying and asked the druggist to sell it cheaper
> or let him pay later. The druggist refused. The husband became des-
> perate and broke into the store to steal the drug for his wife. Should
> the husband have done that? Why or why not?

Kohlberg's theory has many implications for adults working with young
children. Children cannot be expected to understand right from wrong because
they do not have the cognitive ability to do so. They do not do things to be bad.
When they are told something is wrong in a particular situation, they probably
will not transfer the wrongness to other similar situations, and so they may do
it at another time. They are motivated by whether an action brings reward or

LEVEL I: PRECONVENTIONAL (or PREMORAL), Egocentric

Stage 1: PUNISHMENT AND OBEDIENCE ORIENTATION
Obeys rules without questioning to avoid punishment or because it is what authority figures want.
Example: "He shouldn't steal the drug because he'll get caught and go to jail."

Stage 2: NAIVE INSTRUMENTAL HEDONISM
Conforms to obtain reward or have favors returned. (If it satisfies your needs, it's good.) Child thinks of others but first decides what benefits are in a situation for him.
Example: "It's all right to steal the drug because he wants his wife to live."

LEVEL II: CONVENTIONAL, Conformity Orientation

Stage 3: "GOOD-BOY" MORALITY OF MAINTAINING GOOD RELATIONS
Conforms to avoid disapproval by others, behaving in ways that please others. Child begins to have a conscience and to see things from others' viewpoint.
Example: "He shouldn't steal it because people won't think much of his family or him if he does do it."

Stage 4: AUTHORITY AND SOCIAL-ORDER MAINTAINING MORALITY (Law and Order Orientation)
Conforms to avoid censure by legitimate authorities, believing that the social order should be maintained for its own sake.
Example: "He should steal it, but only with the idea of paying the druggist."

LEVEL III: POSTCONVENTIONAL, Individual Moral Principles

Stage 5: MORALITY OF CONTRACT, OF INDIVIDUAL RIGHTS, AND OF DEMO-CRATICALLY ACCEPTED LAW (Social Contract)
Assumes the role of the impartial spectator, judging in terms of community welfare. Laws can be changed as guided by principles of conscience.
Example: "You can't have everyone stealing when they get desperate. The ends may be good, but the ends don't justify the means."

Stage 6: MORALITY OF INDIVIDUAL PRINCIPLES OF CONSCIENCE (Universal Ethical Principles)
Conforms to avoid self-condemnation.
Example: "He should steal it—he has to act in terms of the principle of preserving and respecting life."

FIGURE 10–4
Kohlberg's Stages

punishment rather than whether it is right or wrong. Children will mature and will begin to understand "why." They need explanations in order to understand. Children will eventually begin to develop their own set of moral standards and values. In so doing they will need to know the values of others and the reasons for them. Children need experience in situations requiring decision making, even though cognitively they cannot make a logical decision. Some experience is necessary to learn to make logical decisions.

Problems With Kohlberg's Theory. Children's judgment has been found to become increasingly abstract up to around age 16 (Kohlberg, 1969). It has been found, however, that a child may seem to operate at two or more stages, according to which dilemma he is given. Kurtines and Greif (1974) suggest that the Kohlberg scale doesn't meet the standards usually expected of such a measurement scale. It leaves many of the details of administration to the examiner, uses intuitive scoring methods, and has a reliability that is uncertain because the child's score may fluctuate widely over a short period of time. As a result, they suggest that the instrument for identifying a person's stage of moral development may be the problem more than the theory itself. At any rate, they conclude that "the research done within this framework is beset with a multitude of problems which detract from the model's usefulness" (p. 468).

Gilligan (1982) has argued that women may score lower than men on Kohlberg's scale because they have a greater sense of connectedness with others, acquired at an early age. This sense of connectedness means that women are interpersonally oriented and so will score at stage 3. Men assume their separateness from others and believe formal social rules are necessary to solve the conflicts that will develop between themselves and others with different interests, which leads them to score at stage 4 or 5. Recent literature reviews have found little evidence of women scoring lower than men on Kohlberg's system. What evidence there is tends to disappear when controls are established for the subjects' educational and occupational backgrounds (Rest, 1983; Walker, 1983). As a result Gilligan's arguments for sex-based differences are not well supported.

Three Aspects of Morality

Morality and the value decisions associated with it should not be considered a personality trait, nor is morality a single entity. It has three distinct aspects:

- Moral reasoning
- Self-evaluation
- Conscious resistance to deviant thinking and behavior

Generally, the specific situation seems to affect each person's reaction in each of these aspects of morality. For example, a child may feel guilty after one misbehavior but not after another. Some evidence indicates that more mature styles of moral reasoning are dependent on attainment of certain Piagetian mental operations. Evidence also suggests that growth in moral reasoning is aided by finding that others have different perspectives in morality that conflict with one's own personal perspectives. Finally, some evidence indicates that moral judgments are multidimensional social decisions. These decisions depend on synthesizing several varieties of social information to arrive at conceptions of appropriate and inappropriate behavior (Bandura, 1977).

Self-evaluation has been studied by Hoffman (1977), who views guilt as empathic distress coupled with belief by the person experiencing the guilt that he is responsible for someone else's distress. Parental use of explanations and inductive reasoning helps children learn to accept responsibility for their misbehavior. In inductive reasoning, an individual becomes familiar with examples and nonexamples of something and then uses them to develop a concept or generalization. For example, a parent may talk with a child about a misbehavior, such as jumping on furniture in the living room. The parent reminds the child that he was jumping on the sofa when the parent entered the room and that he had been told not to do so (an example). The parent also asks the child if he remembers jumping on the armchair the previous day and being reminded by the parent that he was not to do so (an example). Then the parent may talk with the child about how he has been permitted to jump and roll on the carpeting (a nonexample). Finally the parent asks the child whether he thinks he is permitted to jump on the loveseat. Why does he think he is/is not permitted to jump on the loveseat? The parent asks the child what he thinks the rule is about jumping in the house. Parent and child agree that the rule is that he must not jump on furniture that people sit on.

Besides adult use of inductive reasoning, Bandura (1977) also suggests that children develop personal standards of appropriate conduct, and that they learn to guide their behavior by rewarding and punishing themselves for attaining or falling short of goals they set for themselves.

When children are tempted to do something they are not supposed to do, the likelihood of succumbing to temptation depends on the following:

- Child-rearing and school experiences
- Understanding of the deviation
- Situational factors

Children whose parents and teachers firmly and consistently insist that they learn and practice habits of self-regulation, who justify their disciplinary action with inductive reasoning, who are warm and communicative, who avoid the use of unnecessarily harsh power-assertive discipline, and who are models of self-controlled behavior are most likely to display desirable conduct when away from adults. Children who think of themselves as intrinsically motivated to behave morally, who anticipate blaming themselves for deviating, who expect pride for good behavior, who know how to talk themselves out of deviating, and who know how to avoid thinking about forbidden activities are better able to resist temptations than children lacking these qualities. Situational incentives and children's moods at the times they are faced with temptations also influence their likelihood of resisting temptation (Perry & Bussey, 1984).

Facilitating Moral Behavior

Research shows that there are developmental changes in the moral judgments children can make, but it is unclear whether their moral conduct correspondingly develops. The question that still is unanswered is whether our ability to recognize what is morally best is translated into action. It does seem that social rules and expectancies become part of social actions quite early in life. Qualitative shifts in cognitive development do occur and do follow predictable sequences. Adults can facilitate children's process of internalizing moral behavior and decision making in these ways:

- Use inductive reasoning with children.
- Verbally attribute prosocial motivation to children.

Even though research results are not clear, adults who work with young children can expect that their cognitive developmental level will influence their ability to understand reasons for moral actions and reasons for rules. Children will continue to need guidance, but it should be guidance resting on the logical reasoning the adult has brought to bear on a situation. Children must not be thought of as more capable of reasoning than they are. Finally, they must not be punished when they cannot understand an action is considered wrong or inappropriate. Explanations and inductive reasoning will do them more good, as will the adult's understanding and appreciation of children's development.

SUMMARY

Children's personal development occurs because of maturation and also because of experience. We all, adults and peers, have some effect on children's development. It is likely that no one person can "take the blame" when social maladjustment occurs because a cumulative effect is occurring. However, children who are experiencing difficulty with one person may not be ready to respond positively to another person. One experience may mitigate against the positive results of other experiences. No one person is totally responsible but neither is any one person totally unimportant when involved in social interactions with children. All adults must accept responsibility for their influence—for their ability to cause change in a child's social development.

REFERENCES

ALLPORT, G. (1958). *The nature of prejudice.* Garden City, NY: Doubleday.

BANDURA, A. (1977). *Social learning theory.* Englewood Cliffs, NJ: Prentice-Hall.

FRENCH, D., BROWNELL, C., GRAZIANO, W., & HARTUP, W. (1977). Effects of cooperative, competitive, and individualistic sets on performance in children's groups. *Journal of Experimental Child Psychology, 24,* 1–10.

GARVEY, C., & HOGAN, R. (1973). Social speech and social interaction: Egocentrism revisited. *Child Development, 44,* 562–568.

GILLIGAN, C. (1982). *In a different voice: Psychological theory and women's development.* Cambridge, MA: Harvard University Press.

GINSBURG, H., & OPPER, S. (1979). *Piaget's theory of intellectual development* (2nd ed.). Englewood Cliffs, NJ: Prentice-Hall.

GOODMAN, M. (1964). *Race awareness in young children.* New York: Macmillan.

GRANT, C. (Ed.). (1977). *Multicultural education: Commitments, issues and applications.* Washington, DC: Association for Supervision and Curriculum Development.

HARTUP, W., GLAZER, J., & CHARLESWORTH, R. (1967). Peer reinforcement and sociometric status. *Child Development, 38,* 1017–1024.

HOFFMAN, M. L. (1977). Moral internalization: Current theory and research. In L. Berkowitz (Ed.), *Advances in experimental social psychology* (Vol. 10, pp. 86–127). New York: Academic Press.

KOHLBERG, L. (1969). Stage and sequence: The cognitive developmental approach to socialization. In D. Goslin (Ed.), *Handbook of socialization theory and research* (pp. 118–140). Chicago: Rand McNally.

KURTINES, W., & GREIF, E. (1974). The development of moral thought: Review and evaluation of Kohlberg's approach. *Psychological Bulletin, 81,* 453–470.

MACCOBY, E., & MASTERS, J. (1970). Attachment and dependency. In P. Mussen (Ed.), *Carmichael's manual of child psychology* (3rd ed., Book 2). New York: Wiley.

MAXIM, G. (1989). *The very young: Guiding children from infancy through the early years.* Columbus, OH: Merrill.

PAGANO, A. (1978). Children learning and using social studies content. In A. Pagano (Ed.), *Social studies in early childhood: An interactionist point of view* (pp. 82–94). Washington, DC: National Council for the Social Studies.

PATTERSON, G. (1976). The aggressive child: Victim and architect of a coercive system. In L. Hamerlynck, L. Handy, & E. Mash (Eds.), *Behavior modification and families. I. Theory and research* (pp. 267–316). New York: Brunner-Mazel.

PERRY, D. G., & BUSSEY, K. (1984). *Social development.* Englewood Cliffs, NJ: Prentice-Hall.

PIAGET, J. (1951). *Play, dreams, and imitation in children.* (C. Gattegno & F. Hodgson, Trans.). New York: Norton.

PIAGET, J. (1954). *The construction of reality in the child.* (R. Cook, Trans.). New York: Basic Books.

PUTALLAZ, M., & GOTTMAN, J. (1981). An interactional model of children's entry into peer groups. *Child Development, 52,* 986–994.

QUILTY, R. (1975). Imitation as a dyadic interchange pattern. *Scandinavian Journal of Psychology, 16,* 223–239.

RAMOS, S. (1975). *Teaching your child to cope with crisis.* New York: David McKay.

REST, J. (1983). Morality. In J. Flavell & E. Markman (Eds.), *Carmichael's manual of child psychology* (4th ed.). New York: Wiley.

ROSS, H., & GOLDMAN, B. (1977). Establishing new social conditions in infancy. In T. Alloway, P. Pliner, & L. Krames (Eds.), *Attachment behavior.* New York: Plenum.

SEARS, R. (1963). Dependency motivation. In M. R. Jones (Ed.), *Nebraska symposium on motivation. 2.* Lincoln, NE: University of Nebraska Press.

SINGLETON, L., & ASHER, S. (1979). Racial integration and children's peer preferences: An investigation of developmental and cohort differences. *Child Development, 50,* 936–941.

SMILANSKY, S. (1968). *The effects of sociodramatic play on disadvantaged preschool children.* New York: Wiley.

SUNAL, C. (1986). Parent involvement in social studies programs. In V. Atwood (Ed.), *Elementary school social studies: Research as a guide to practice*. Washington, DC: National Council for the Social Studies.

WALKER, L. (1983). Sex differences in the development of moral reasoning: A critical review. *Child Development, 54*, 1103–41.

11

THE CHILD'S SENSE
OF HISTORY

One day 4-year-old Alisa asked, "Grandma, were there cars when you were little?" Young children are interested in the past. Their interest is strong even though they cannot understand time as adults do (Piaget, 1970). They are interested in exploring past events that were personally experienced by an adult who is important to the child.

Alisa's grandmother replied to her question by talking about the first car she remembered her parents having. She showed Alisa an old photograph of the car and, on another day, took her to see antique cars in a parade. Since then Alisa has maintained an interest in old cars. Two factors are important in the manner in which Alisa's grandmother handled her question. First, she capitalized on Alisa's interest by relating cars to the grandmother's experience as a little girl. Their interaction revolved around the personal experiences of an individual familiar to Alisa. Second, Alisa's grandmother followed up on the initial interest by finding an old photograph and by taking her to see antique cars in a parade. Alisa's question was answered with a specific "yes" and then followed up with experiences that allowed Alisa to use her senses to make many observations related to her initial question.

Watt (1972) has defined history "in terms of response: to say that history is that to which people respond historically, and that historical response is an emotional or intellectual reaction to the knowledge, or the belief that certain things happened in the past. Such a response is ... a sense of the past." (p. 43) Alisa's grandmother responded to the intellectual and emotional content of her granddaughter's question. She stimulated further intellectual and emotional reactions in her granddaughter, enlarging her "sense of the past."

TIME

Children's exploration of history is affected by their conception of time. Children make what adults consider to be "errors" in working with time. Alisa may seriously question whether there were cars when her grandmother was a child because her grandmother is surely old. Dramatic errors in the estimation of time usually are few by age 8, when the basic thought processes of the concrete operational period enable children to better understand the passage of time. The comprehension of time by preschool and primary-grade children is affected by the characteristics of their preoperational thought (Figure 11–1). Two characteristics of thinking influence children's understanding of time: centration and reversibility.

Centration

Centration is the centering of attention on one feature of a situation to the exclusion of all others (Piaget, 1964). Children focus on part of an event, on a particular slice of time. Such focusing results in children's acquisition of a kaleidoscope of individual scenes usually having no relationship in time. Therefore, little structure is available with which to impose a time sequence on children's experiences. When children do try to link experiences together, transductive thinking occurs. In transductive thinking preoperational children link experiences together as is, with no time sequence logically imposed. The result is a stream of events that the child understands as connected but that do not actually have any cause and effect relationship (Ginsburg & Opper, 1982).

Reversibility

Reversibility involves the understanding that something that has been changed can be mentally, and sometimes physically, returned to its original state by reversing the process of change. For example, a ball of clay that has been rolled

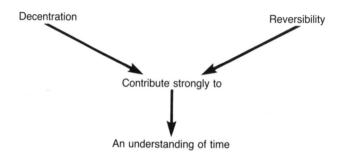

FIGURE 11–1
Characteristics of thinking that lead to understanding time

out into a long, thin rope can be rerolled into a ball (Stassen Berger, 1980, p. 552), a physical reversal. Although young children observe such a reversal and even carry it out following someone's directions, they are still fooled by the way the clay looks. The rope stretches out and looks longer so it seems to have more clay. Young children can't mentally follow the rolled-out clay back to its start, the clay ball. Older, concrete operational children can quickly mentally reverse the process and visualize it.

Reversibility is essential to an understanding of time. Reversibility can occur with both physical actions and mental actions—thoughts not related to any physical activity. An example of reversing a mental action occurs when we think through a problem to its solution and then retrace the steps we took to arrive at the solution, looking for any errors we might have made. Centering interferes with reversibility. When children devote all attention to one point in time and ignore other points along the way, they cannot retrace their mental steps. Retracing can't occur because some of those steps were not stored in memory. They were ignored as others were centered on. The development of reversibility occurs after the child has begun to *decenter*, that is, to move away from centering as a characteristic of thinking. Reversibility is important to an understanding of time sequence and is part of the reason why logical understanding of time doesn't appear until middle childhood (Piaget, 1970).

Other characteristics of preoperational thought have some influence on young children's conception of time, but centering and a lack of reversibility are probably the major factors involved in children's conceptions of time.

Children's Capabilities

Understanding the limitations of young children's ability to understand time is necessary, but an understanding of their capabilities is also important. By ages 3 and 4, young children know there was a yesterday and are aware of a tomorrow. They also have a conception of age as related to time. They can correctly identify a 20-year-old as younger than a 40- or 60-year-old (Jantz & Seefeldt, 1976), although specific errors do occur. At ages 4 and 5, they begin to discern an order in important days in their lives: birthdays, Halloween, Valentine's Day, and so on. As they begin to discern an order they often ask, "When is (holiday) coming?" Then, "What comes next?" They are beginning to sequence events over a longer period of time because they perceive that such a sequence exists. Around age 7, as children move into concrete operational thinking, more accurate conceptions of time are built and longer periods of time are understood.

Levstik (1986) reminds us that children also are capable of an emotional response to historical events when those events are told as a story. Young children's interest in fantasy, nursery rhymes, and fairy tales demonstrates their ability to react to stories that are not limited to the here and now (Levstik, 1986). Young children enjoy historical fiction and will gradually move on to biography and nonliterary sources to verify their perceptions as they mature (Levstik, 1986, p. 74).

HISTORY EDUCATION

Definition

"Working with events in times past" is a definition of history education that can be used by early childhood programs. Another related relevant definition is "experiencing parts of times past" (Sunal & Warash, 1987).

Characteristics

Laville and Rosenzweig (1982) suggest that history education has a humane function. It centers on making people more independent, free, reflective, and critical. For this purpose, we need most of all to teach children processes rather than a package of facts. This doesn't mean children should not learn facts about the past nor does it mean that we cannot decide that some facts are more important than others. It does mean that facts should be presented as instruments used in social analysis—as part of a system and sometimes as results of social analysis. History becomes open to discussion and reevaluation. It is not closed up with the decisions all made before children ever get to work with it (pp. 57–58).

Instruction

This open view of history education emphasizes thinking (Figure 11–2). It is compatible with the active role Piaget (1964) and McKenzie (1986) have suggested for teaching and learning. With young children, it assumes the child is thinking and building on that thinking no matter what limitations exist. For very young children, history education focuses on experiences with history that add to children's storehouse of learned facts and strengthen their learning processes, such as observation. These facts can eventually be used by children to make inferences related to historical situations. With young children the presentation of a "package of facts" frustrates the learning process. It is true that children are avidly acquiring

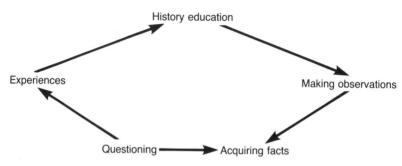

FIGURE 11–2
History education for young children

facts, but this acquisition occurs only when they experience facts in some active manner.

Children's investigation of history best occurs when they are involved with either loved, familiar people like grandparents or with impressive strangers who attract their interest, such as a visitor dressed in a brightly colored Revolutionary War uniform. Bandura's (1977) modeling theory suggests that children don't learn equally well from everyone. They are more likely to imitate the behavior of others if they particularly admire and identify with them. If these admired people try positively to reinforce children for what they do, the effect will be stronger. Evidence has accumulated that children may model parents, peers, teachers, and sports, movie, literary, and historical figures (Stassen Berger, 1980). Modeling theory has implications for history education because models can be a valuable part of children's experiences with history if the power of a model's influence on children is recognized and appropriately utilized.

History education is active and emphasizes questioning, interpretation, and knowledge of the social facts of the past and present. It should also be based on real problems for which children have contemporary concrete referents in their own environment (Laville & Rosenzweig, 1982, p. 3). The adult's role is active and responsive to children, with an emphasis on the encouragement of questioning and social interaction.

TOPICS IN HISTORY EDUCATION

History education for young children often begins with experiences related to an individual children know. Such experiences can open up many avenues for continuing exploration leading from the original experience. Topics for young children's history education can include any area, but they often center on the following:

1. Past events (e.g., a birthday party that occurred when grandmother was 7 years old)
2. People in the past who behaved as we do today (e.g., singing and making noise to celebrate a special family event—such as a birthday)
3. Change (e.g., in automobile design)
4. An introduction into what time means (e.g., Alisa's grandmother as a little girl when a remembered birthday party occurred)

Choosing a Topic

How does one choose a topic? In the home, such choices usually occur naturally within the context of daily activities and discussions. In a school setting, where there are children from many homes, topics of interest often vary widely from child to child. Some topics do interest most children, however, and these are the topics many teachers select. Care must be taken that a topic is not imposed on a group of children who are, in this instance, reluctant or uninterested. Such frequently occurring topics as "George Washington and the cherry tree" may be questioned if the criteria to be used are (a) natural occurrence and (b) familiarity. Children living in Virginia may find the topic of interest, especially if they can go on a field trip to Mount Vernon. Children in Michigan's cherry orchard counties may also find the topic of interest. Children in southwest Texas, however, may find little that is familiar in this topic. All young children are likely to be unable to understand the moral of the story because they don't understand the concept of a lie. So the question arises again, particularly when a group of young children is involved: "How does one choose a topic?"

The reasons for asking the question should be examined. For sensorimotor and preoperational children, content learning is not important. It may occur, but children's activity is not directed toward its acquisition. The processes of thinking that young children develop are more important. History itself as a content topic is inappropriate for very young children. Therefore, the four topics cited earlier are general. They encourage the use of processes—of patterns of understanding one's world that can be applied to many specific topics, such as changing automobile design. For very young children, the adult's question should actually be: "What topic is a naturally occurring familiar one that (a) lends itself to children's active exploration via their senses and (b) also allows them to organize and classify the information gained from their senses and from active exploration?"

An alternate, or additional, question may reflect Levstik's (1986) comments regarding children's ability intellectually and emotionally to enjoy stimulating literature about faraway times and places. Such historical literature may not focus on topics that are naturally occurring in the child's environment nor familiar, but it is intellectually and emotionally stimulating. Such a story or nursery rhyme often has rhythmic qualities that can be actively explored and enjoyed by young children. This question therefore is, "What topic is found in a story the children enjoy?"

For later primary-grades children, who are concrete operational thinkers, individual topics should be considered as part of a whole that contributes to their understanding of history. These children should actively explore topics in ways that enable them to develop fundamental historical concepts. Sample concepts include:

- Chronology
- Cause and effect
- Colony

Sample generalizations that may be inferred include these:

- We all experience change.
- Historical events are often influenced by key individuals.
- The everyday experiences of ordinary people have had an impact on how societies have changed.

Planning for children's experiences with history requires active listening on the adult's part. The best way to begin is to spend some time really listening to the questions being asked by young children. Areas children demonstrate active interest in are starting points. Choices should be made on the basis of topics that offer an opportunity for concrete, sensory experiences and for the organization of information gained from these experiences via classification and, eventually, concept formation. A topic such as "Indians" may be limited when concrete experiences are required. This topic may also lend itself to stereotyping when the range of concrete experience possible is very limited. An effort must be made to brainstorm many possibilities for concrete experiences with a topic that seems limited.

Some classroom teachers have basal social studies texts available. These are likely to contain limited specifically historical content. Other content in the basal text is likely to lend itself to historical considerations if the teacher approaches it creatively. A focus on investigating the local neighborhood, for example, might be extended to a consideration of the history of the neighborhood. Were the first homes built long ago or rather recently? Did that building on the corner across the street from the school once have a store on the first floor? How can we find out? Although a basal text may dictate topics to be studied, the teacher can insure that the topic is explored broadly and that children's interests are attended to and stimulated.

Types of History

The adult's definition of history often becomes a limitation on the choice of topics. Most adults think of history in terms of presidents and generals (Krug, 1967). Teachers of young children translate presidents into "George Washington and the cherry tree" and generals into events such as Independence Day. Pilgrims and Indians often fill out this set of topics for historical studies. History is often approached as political history. But history is also social and technological.

Social and Family History. Social history is the history of all people, not just politically famous people (Krug, 1967). A basic question asked by the social historian is "What was it like to be _____?" Examples of this are:

> *"What was it like to be a child on a New England farm in the early colonial period?"*

> *"What was it like to be an African-American child on a rice plantation in Louisiana in 1880?"*

> *"What was it like to be a Depression-era child in Detroit?"*

Another question is "How did _____ contribute to the economic (cultural, political) life of the country?" For example,

> *"How did the work of women contribute to the economic life of early colonial America?"*

Family history is a part of social history. Family history is of great interest to young children. It can discuss familiar, loved people who are important to children. It can discuss events that children can concretely relate to familiar people and places and to experiences that are often not too different from those the children have had. Social history in general often has some or all of these attributes, which make it a most relevant history for young children.

Technological History.   Technological history is another form of history that young children usually find interesting. Young children often express lively interest in awesome representatives of older technologies such as steam-driven locomotives; river steamboats; the complex gearwork, pulleys and belts in old factories; and large hand weaving looms.

David, as a 3-year-old, visited the train museum in Baltimore. The museum houses steam locomotives and an enormous toy railroading set, and is an actual railroading center. There are lots of tracks, repair sheds, and a roundhouse. All of this makes up the museum and much of it can be visited. The total atmosphere of the site seemed to enthrall David. Afterward, he was interested in any book that had "train pictures." He loved children's stories about trains, such as *The Little Engine That Could.* Fingerplays such as "Choo-choo-choo, the train went up the track . . ." were favorites. Of course, he wanted a train set. He continued his train interest and soon could identify all sorts of historic trains from their pictures. He was fascinated by pictures of very early trains whose cars were really carriages adapted to ride on train tracks. To David, the history of the train was endlessly interesting. One part of technological history had captured his interest. David was fascinated by trains, Mariam was interested in cameras, Jenny in hand looms, Asa in trucks, Adolfo in lights and switches, Marjorie in buses. Their interests suggest lots of topics to pursue in technological history education.

Social history, technological history, and political history are all specific types of history. They can be viewed as separate, but they are also interrelated. Their interrelationship implies the necessity to understand history as more than politics. History is about families and machines, farmers and generals, children and their toys. History education should include each of these types of history and should try to bring them together so that their interrelationships can be explored.

TEACHING TOPICS

Preoperational and Sensorimotor Children

Once a topic has been chosen, then what? With preoperational and sensorimotor children, open exploration should be used to introduce a topic. If the topic is transportation and, more specifically, cars, children could start by visiting the center's parking lot or a nearby street. They should touch, sit in, and ride in different kinds of cars: big ones, small ones, station wagons, sedans, old cars, new cars. A visit to an automobile sales showroom and an automobile junkyard would be fun and thought provoking. Back at the center children could be given models of antique and modern cars to play with. Later, pictures of additional models of cars might be introduced. The children could classify the cars. Further trips to broaden the base of the children's experience could include a visit to a nearby garage to look at a car's engine and underside, a trip to a museum to see antique cars, a trip to an assembly plant to watch new cars being put together, and a visit to an auto parts store. Children might eventually organize pictures or models of cars into groups. Some children might be able to organize them into a simple time line of the history of cars.

Teacher-guided exploration can occur on field trips as the teacher asks questions related to what is being seen and draws children's attention to things they haven't noticed. Children can be given an opportunity to classify both during and after their trip.

Concrete Operational Children

Children who are concrete operational should be given lots of data relating to a topic, such as cars, to work with. For example, if they visit a museum to look at old cars, they can afterward work with pictures of many old cars. The children make observations of both the real cars and of the pictures of old cars. These observations are shared with their classmates. As the observations are made, the teacher records them on chart paper. To help the children begin to discern patterns in the evolution of automobile design, the teacher can provide additional photographs and some models of old cars. As students examine these, their observations are recorded.

The children at one school noticed patterns emerging. They noted that, when arranged in a time sequence, cars became more "closed up." That is, a roof and roll-up windows were added to all cars except for convertibles. The occupants of a car were eventually no longer exposed to the weather as they drove along. The children also noticed a gradual smoothing of design. That is, the running board disappeared, headlights became incorporated into the body of the car, and there generally were fewer protuberances on a car. The teacher wrote children's comments on chart paper as they identified these two patterns. Library research and interviews with family members and two automobile dealers provided the children with information that supported the two patterns they had noted in the data. The students refined the statements until they had developed two generalizations:

- As people got used to cars, they wanted to be more comfortable in them, and so cars became more closed up.
- To make cars go faster, they were designed so they were smoother.

After these generalizations had been arrived at, the teacher extended the children's activity by encouraging them to go out to the school's parking lot. There they looked over cars produced in the past few years and decided their generalizations applied to the cars in the parking lot. All the cars were closed up and were smooth (had few protuberances).

The topic of "cars" was one for which lots of data were available. Many historical topics are more difficult to study because less data are available. For example, if children are exploring the experiences of slave children in their state during the 19th century, they are likely to have few memoirs or letters to work with. Their resources may be mostly census figures and other data that do not address the experience of slavery, but rather verify its existence. In such cases the few pieces of data that do address the experience should be used and their limitations noted. Children can be encouraged to build concepts and general-izations about the experience. But they must also be encouraged to infer the limitations that scarce data impose.

PEOPLE AS RESOURCES

In exploring any topic in history education, people are especially rich resources for children. Family, community, technological, and national history assume a sense of reality when described by an individual who lived that history. As an adjunct to having visitors come to the classroom, reproductions of paintings can also be used to bring people and events from the past into the classroom (Sunal & Hatcher, 1986).

Tape Recordings

Some teachers have tape-recorded stories told by people both in the classroom and privately at the person's home. Many times these stories are popular and are played over and over. Taping in the classroom has its good and bad points. Background noise is difficult to control, so the resulting tape may be hard to understand because of a chaos of noises. These noises can be controlled if the speaker is in a small room with a limited group of children. The tape will still have children's comments on it but these may highlight important and intriguing parts of the story. Children enjoy listening to a tape on which their comments are also recorded. If it's a really interesting story, they'll keep on listening to it as well as to extraneous comments accompanying it (Mehaffy, Sitton, & Davis, 1979). Private recording is more likely to result in a clearly recorded story. Because most of us aren't used to recording, we rarely have perfect diction, pitch, and so on. If the story is good, a few imperfections won't matter. The bad point about private recording is that it separates the person from the story. The children hear it but don't experience its telling. The interest level may not be as great, as a result.

USING EACH CHILD'S PERSONAL HISTORY

The child's past, the child's heritage, the child's family history, and other chil-dren's family histories are all effective approaches to history education with young children. What about specifics? Each child might be asked to build a limited family tree going back to grandparents. A family tree can lead to discussion of family size. It can also encourage investigation of family relationships. Discussing where family members live and have lived is another natural extension. Finally, what families do and have done together can be discussed.

The Life Span

An additional approach works with building children's concept of the life span. The concept of the life span will contribute to building children's sense of personal history, which can in turn be used to build a wider sense of history.

Infancy makes a good starting point. Children enjoy visits to their class by infants. They can be encouraged to talk about how they differ from the infant and can be given an opportunity to examine diapers, bottles, and infant clothing. This is also a good time to have them bring in their baby pictures.

Later, children can move from considering what has been, infancy, to what will be, middle childhood. Emphasis might be placed on how children in upper elementary grades differ from young children. A visit to a sixth grade classroom or a junior high school should be interesting. Middle grades students can visit in return and read a story, play a game, or do some other activity with the children. They can talk about their favorite snack, television program, hobby, and so on.

Many children will be familiar with adolescent baby-sitters but are not aware of what they do when they're not baby-sitting. A visit to a high school may be possible, perhaps through arrangements with a child development class being offered for high school students. During the visit the children might eat a snack in the cafeteria or visit the greenhouse or planetarium, a shop class, or a practice session of the chorus. High-school students could pay return visits to the children. Foods-class students might cook something with the children. Lots of possibilities exist.

Children should talk with young, middle-aged, and elderly adults. Children should be specifically involved with an age group that seems to have few representatives in their neighborhoods. Activities with adults can include talking about how they occupy their time and about their favorite games, clothes, foods, and so on. Children should spend some time becoming acquainted with adult activities. Adults of all ages may jog, cook, or read. Talking to adults, watching them, and visiting places where they work and play will help children understand similarities and differences among adults.

The conception of the life span is basic to children's sense of history. The life span is the central part of a person's own history. It is extended into the past by ancestors and into the future by descendants and by those who have been influenced by the person. As children begin to develop a sense of their current place in the life span, judgment of others' places in their life span becomes possible.

ACTIVITIES WITH TIME

Activities building a sense of history also build an understanding of time. With very young children, concepts important to understanding history are "before" and "after." Adults can build an understanding of these concepts by using them in referring to daily routines. For example, "Wash your hands before you eat lunch." This statement encourages the development of a personalized concept on a level easily grasped by many young children. Adults should identify words commonly used to convey time and/or assume an understanding of time. After identifying them, adults should try to use such words with children in situations that include concrete experiences with the term.

Marking Time With Shadows.   The passage of time can be examined on a daily basis using outdoor shadow clocks and shadow games (*Early experiences*, 1977). Children can draw a small "x" on a concrete playground area. As a child stands on her "x," another child traces her shadow with chalk on the concrete. This drawing is labeled with the time of day. The process is repeated hourly. With each passing hour, the children will notice their shadow has moved and changed in size (Figure 11–3). The passage of time can be determined by the direction and size of the shadow. Early shadow clocks were developed in this manner.

Shadow games can be added to enhance children's understanding. These can be played at times of the day when different sizes of shadows occur in order to extend the children's experience with the changing of size and position of shadows throughout the day. For example, shadows are short at noon so jumping on another child's shadow is difficult. Games include having children try to jump on one another's shadows and arranging shadows so the shadows are holding hands or forming alphabet letters.

Building an awareness of the passage of time is easier when there is concrete evidence of change. Shadow study allows children to see something happening. They begin to understand a relationship between snack time and a certain type of shadow and between lunchtime and another type of shadow. Shadow length is a means of classifying time. For example, "short shadow" is lunchtime. Shadow play should continue over a period of time and then be repeated occasionally.

Marking Time With the Moon.   Longer lengths of time can be studied through observation of the changing moon in the daytime sky. The children can look for the moon periodically during the day while standing in the same spot. The spot can be a circle with their name written in it. Then, they should draw it on a map of their play area. They might note that it is over the slide set at noon and over the sandbox at 2 p.m. When the activity is repeated the next day, they will notice a change in the moon's position. They will observe a change throughout the day and over a period of several days. If the activity is repeated over several months, the children will see a repetition of movement. Comments may be heard such

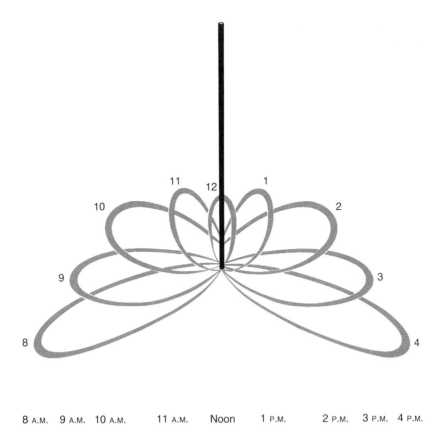

8 A.M.   9 A.M.   10 A.M.   11 A.M.   Noon   1 P.M.   2 P.M.   3 P.M.   4 P.M.

FIGURE 11–3
Drawing of the shadows produced by a stick from 8 A.M. to 4 P.M.

as, "Hey! Look! It's on top of the sandbox again!" Moon watching is possible at all ages. But mapping the changing position of the moon is difficult for early preoperational children, usually under age 4½. Simply going outside and finding the moon is the best activity for the youngest children because the daily change is an obvious one. Three-year-olds will find that there has been a major change in position if they find the moon at 3 p.m. one day and then look for it at 9:00 a.m. the next day.

Old Methods of Marking Time.   Many old methods of marking time, such as sand clocks and shadow clocks, are concrete. Early methods of telling time were used by people who usually were uneducated, so they tended to be based on some kind of physical observations and were not very abstract in their simpler forms. Many of them are easily understood by late preoperational and early concrete children. The adult should realize that even simple, observational methods became quite sophisticated over the centuries. So, in using an old method of marking time with young children, the adult should make certain it is an "unimproved" basic version. In using an unimproved version, children will be living history—the history of timekeeping.

Time Lines. In teaching concepts of time, simple, pictorial time lines can be used effectively. A birthday time line with children's pictures on it can depict birthdays from January through December. Time lines over a longer span can also be built using pictures over the important dates. The time line should have a specific topic and should not contain a large variety of subdivisions.

Current Events. Today's current events are tomorrow's history. Circle time is a good opportunity for children and teacher to talk about news events. Children's interest in the news will be sharpened and perhaps they may begin to make some sense of it (Ellis, 1977). Reflecting on last week's current events offers children an opportunity to develop their sense of the passage of time. If parents are informed of current events activities, they can work at home with their children to build better awareness of current events.

Marking Time and Celebrating History With Holidays. Ellis (1977) suggests that holidays are big news to young children. Current events time can be used to review the history and traditions of holidays. Celebrations can include lesser known holidays. The following are suggested as possibilities for historical investigation (pp. 320–321).

Martin Luther King's Birthday	Flag Day
March of Dimes Week	American Indian Day
Fire Prevention Day	Brotherhood Week
Black History Week	Columbus Day
United Nations Day	Conservation Week
Veteran's Day	Kindness to Animals Week
May Day	Susan B. Anthony's Birthday
Mother's Day	Presidents Day
Citizenship Day	Bill of Rights Day
Father's Day	Grandparent's Day

What other holidays can you add? Holidays are a special sort of current event that usually has an interesting history if it has not become stereotyped, as has happened with some holidays commonly observed in programs for young children.

Learning About the Concept of Change. Over the course of time things change. History identifies and examines changes that have occurred. The pace of change seems to have been increasing throughout this century. Young children need to become aware of change as it occurs in their social world and need to be helped to learn to cope with it. In their daily activities very young children can work with understanding the concept of change by considering the following questions:

> *"Is something different here?"*
>
> *"What is changing?"*
>
> *"What caused the change?"*

Primary-grades children might also ask "What does this change cost us?" and "Is the change worth what it costs?" (Sunal, 1981).

SUMMARY

"Did you play hide-and-seek when you were 6 years old?" The interest in history is there. So is an early form of a sense of history. What young children need is the opportunity to extend their sense of history. That opportunity can be built from little things—from old valentines and from a ride on Grandpa's shoulders like the one Mom had when she was 4 years old. The experiences provided make a difference; they build and they provide something to build on.

REFERENCES

BANDURA, A. (1977). *Social learning theory.* Englewood Cliffs, NJ: Prentice-Hall.

Early experiences. (1977). New York: MacDonald Educational.

ELLIS, A. (1977). *Teaching and learning elementary social studies.* Boston: Allyn & Bacon.

GINSBURG, H., & OPPER, S. (1982). *Piaget's theory of intellectual development* (3rd ed.). Englewood Cliffs, NJ: Prentice-Hall.

JANTZ, R., & SEEFELDT, C. (1976). *Curriculum guide: Children's attitudes toward the elderly.* College Park, MD: University of Maryland Center on Aging.

KRUG, M. (1967). *History and the social sciences.* Waltham, MA: Blaisdell.

LAVILLE, C., & ROSENZWEIG, L. (1982). Teaching and learning history: Developmental dimensions. In L. Rosenzweig (Ed.), *Developmental perspectives on the social studies.* NCSS Bull. No. 66. Washington, DC: National Council for the Social Studies.

LEVSTIK, L. (1986). Teaching history: A definitional and developmental dilemma. In V. Atwood (Ed.), *Elementary school social studies: Research as a guide to practice.* NCSS Bull. No. 79. Washington, DC: National Council for the Social Studies.

MCKENZIE, G. (1986). Learning and instruction. In V. Atwood (Ed.), *Elementary school social studies: Research as a guide to practice* (pp. 119–136). NCSS Bull. No. 79. Washington, DC: National Council for the Social Studies.

MEHAFFY, G. L., SITTON, T., & DAVIS, O. L., JR. (1979). *Oral history in the classroom.* How-To-Do-It Series 2, No. 8. Washington, DC: National Council for the Social Studies.

PIAGET, J. (1964). *The early growth of logic in the child* (E. A. Lunzer & D. Papert, Trans.). London: Routledge & Kegan Paul.

PIAGET, J. (1970). *The child's conception of time* (A. Pomerans, Trans.). New York: Basic Books.

STASSEN BERGER, K. (1980). *The developing person.* New York: Worth.

SUNAL, C. S. (1981). The child and the concept of change. *Social Education, 45,* 438–441.

SUNAL, C. S., & HATCHER, B. (1986). *How to do it: Studying history through art.* Washington, DC: National Council for the Social Studies.

SUNAL, C. S., & WARASH, B. (1987). A long time ago: Teaching history to young children. *Dimensions, 15,* 4–9.

WATT, D. G. (1972). *The learning of history.* London: Routledge and Kegan Paul.

12

THE YOUNG GEOGRAPHER

Young children seem to move in every possible way, physically interacting with the space around them. Perceptual-motor research (Barsch, 1967) has examined the developmental implications of this movement. This research implies that early geography activities should be based on the assumption that children's movement helps them acquire information they need to develop geographic concepts.

Much of children's movement is spontaneous and does not follow a carefully structured sequence. This is the sort of movement found in everyday experiences. It is generally not carefully organized by adults. This movement generates a wide range of information, some of which will be applicable in forming geographic concepts (Sunal & Sunal, 1978a).

DEFINING GEOGRAPHY

Children must develop a repertoire of space concepts that they can easily use before they are able to map the environment. Geography is an explanation, a description, and a structuring of an interaction between objects physically existing in space. Borchert (1983) has described it as one way of selecting things to observe in the world around us, assembling the observations, and thinking about them. Borchert also states that these observations are descriptions of the physical and cultural features of human settlements and their natural settings. The discipline considers data in terms of geographic patterns and changes in pattern (Borchert, 1983). Geographic concepts are rooted in space concepts.

SPACE CONCEPTS

Early Development

Space is explored early in development so that, by the third month, babies are coordinating eyes with hand and foot movement and investigating space through this coordinated movement (Piaget & Inhelder, 1967). Children soon learn to distinguish the faraway object from one nearby. They also define the external outlines of objects and differentiate small, large, and medium-sized objects. By approximately age 2 they develop an experience-based understanding of space in terms of their senses and motor activities (Piaget & Inhelder, 1967).

Early understandings of space provide information from which the representational mapping of space can be developed, beginning around age 2 (Laurendeau and Pinard, 1968). These representations initially probably are simply rough approximations because young children's thought is limited and somewhat inflexible. Also, young children construct their mental image of space piecemeal. This image is not really one image; rather, it is a mosaic of images. Each part of the mosaic is fragmentary. Each is distinct from the others. Each is dependent upon the dominant perceptions provided by personal experience (Sauvy & Sauvy, 1972).

Topological Space

A mosaic of images is what Piaget and Inhelder (1967) are referring to when they describe children's interest in topological space. Topological space means that, for young children, the only really meaningful spatial relationships are those of a particular kind. These include neighborhood, or proximity; enclosure (in two dimensions) as occurs in a drawing of a square with the inside enclosed by the lines of the drawing; envelopment (in three dimensions) as occurs when a child sits in a box completely surrounded by the box; continuity; separation; and order. For example, the young child will carefully place blocks next to each other, making sure that each touches its partner. Yet the child will aim the line of blocks in any direction and will often end up with a wandering line going to no place in particular. The attention to detail is there but the holistic view is not. These detailed relationships do not allow children to understand space in terms of Euclidean geometry. An object is not seen as being composed of points that are at invariant distances from each other as, for example, in a square. Nor do children understand placing an object precisely in a frame of reference. Very young children can be introduced to topological space because it does not require reference to straight lines nor does it require measurement (Sauvy & Sauvy, 1974).

Projective and Euclidean Space

From the age of 4 or 5, projective space and Euclidean space begin to be sketched in against this background of topological space. The predominance of topological considerations continues until the child begins to achieve concrete operations at around age 7. For example, a child who can distinguish his right from his left hand usually cannot correctly distinguish the right and left hands of a child facing him. Laurendeau and Pinard (1968) suggest this occurs because the child's thought is still centered, and he is not yet integrating the parts of the whole situation nor is he able to use reversibility. Projective relations, involving straight lines and perspective, begin development but are not thoroughly accomplished before age 7. Euclidean geometric relationships are present only in the form of a rough sketch in young children. Maps, graphs, and diagrams incorporate topological, Euclidean, and projective concepts. They provide a variety of information dependent upon them.

EGOCENTRISM

As children strive to structure and understand relationships occurring in the space around them, their efforts can be limited by their egocentrism. Egocentric individuals perceive the world from their own point of view and cannot usually take the perspective of others (Seifert & Hoffnung, 1987). Young children are able in specific, very familiar situations to understand another's point of view (Selman, 1980; Liben, 1978). Donaldson (1979) has reported that children are not egocentric when the tasks they are given are relevant to their experience. Opportunities to try to understand spatial relationships confront the child with different viewpoints, which results in efforts to resolve the confusion that can be produced by different viewpoints. In making this effort children move toward understanding. As they move toward understanding, egocentrism appears less frequently (Flavell, 1977).

SPECIFIC AREAS OF TOPOLOGICAL STUDY

Because topological space concepts are grasped first by young children, they should serve as the starting point for geographic activities (see Figure 12–1). Activity should progress from work with children's self-image outward. Children need to understand concepts such as "up" and "down" and "back" and "front" in relation to their own body before trying to apply them to the space they live in (Piaget & Inhelder, 1967; Barsch, 1967). As children progress outward, they need ample opportunities to experience their surroundings concretely.

Eight topological concepts are basic to geographic skills (Sunal & Sunal, 1978b):

1. Continuity and discontinuity
2. Closed curve
3. Boundary and region
4. Exterior and interior
5. Holes
6. Order
7. Point of reference
8. Direction.

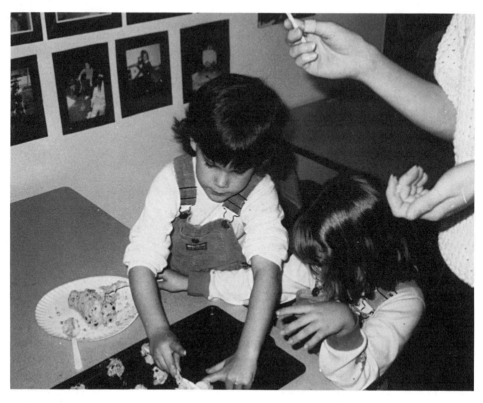

FIGURE 12–1
Cookie making provides many opportunities to explore topology.

Continuity and Discontinuity

Continuity and discontinuity can be understood by imagining that someone has painted the curb on a block yellow. If you stand in the middle of the next block, the yellow curb looks like a yellow line beginning at a lamppost and ending at a litter basket. The line is continuous, with no breaks in it, and has definite beginning and ending points. Now suppose that Ann brings out her tricycle and places it on the yellow line. Starting anywhere on the line, you can walk along it, approach the tricycle, arrive in its neighborhood, and reach it. As you continue along the line you will, for a moment, be in the tricycle's neighborhood, but on the other side of it. Then you will finally leave it behind. Next, Ann brings out a wagon and a large ball, which she sets on the line near the tricycle. Now the tricycle has neighbors on the line on either side of it. The line continues on and is understood to be continuous even though these objects are on it. Now, suppose that a section of the yellow painted curb crumbles. When it crumbles it breaks up the continuous line into two separate lines beginning and ending at the crumbled section. A discontinuity has been introduced.

What are some experiences that can present clear instances of continuity and discontinuity? Children usually follow the same path to the bathroom, eating area, and outside playground. They walk or ride in a car or a bus to school along the same path. These daily activities can be used as a beginning point. Children might chalk or tape a line on the floor indicating the path they follow to the bathroom or eating area. Then they can mark it on a drawing of the route. This activity can be repeated with many familiar paths. Eventually children can be asked to draw a line indicating a continuous path on a drawing of two familiar places, such as the classroom door and closet.

Discontinuities can include a big puddle on the sidewalk that the children are asked to go around. Or Dennis has built a block tower right in the middle of the usual path to the sink. Discontinuities break up usual patterns and should be noted and discussed. They can also become the focus of a path-drawing activity in which the children draw in the obstacle. As children begin to translate their paths into two-dimensional drawings, they move toward an understanding of the use of maps such as road maps, which are maps of continuous and discontinuous paths.

Closed Curve

A concept related to that of continuous and discontinuous lines is the closed curve. A closed curve can be compared to the outline of a swimming pool. There is no end point. Wherever a person begins walking around the pool, he can travel its whole length without encountering any discontinuities. Sometimes the path of a closed curve crosses itself, as in the figure "8," without a discontinuity. The walker is able to continue right along and return to the point at which the walk began. A closed curve is essentially a continuous line whose two end points have been joined together. Children's environment contains many closed curves. The edge of Johnnie's bathtub and the edge of the fountain in the park are closed curves. On a larger scale, the freeway near Ann's grandmother's home in Washington, D.C., forms a circle around the District of Columbia and is aptly called a beltway. On an even larger scale, the boundaries of a state or nation form closed curves. Young children's experiences with closed curves on a smaller scale provide them with an opportunity to develop the foundation for understanding larger closed curves such as those represented by the boundaries of a nation.

Interior and Exterior, Boundary and Region

A closed curve defines two spatial regions, an interior and an exterior. Neither region shares anything with the other. The closed curve creates a division between them, just as a fence divides the park inside it from the streets outside it. The concept of a boundary easily becomes part of an investigation of interiors and exteriors because the boundary is the closed curve dividing the two regions.

A Game.   Boundaries and regions and exteriors and interiors are concepts that are involved in the game "Crossing the Barriers." Children play on teams. Each team wears its own color armbands and matching hats. Teams take turns moving about; for example, moving from the snack area to the block area or from the swing set to the sandbox. As the children take turns they encounter barriers that have a team color on them, such as a piece of rope or a wood plank. When children meet and pass a barrier with their color on it, they take off their hats. When the children encounter a barrier with another team's color on it, they put their hats on. Children are always "hats off" in a certain region, and soon they discover this. The barriers can help them define the boundaries of that region and determine whether they are in the interior of it. This game can be transferred to paper with the barriers represented by different colored paper strips. Colored counters represent the children. Activities such as "Crossing the Barriers" help children develop a basis for understanding boundaries and regions depicted on maps and globes.

Opportunities for Activities. Lots of opportunities occur for discussion of boundaries and regions and exteriors and interiors. Very young children often argue about their space, a place they have defined as their territory. For example, Laura and Lana argue over a comfortable armchair. When one of them is sitting in the chair, the other may try to push her out. Getting the other child off onto the floor or up on an arm of the chair has become the mark of gaining possession of it. Laura and Lana have staked out a region with mutually recognized boundaries.

Sand and clay modeling tables offer many opportunities to work with regions and boundaries and exteriors and interiors. A version of "Crossing the Barriers" can be played in which all the sand toys of one color, shape, or purpose are used in one region and not in another. Later, an adult can make a simple drawing of the region the child made in sand or clay. Areas within the region can be labeled according to the child's directions.

A political map can be introduced to the children at this point. A good choice would be a map of the United States: (a) with states clearly marked out and (b) showing each state in a color different from its adjoining states. Children can then easily distinguish the boundaries and the regions within them.

Interiors and exteriors are closely linked to boundaries and regions. Children enjoy climbing on a box and playing in it, exploring its interior and exterior. They begin to understand that interiors and exteriors are separate but necessarily interrelated. Some authors of children's books such as Mitsuma Anno have explored the interior—exterior relationship and used it to create complex drawings about what seem to be simple topics in, for example, *Anno's Alphabet* (Anno, 1975).

Stages in Understanding Exteriors and Interiors. Children should start with exploring interiors and exteriors, using their whole body as they do when playing with a large box. Then they can be offered opportunities to work with interiors and exteriors in a more abstract way. First, they can work with dolls placed inside and outside something, such as a shoebox. They can paint the interior of a shoebox in one color and choose another color for the exterior. Next, photographs can be examined of the children inside an object, such as a tire tunnel, and also lying on the outside of it. They introduce two-dimensional interior and exterior views and move children into a much more abstract activity. Finally, children might be shown drawings of boxes and other objects and asked to place a cutout figure inside the box or outside it.

Holes

After working with boundaries and regions they created, children can investigate the concept of the hole. Holes break up the continuity of a region. They represent a closed curve introducing a new, different region inside the curve. The water in a pond is a very different region from the fields surrounding it. When a region, such as a piece of paper, has a hole punched in it, some of the area is lost to the region. The hole is a new region. Besides a loss in area, the new region is no longer connected to the old region. The boundary between them is the edge of the hole. Maps depict the breaks in continuity in a region. A lake is shown so that it may be understood as representing a separate region surrounded by another region. Before the concrete operational period children will usually not understand how diverse regions are connected or the existence of regions within regions.

They can, however, observe holes and investigate the characteristics of regions within regions. A hole in a sock through which a part of their heel shows is usually quite interesting to children. Water in a puddle can be splashed and examined, as can the asphalt surrounding it.

Order

Order requires that objects be presented in the arrangement in which they occur. If a bush, tree, and sandbox are to be mapped, the viewpoint is determined and then the appropriate order is faithfully reproduced. The viewpoint must be decided first. An observer standing by the bush views things in the following order: first, bush; second, tree; third, sandbox. An observer standing by the sandbox views things in the reverse order: sandbox, tree, bush. All mapping involves determining a viewpoint and then striving faithfully to represent the resulting order. This is why maps often contain an arrow pointing to an "N" (north). The reader uses this symbol to determine the map's viewpoint. Order depends on viewpoint but is important in itself. It is particularly important when a complex set of objects is being mapped. Order is investigated by children when they physically explore their environment. They quickly spot a change in the order of a familiar environment as, for example, when a chair has been moved to a different location in a room. Children can use maps in which two or three objects in the environment have been drawn. For example, children could be given a playground map on which the bush, tree, and sandbox have been drawn. Day after day a new map can be presented to the children in which the order of the objects remains the same but the distance between them is increased. Children's attention should be drawn to the space as being the only difference. It will be noticeable if these successive maps are displayed alongside each other. Order becomes the important characteristic of such maps.

Point of Reference

Point of reference is related to the concept of order and begins with the child. The child is the first and most meaningful point of reference for perceiving space. With young children the goal in studying point of reference is to encourage them to experience many points of reference. Several points of reference should be experienced using the same set of variables. For example, a region in Johnnie's school playground contained a tree, a fallen log, and a small pond. Over several days, Johnnie and his teacher looked at and talked about the same general view from different locations in the tree, on the fallen log, and at the pond's edge. Johnnie noted different items from each location.

If the child appears ready, a transition can be made using discussion of photographs, such as one of Johnnie in the tree and by the pond. More abstract activity could follow, using a drawing of the pond, tree, and fallen log, on which the child draws himself. This might be followed by a language-experience story describing what the child saw from different locations.

Direction

Direction is a concept that is difficult for young children. Researchers have found children can learn the cardinal directions (north, south, east, west) at age 5 (Atkin, 1981). Learning activities must be carefully sequenced and tightly structured. Prior experience with moving in different directions and in changing and labeling directions is most appropriate. Ann enjoys standing at the beginning of a sidewalk tire mark and acting out the skid. She usually moves in the direction in which the traffic flowing next to her is moving. Her parents attach labels to her movement such as "going forward" or "going uptown." They tell Ann her grandmother lives "south" of where they live.

BLOCK PLAY FOR TEACHING GEOGRAPHY

Blocks teach topological concepts and prepare children for projective and Euclidean space concepts. Block play encourages children to experience various perspectives as they examine a block tower they have built from different points of reference. Block play also encourages children to build continuous lines, then remove a block and create a discontinuity. Children can create a closed curve with blocks and then sit inside the area it defines and experience being in the interior of the curve. By climbing outside the closed curve of blocks, they can experience being on the exterior of the region defined by the boundary line, which is the closed curve. Children can build block roads and drive cars in different directions. Blocks lend themselves to experiences that explore many space and geographic concepts. They are an essential element of geographic activities in the early childhood years.

TRANSITION TO MAPS

A transition from physically experiencing space concepts to using maps representing the relationships of entities occurs in six steps (Gerhardt, 1973). These are:

1. Physical experience with space concepts
2. Photographs of children's experiences
3. Three-dimensional miniature models
4. Two-dimensional paper cutouts
5. Line drawings
6. Miniaturization of line drawings

After physical experience with space concepts, photographs of children's experiences can be examined. Then a map of an area can be constructed using three-dimensional models closely representing the real thing. There are many such models. Commercial toys are available that are recognizable models of children, dogs, schools, barns, and so on. These can be used to recreate the child's classroom, bedroom, or the kitchen table at breakfast time.

Preoperational children find the transition to three-dimensional models an easy one to accomplish. They more readily grasp the idea of reduced scale when three-dimensional models are used. A map of the children's play area, with miniature models of, for example, a tree, bush, and sandbox, could be used. Children could then replace the miniature with such nonthematic concrete materials as blocks and cardboard boxes as they move a step closer toward two-dimensional representation of objects.

A next step in the transition to maps is the use of three-dimensional models that are not thematic. Thus, an oatmeal box represents a tunnel, a silo, or a tower of Detroit's Renaissance Center. A tuna-fish can might represent the above-ground pool in the backyard next door. A series of shoe boxes lined up next to one another makes an excellent model of Baltimore's rowhouses. These models are more abstract than are the lifelike models used earlier, but they are close enough to the real object that usually children quickly understand them as representing the object.

The transition to two-dimensional representation occurs next. This is more difficult for children because it requires abstraction—the ability to form a three-dimensional mental image when only two dimensions are represented. Paper shapes replace the oatmeal boxes, tuna-fish cans, and shoe boxes. Now the "tree" is a circular brown paper cutout, the sandbox is a rectangle, and the bush is a free-form flat piece of paper.

Next in the transition to two dimensions is the use of line drawings instead of paper shapes. The shapes can be traced on a posterboard. Children match the paper cutout to the line drawing. Finally, miniaturization of line draw-ings occurs as the children are ready, producing a recognizable map. As the process moves through the sequence, it becomes gradually more abstract. Each step should be expected to represent greater cognitive maturity.

Choosing Maps and Globes

When children are able to move through all six steps of the mapping sequence, they are also ready to use commercial and homemade maps and globes. Maps with raised contours are most appropriate for young children. They can feel the recessed and raised areas to determine similarities and differences among geo-graphic regions. Children particularly enjoy making their own maps. Flour and salt mountains, lakes, and streets are fun to build. When commercial maps are used, maps of the same scale should be used as much as possible. Maps con-taining two different scales, such as a state map with an insert containing an enlarged city map, should not be used because such differences may confuse children (Towler and Nelson, 1969).

The Globe

Beginners', or simplified, globes are best for preschool-primary-grades children. These globes show bodies of water and land masses. Generally they use only a few colors. Few details beyond the continents, countries, large cities, and large bodies of water (such as the Great Lakes) are given. By identifying major features, these globes are a useful teaching tool that does not overwhelm children with detail. The globe should be present in the classroom and used often as geographic information is discussed during circle time, current events, storytelling, and so on (see Figure 12–2). As the globe is used informally, children should consider its roundness and be informed that it is a model of the round earth. They can learn that bodies of water are typically shown in blue and that other colors delineate land masses. They can compare the areas covered by land masses and water. Cities and countries in the news can be located, as can the top and bottom (poles) of the earth. Young children should have an opportunity to explore and discuss:

- The globe's use as a model of the earth
- The globe's shape
- Land masses and bodies of water shown on the globe
- Locations of cities and countries
- The poles
- Special features, such as the equator

Map Symbols

As children make the transition to the use of maps, they are introduced to symbols. For example, they use a circle to represent a pond. Once they understand

FIGURE 12–2
Finding a place on the globe makes it more real.

the concept that an abstract symbol can stand for a real feature of their environment, they are ready to begin exploring the symbols used on maps. They might start with the use of large circles to identify large cities and small circles to identify small cities. Their attention might be drawn to cities represented by stars. These are used to identify special cities—capital cities. Map symbols should be introduced slowly, so that children have ample time to work with each new symbol.

Concrete operational children develop the ability to work with directional symbols. Preoperational children should go outside and look for the moon in the daytime sky, observing its movement throughout the day and over a period of days. Its location should be recorded hourly on a map of the playground so that the movement becomes obvious. The children should also study the sun on an hourly basis on a sunny day. This can be done by drawing a large X in chalk on concrete. A child stands on the X facing in a specified direction. His shadow is traced by another child. After an hour passes, the child goes outside, stands on the X facing in the specified direction, and his shadow is drawn again. The process is repeated hourly during the school day. The sun's movement becomes obvious through this activity.

More mature children can learn that their shadow points north at noon. If they face the direction of their shadow, north, and stretch out their arms, their right arm points east, their left arm points west, and their back is south. These cardinal directions can be painted on the playground for permanent reference. Eventually the children can be taught to use "N" to stand for "north," "E" for "east," and so on. Finally, maps of the playground can be made with the directions written in. The cardinal directions should also be posted on the walls of the classroom. Activities can incorporate use of the directions. Classroom maps can also be made with the directions written in.

Research on Geography

Buggey and Kracht (1986), in a review of research on geographic learning, reported studies indicating that primary-grades children learned various map-reading skills if they were taught these skills in carefully sequenced instruction (Atkin, 1981; Rice & Cobb, 1978; Blaut & Stea, 1974). There is some evidence that children could learn ideas about:

- The earth's shape
- The globe as a model of the earth
- Directions
- Orienting a map
- Distance and scale
- Symbols and location
- The earth–sun relationship

Herman (1983) has suggested that children in kindergarten through grade 3 should focus on the following:

1. Explaining how people and places (regions) differ from one another at various levels—local, national, world
2. Describing and appreciating the relationship between the physical and cultural worlds (human–land relationships, including environmentalism and conservation)
3. Identifying problems resulting from physical and economic factors, including population distribution and density

Research is not conclusive about the best grade level to introduce specific concepts and skills. It does suggest that primary-grades children can learn a variety of geographic skills and concepts. It also suggests that careful presentation and sequencing of activities in small steps is most important (Buggey & Kracht, 1986).

SUMMARY

Teachers should initiate geographic experiences with young children by providing motor experiences inside and outside of the classroom. These can be followed by a transition in mapping experiences, which moves from work with photographs and three-dimensional miniatures and models, to two-dimensional paper, and finally to work with lines. Because not all children will be able to progress to lines, opportunities should be offered at all levels in each area of study. Maps and globes must be present in the classroom and need to be referred to frequently. Although preoperational children cannot be expected to interpret commercial maps easily, they can work with student and teacher-made three- and two-dimensional maps. Such maps can, for the most part, center on themes familiar to the children and should originate in actual exploratory work done inside and outside the classroom by the children. More cognitively mature children will be able to work with simple commercial maps and globes.

Adults working with young children should plunge into geographic activities from the very beginning. Motor activity and topological studies form a base from which teacher and children can build a geography program of progressive sophistication. This program should develop and enlarge relationships explored by children during a variety of concrete experiences. Young children can, and should be encouraged to, discover the purpose and use of maps.

REFERENCES

ANNO, M. (1975). *Anno's alphabet.* New York: Crowell.

ATKIN, C. (1981). Introducing basic map and globe concepts to young children. *Journal of Geography, 80,* 228–233.

BARSCH, R. (1967). *Achieving perceptual–motor efficiency. A space-oriented approach to learning* (Vol. 1). Seattle: Special Child Publications.

BLAUT, J., & STEA, D. (1974). Mapping at the age of three. *Journal of Geography, 73,* 5–9.

BORCHERT, J. (1983). Questions students ask. *Journal of Geography, 82,* 43.

BUGGEY, J., & KRACHT, J. (1986). Geographic learning. In V. Atwood (Ed.), *Elementary school social studies: Research as a guide to practice* (pp. 55–67). NCSS Bull. No. 79. Washington, DC: National Council for the Social Studies.

DONALDSON, M. (1979). *Children's minds.* New York: Norton.

FLAVELL, J. (1977). *Cognitive development.* Englewood Cliffs, NJ: Prentice-Hall.

GERHARDT, L. (1973). *Moving and knowing. The young child orients himself in space.* Englewood Cliffs, NJ: Prentice-Hall.

HERMAN, W., JR. (1983). What should be taught where? *Social Education, 47,* 94–100.

LAURENDEAU, M., & PINARD, A. (1968). *Les premieres notions spatiales de l'enfant.* Montreal: Delachaux & Niestle.

LIBEN, L. (1978). Perspective-taking skills in young children: Seeing the world through rose-colored glasses. *Developmental Psychology, 14,* 87–92.

PIAGET, J., & INHELDER, B. (1967). *The child's conception of space.* New York: Norton.

RICE, M., & COBB, R. (1978). *What can children learn in geography? A review of the research.* Boulder, CO: Social Science Education Consortium.

SAUVY, J., & SAUVY, S. (1972). *The child's discovery of space.* Baltimore, MD: Penguin.

SEIFERT, K., & HOFFNUNG, R. (1987). *Child and adolescent development.* Boston: Houghton Mifflin.

SELMAN, R. (1980). *The growth of interpersonal understanding.* New York: Academic Press.

SUNAL, C. S., & SUNAL, D. W. (1978a). Space concepts for young children. *Day Care and Early Education, 5*(4), 33–41.

SUNAL, C. S., & SUNAL, D. W. (1978b). Mapping the child's world. *Social Education, 42,* 381–383.

TOWLER, J., & NELSON, L. (1969). The elementary school child's concept of space. In W. Herman (Ed.), *Current research in elementary social studies* (pp. 78–89). New York: Macmillan.

13

THE YOUNG CHILD AS A CONSUMER

Cynthia Szymanski Sunal and Barbara Hatcher
West Virginia University and Southwest Texas State
University

"Let's face it, I always want to buy more than I have the money to buy it with, or, you could say I have chocolate tastes but a jelly bean budget." This comment states the focus of consumer education and the related study of economics. It is the universal problem of a person's desire to satisfy unlimited wants with limited resources (Maxim, 1977, p. 31).

Children live in a world that works hard at increasing their wants, no matter how limited their resources. Even at an early age children are consumers and a vital part of the economic system. Who hasn't witnessed unhappy children in conflict over their parents' unwillingness to purchase an expensive toy? Children are exposed to other types of economic activities as well when they note a tip left for the waitress or see their parents cash a check. They are experiencing economic decision making in action when they hear adults discuss the payment of a big electric bill. Although children have many opportunities to experience economic concepts, a lack of explanation and understanding of basic principles can leave them bewildered.

Hartoonian (1981, p. 13) suggests that economics basically involves a series of decisions. He describes this series as beginning with relatively unlimited wants and relatively limited resources, which creates problems of scarcity and the need for choices. Because of the tension between unlimited wants and limited resources, an economic system must answer five basic questions:

1. What to produce?
2. How to produce?
3. How much to produce in the short run?
4. How much to produce in the long run?
5. How to distribute output?

What are the essential economic concepts children can understand? How are these concepts presented to children? What principles should guide the teacher's lesson planning? Kourilsky and Hirshleifer (1976) have identified nine concepts as comprehensible to kindergarten and primary-grades children:

1. Scarcity
2. Decision making
3. Opportunity cost and cost-benefit analysis
4. Production
5. Specialization
6. Distribution, consumption, savings
7. Demand and supply
8. Business organization and business venture
9. Money and barter

Kourilsky (1985) introduced these and other basic concepts to young children through concrete experiences, learning centers, simulations, and other strategies.

How are these concepts presented to children? What suggestions do we have from research on appropriate instructional strategies for pupils? Yeargan and Hatcher (1985) found abstract economic concepts should be presented in real-life settings. Schug and Beery (1987) suggest:

> Economic education can begin with a focus on the everyday experiences of children. Learning activities can be designed to help young people become aware of economic decisions they make. Scarcity, for example, is a fact of life in many classrooms and can be used as a learning experience for children. (p. 364)

They recommend the use of neighborhood field trips to the bank, fast-food restaurant, specialty import shop, farmer's market, retail store, local manufacturer, shoe repair shop, or print shop as places where children can learn real-world economics. In addition, teachers who are alert to economic principles may reinforce these concepts throughout the curriculum. For example, economic concepts such as working, shopping, and trading are frequent topics in children's poems, songs, and stories. By questioning students and designing learning activities, teachers can extend economic understanding through literature. Darrin (1968) concludes that economic principles should be integrated throughout the curriculum.

KEY CONCEPTS

With the suggestions from research, we have selected the following economic concepts for use with young children. We believe they are important and developmentally appropriate:

1. Wants and needs
2. Scarcity

3. Identifying resources
4. Planning
5. Ordering goals
6. Goods and services
7. Buyers and sellers
8. Producers and consumers
9. Money
10. Making choices

Wants and Needs

With young children, experiences with wants and needs should focus on identification. Limitations in the reasoning abilities of young children prevent them
from understanding and attempting to answer the complex question, "How can
we balance the things we need with the things we want, and with what is
available?" Because of these limitations, a hierarchy can be identified that begins
with the awareness of wants and needs, moves to the identification of wants and
needs, and culminates in the formulation of an appropriate balance between
them. This can be incorporated into ongoing activities with questions such as:

1. Is this something you have to have? Is this something your
friends have to have? Is this something everybody has to have?
2. Do you eat it, wear it, live in it?
3. Do you need it to live?
4. Who gives it to you?
5. Could you get it by yourself? (Michaelis and Keach, 1972,
p. 153)

Eventually the child will be capable of classifying familiar items as a need or want
(see Figure 13–1). Ms. Secreto, a kindergarten teacher, planned for activities related
to wants and needs by placing items in bags and having groups of children
examine and sort them as they wished. Later she asked each group to sort the
items into a needs group and a wants group. At the completion of their work,
the children formed a circle. She then sent a representative of each group back
to the items to select one from each category. Ms. Secreto asked each child to
tell the class about the item needed and the item wanted. Next, she gave each
child a picture. The children were to decide whether it was a need or a want.
The children with needs pictures went to one side of the room. The pupils with
wants pictures went to the other side of the room. As a concluding activity, Ms.
Secreto asked the children to find something in the room that was needed. The
children were able to select an item and explain why it was needed. Ms. Secreto
arranged for bags of items to be used several times until the children could
differentiate between wants and needs. Additional activities encouraged the children to consider whether something was a want or a need in a particular instance.
For example, a heavy, warm pair of blue jeans can be a need in winter, but an
uncomfortable, though fashionable, want in summer. Ms. Secreto found her chil-

FIGURE 13–1
A classroom store can sell many items.

dren enjoyed reading Arnold Lobel's *On Market Street*. This is an alphabet book in which a child decides what to purchase, from A to Z. She used the book to help her pupils classify items according to wants and needs. As an extending activity, her students made their own ABC picture books and arranged the pictures into wants and needs.

Scarcity

Scarcity is involved in problems centering on wants and needs. Children are directly affected by simple shortages in items they use in the classroom frequently. For example, there may be a shortage of scissors, crayons, or wheel toys. Children have to wait for a turn or bargain for an early opportunity to use the item.

To illustrate the concept of scarcity, Ms. Secreto worked with the children to identify items of which "we have plenty" and of which "we need more." These items were classified as needs or wants. Items that were scarce in the classroom were put on one of two lists, "Things We Need to Buy" and "Things We Want to Buy." As the class acquired needed items, they were checked off on the list. When all the list was checked off, votes were taken on what to purchase first from the "wants" list.

As recommended by Schug and Beery (1987), Ms. Secreto found children's literature was useful in reinforcing economic understandings in her classroom. She read the following stories to illustrate the concept of scarcity as a basis for decision making: *Stone Soup* by Brown, *The Little Match Girl* by Anderson, and *Seven Little Popovers* by Eastwick. Popular folk and fairytales such as *The Three Wishes* and *The Fisherman and His Wife* offered other possibilities.

Identifying Resources

Children should identify resources needed to reach a goal or produce a product or service. Recognizing the factors of production is an important part of consumer education because it requires thinking about a problem rather than acting on impulse. An adult working with children to identify resources should be familiar with the major categories of resources, although young children may not explicitly be taught these terms. Resources related to production are called factors of production, or productive resources. These include:

1. *Human resources.* Included are people and their physical and mental abilities involved in producing a good or service.
2. *Natural resources.* These are the gifts of nature used to produce goods and services. They include land, minerals, water, oil, fertility of soil, timber, and so on. Some of these are used up in the process of production.
3. *Capital resources.* These are usually the means of production and were created by people's past efforts; for example, hammers, saws, bulldozers, cranes, sewing machines, tractors, and hoes. They are used in the further production of goods and services.

To help children recognize the factors of production, Ms. Secreto consistently encouraged the children to identify items needed to complete a task. When Paul wished to paint a picture of a truck, she worked with him to specify items he would need for the task. He recognized the need for paint, an easel, paper, paintbrush, and paint shirt. These were essential resources needed to produce the picture. Ms. Secreto pointed out that his work or effort was also essential.

After working with the children to identify resources needed to complete a project, Ms. Secreto used another strategy. She presented the children with a set of resources: a set of Tinkertoys and several egg cartons. The children made these resources into toy trucks, cars, trains, and tanks. This second strategy of deciding what could be made with the resources presented the children with a more demanding problem. They had to determine what to produce from the available resources. This activity introduced the concept of opportunity cost. A decision to produce one good or service with the available resources means giving up the possibility of producing something else. When Paul chose to make a truck, he gave up the opportunity to make a wagon, a car, or another item.

Planning

Planning is an essential part of consumer education because impulsive buying and decision making lead to poor consumer choices. To give children skill in planning, Ms. Secreto provided opportunities for students to arrange and reorganize their work periods, to design a new classroom floor plan, and to make decisions about special events and class parties. For example, the children designed a new arrangement for the art area. They tried it out and evaluated the new floor plan for convenience. Other planning experiences included reorganizing lunchtime activities and reordering the day's events.

Ms. Secreto offered opportunities for individual planning, too. Children listed the necessary steps to complete a task. Stick-figure drawings were used to illustrate the activity, and each child identified the necessary steps in the process. For example, Paul listed the following steps to build his egg carton truck:

1. Gather resources for building: egg carton, scissors, Tinkertoy rods, Tinkertoy circles.
2. Punch holes for Tinkertoy rods.
3. Put rods through holes.
4. Attach Tinkertoy circles to ends of rods.

He identified and sequenced the essential steps successfully, but many of his classmates included nonessential items in their planning. When their plans were followed, the children discovered that many of their steps were unnecessary.

Ordering Goals

Ordering goals is a necessary part of wise decision making. An adult recognizes that the refrigerator is operating poorly and will have to be replaced. At the same time, the television is in need of repair. Both items cost too much to replace at the same time. So goals need to be ordered. Which item is essential? Which one can be repaired at minimum expense to ensure lasting use? Consumers must address these questions when making a decision. The ordering of goals organizes one's needs and wants. It helps individuals cope with the scarcities that will always be present.

Children need to learn to order goals, too. However, this is difficult for them (Inhelder & Piaget, 1958). Children could practice the ordering of goals by first practicing on familiar and immediate short-term objectives. For example, on a trip to the zoo, the children may be asked, "Do we go to see the elephants or the monkeys first? If we go to the elephant house, we can watch the elephants play in the water. However, if we go to the monkey cage, we can observe them eating. What shall we do?" Children have to order their goals. Both goals would be achieved, but one would come before the other. Simple decision-making experiences can involve playground games, stories to be read to the class, and learning activities in the classroom.

Goods and Services

Children should learn to distinguish between goods and services. Young children quickly understand the need to purchase goods. This is less abstract than is the purchase of services. Some services, like obtaining a haircut, are more concrete than others.

The term *goods* can be defined as "things we buy" whereas *services* are "things people do for us." The concept of services was introduced in one classroom via a visit to a garage that serviced trucks. The mechanic introduced himself and told the children that he repaired broken trucks. He explained that trucks are hard to repair because of their size. A large garage is needed to work on them and often special tools are needed. His job is to help the truck owners by doing the work for them. Then they pay for his services. The children watched as tires on the truck were replaced. He wrote a bill, presented it to the truck owner, and was paid for his services. The teacher explained that the mechanic's work was called a service. A service is work performed by an individual who does not produce a product, but performs a needed task. Money is usually exchanged to pay for the work. Richard Scarry's *The Busiest People Ever* is an excellent way to illustrate how people provide goods and services. Children enjoy the cartoon animals performing various tasks. Children can recreate the characters as pop-sicle-stick puppets and group the puppets according to the services they provide.

Buyers and Sellers

Intertwined with the concept of goods and services are the concepts of buyers and sellers. Young children should work with the definition of *buyer* as the person who receives and pays for both goods and services. The *seller* is the person who gives the buyer the purchased goods or who performs the service for a remittance.

When working with goods and services, children should notice that money is exchanged. Both buyers and sellers should be identified. It is also important for children to be buyers. A field trip to the store to purchase items for the mid-morning snack is an appropriate experience. Children should select the items and give the money to the clerk and accept the change. They need to experience the buyer's role. Children also need to have the opportunity to sell items. For example, a first-grade class borrowed money from their teacher to purchase packages of radish seeds. The radishes grew and were harvested. The children sold them every other day for two weeks. At the end of the period, the revenue from the sales was counted, and the teacher's loan money was subtracted and returned. The profits from the sale were distributed to each child. The pupils participated in a real-life selling experience. Equally important, they used their profits to become buyers at the local ice-cream shop. Third graders participated in a similar experience when they opened their own cupcake factory (Yeargan & Hatcher, 1985). Research has shown that these and similar experiences enable children to master economic concepts (see Figure 13–2).

FIGURE 13–2
Cookies we've made are sold in the classroom store.

Producers and Consumers

A class project such as radish growing can reinforce an understanding of the concepts of producers and consumers as well (Sunal, Warash, & Strong, 1988). Children in the radish project produced a product, and they also used their profit to be consumers. Richmond (1979) describes the *Kids Kountry Kookbook* as a valuable strategy to enable her pupils to directly experience the role of producers. Richmond's third and fourth graders began with plans for a mimeographed cookbook of favorite local recipes. When the newspaper printed a story about the project, recipes were submitted from throughout the county. Orders for the cookbook were requested. The project grew and grew. A bank account was established, the cookbook was professionally printed, shares were sold in the cookbook corporation, newspaper ads were published, and all the cookbooks were sold.

Younger children may not be involved in such a complex project, but they could participate in a variation of it. For example, they could use pictorial recipes or, as Warash (1988) suggests, the children could dictate and publish their version of favorite recipes. Here are two delightful examples:

Thanksgiving Turkey

You buy a turkey at the store.

Let it get soft.

Put bread and onions and stuff in it.

When you're real hungry take it out and eat it.

Brownies

Get lots of sugar and some chocolate.

Put it in a bowl and mix it all up.

Put it in a pan.

Lick the bowl, Yum! (Warash, 1988)

The children's cookbook can become a sales item at a school fair, during a parents' night, or other event. A one-time sale is best with children taking turns selling (5 to 10 minutes each). Adult supervision may be needed to assist with change. Profits from the sale can be used to purchase books for the classroom, the adopt-a-pet program at the zoo, a class picnic, and so on. This is an excellent way for children to experience both the producer and the consumer relationship.

Money

Although young children cannot comprehend an abstract definition of money as a medium of exchange, they can comprehend that money makes it possible to obtain goods and services. The identification of basic money units should be presented to children. A real understanding of the value of money will not be achieved until the elementary grades (Piaget, 1929). Value is complex, because it is abstract and requires an understanding of numbers, addition, subtraction, and other concepts.

The naming and recognition of monetary units is an appropriate goal for young children. Paul's father played a weekly game with him called "allowance." Each Saturday he reached into his pocket and selected some coins. If Paul could identify them, he could keep them for his allowance. After identifying as many as he could, Paul counted them with his father. Paul quickly learned to recognize and name coins. Then his father added another requirement. Paul had to tell how much each coin was worth: one cent, ten cents, and so on. This took longer to learn. Paul did not really understand the concept of value, but he made a beginning.

Making Choices

The purpose of consumer education is to help individuals make the best possible choices with their limited resources. Many consumer education activities encourage children to make choices; for example, identifying items they need and want most, and making a choice of which to purchase.

TEACHER RESOURCES

The Joint Council on Economic Education is an excellent source of information on economic education. The Joint Council produces economically sound materials for students of all ages, kindergarten through college. It also sponsors workshops for teachers throughout the country. The address is:

> *Joint Council on Economic Education*
> *2 Park Avenue*
> *New York, New York 10016*

Useful materials from the council at no charge include the following:

Checklist of Economic Education Materials for Teachers
    Published twice a year by the Joint Council, this lists all available publications and media materials. It can be obtained free from the Public Information Department of the council.

Update
    A quarterly newsletter, this publication is designed to keep readers abreast of developments in economic education programs. It is available free from the Public Information Department of the council.
Other, generally low-cost, materials relating to economics and economic education are:

The Elementary Economist. Joint Council on Economic Education.
    Curriculum strategies for teaching economics ideas K–6 are described in the newsletter. Cost is $15 per year for three issues. A package of all back issues can be purchased for $12.50, a bargain!

Headstron, J. (1977). *Framework for Teaching Economics: Basic Concepts. Selective Bibliography in Economic Resources.* Boulder, CO: Social Science Education Consortium, Inc., and ERIC/CHESS.

Annotated materials for teaching and learning economics, such as textbooks, audiovisuals, and print materials, are included in this resource, Part I of the series, *Strategies for Teaching Economics, Primary Level (Grades 1–3): Master Curriculum Guide in Economics for the Nation's Schools.*

Hendicks, R. H., et al. (1986). *Learning Economics Through Children's Stories.* 5th ed. New York: Joint Council on Economic Education.

This publication contains an annotated bibliography of children's books illustrating economic principles. The economic concepts are identified for each listing.

Piggy Bank (Grades K–3). (1984). New York: Joint Council on Economic Education.

This is a software game with 5 levels of difficulty. Players can choose the level at which they wish to play. Students practice using number facts by counting various combinations of coins. Extension activities introduce attributes of money as well as concepts of exchange and saving. Sound option. Color available.

Schug, M. (Ed.). (1986). *Economics for Kids: Ideas for Teaching in the Elementary Grades.* New York: Joint Council on Economic Education and National Education Association.

Written for classroom teachers, this practical guide presents ideas and information on when, what, and how to teach economics to young children. It features 15 teaching activities and 4 simulation games plus suggestions for using the community as a resource.

Silk, L. (1978). *Economics in Plain English.* New York: Simon & Schuster.

This is a concise explanation of economics in readable format. Terminology is explained and economic philosophies are discussed.

Strategies for Teaching Economics, Primary Level (Grades 1–3): Master Curriculum Guide in Economics for the Nation's Schools, Part II, Vol. 1. (1977). New York: Joint Council on Economic Education.

This volume provides lessons that present economic concepts for primary-grades children. The lessons relate to basic economic concepts identified in Part I of the series.

SUMMARY

Formal lessons in consumer education and economics are inappropriate for young children. Rather, concepts that are developmentally appropriate should be identified and then integrated into classroom experience. There are many opportunities daily to address wants and needs, scarcity, choices, resources, planning, and ordering goals. In addition, adults should provide experiences for children to observe the production of goods and services in the community, buyers and sellers in the marketplace, and the use of money as a medium of exchange. The daily experiences of her students in the classroom, their homes, and their community can be viewed from an economic frame of reference. A sensitivity to economic principles in everyday events will enable teachers to take advantage of opportunities to make those principles comprehensible and captivating.

REFERENCES

DARRIN, G. (1968). *Economics in the elementary school curriculum: Study of the District of Columbia laboratory schools.* Doctoral dissertation, University of Maryland, College Park, MD.

HARTOONIAN, H. (1981). Development of decision-making ability through the use of economic content. In S. Symmes (Ed.), *Economic education: Links to the social studies.* Washington, DC: National Council for the Social Studies.

INHELDER, B., & PIAGET, J. (1958). *The growth of logical thinking from childhood to adolescence.* New York: Basic Books.

KOURILSKY, M. (1985). *Children's use of cost-benefit analysis: Developmental or nonexistent.* Paper presented at the annual meeting of the American Educational Research Association, Chicago, IL.

KOURILSKY, M., & HIRSHLEIFER, J. (1976). Mini-society vs. token economy: An experimental comparison of the effects on learning and autonomy of socially emergent and imposed behavior modification. *Journal of Educational Research, 69,* 376–381.

MAXIM, G. (1977). *Methods of teaching social studies to elementary school children.* Columbus, OH: Merrill.

MICHAELIS, J., & KEACH, E. (1972). A unit on interdependence for four-year-olds. *Teaching strategies for elementary school social studies.* Itasca, IL.: Peacock.

PIAGET, J. (1929). *Judgement and reasoning in the child.* (M. Warden, Trans.). New York: Harcourt Brace.

PIAGET, J., & INHELDER, B. (1958). *The growth of logical thinking from childhood to adolescence.* New York: Basic Books.

RICHMOND, C. (1979). Kids country kookbook. In A. Nappi and A. Suglia (Eds.), *Economic education experiences of enterprising teachers* (pp. 7–12). New York: Joint Council on Economic Education.

SCHUG, M. C., & BIRKEY, C. J. (1987). *Teaching social studies in the elementary school: Issues and practices.* Glenview, IL: Scott, Foresman.

SUNAL, C., WARASH, B., & STRONG, M. (1988). Buy! sell! produce!: Economic education experiences for young children. *Day Care and Early Education,* 146–164.

WARASH, B. (1988). *West Virginia University nursery school children's recipes.* Morgantown, WV: West Virginia University Nursery School.

YEARGAN, H., & HATCHER, B. (1985). The cupcake factory: Helping elementary students understand economics. *The Social Studies, 76,* 82–84.

14

THE CHILD'S AWARENESS OF AGING, THE ELDERLY, AND DEATH

Mary E. Haas and Alice Galper
University of West Virginia and Mount Vernon College

Put yourself in the role of the teacher in each of the following situations.

1. You ask the children about their fathers' occupations. One little boy answers, "My father doesn't work anymore. He died."
2. You overhear children talking in the household corner. Robert says, "I'll be a boy or the father, but I won't be a dumb, old man!"
3. You are the first-grade teacher. On the weekend following Thanksgiving you receive this call from your principal: "I'm calling because I have some bad news that I think you should know before coming back to school. Mr. Franks, our kindergarten teacher's husband, called me a few minutes ago and told me that Joan was killed in an automobile accident this morning while driving to the store. We are calling all of the parents of the kindergarten children. You may want to call your students' parents too. I plan to visit every classroom Monday morning to answer any question you or the children may have about the arrangements."

How do you think you would feel? How would you respond to the student(s)? What would be your motivation for your response?

In concretizing the definition of social studies, we ask students to identify patterns in their lives and to examine natural human activities and feelings. We also expect students to begin to analyze and develop their values with an emphasis on human dignity. With these ideas in mind, the rationale for studying the topics of aging, the elderly, and death becomes clear.

All citizens need to learn to understand their roles in society. A logical place for the child to begin is with the concept of the life cycle, which includes growth, change, and death. As 4-year-old Michael says to his day-care teacher, "There is always a beginning and an ending, and things happen in between." As children mature they need to become more aware of what they realistically can look forward to during their lifetime. The child does this through observation and modeling the behaviors of elders and through interacting with peers and adults.

In a lifetime people encounter many highs: accomplishments, recognitions, and new beginnings. Schools give much reinforcement and recognition to these positive experiences. But people's lives also include many lows: difficulties, disappointments, tragedies, and endings. Unfortunately, both adults and schools frequently neglect to give any positive support to help children face these types of situations. By avoiding these lows, the curriculum given to children becomes one that fails to educate the whole person. In avoiding helping children through the low points of life, many children are left to educate themselves with a catch-as-catch-can curriculum.

The literature indicates that children as young as 3 years of age are able to articulate their attitudes toward the elderly and the aging process. Sadly, they are developing negative and stereotypic views toward the elderly and the aging process that influence their own views of growing old. Many see old age as a time of inabilities and illness.

Changes in life span and lifestyles of Americans have separated many of the young from encountering the elderly and from encountering death during their youth. Young children learn about a youth-oriented society from the media and hear many negative and stereotypic statements about the elderly. They also learn of death through the media. The media's curriculum is a one-way curriculum with negative messages. Often these fragmented messages are internalized and interpreted with little or no help from a concerned adult.

Those who plan to become teachers believe that they will be teaching such traditional subjects as reading, history, and mathematics. However, the teacher soon realizes that other things enter into the curriculum that they as teachers feel unprepared to teach. In this chapter, children and their attitudes toward death, aging, and the elderly will be examined. Ideas will be presented illustrating ways to integrate these topics into the existing curriculum. Suggestions also will be made as to how the teacher can prepare to deal with these topics when teachable moments arise with either individual students or the entire class.

HOW CHILDREN VIEW AGING AND THE ELDERLY

"Stereotyped views of the elderly are prevalent and are uncovered in various studies" (McTavish, 1971, p. 90). Among the children's views are that old people are generally ill, tired, not sexually interested, mentally slower, forgetful and less able to learn new things. The elderly are also seen as grouchy, withdrawn, feeling sorry for themselves, less likely to participate in activities other than religion, isolated in the least happy or fortunate time of life, and generally unproductive.

Trebig (1974) suggests that the language used in socializing children plays an important part in the formation of children's attitudes toward "old" people. Of the 85 children ages 3, 4, and 5 interviewed, the overwhelming number of responses to the word "old" were negative and the children also indicated that they did not want to get "old" someday. Because many young children said they did not know any old people and rarely see their grandparents, Jantz, Seefeldt, Galper, and Serock (1976) concluded that parents, teachers, and policymakers should be concerned about the extent of age segregation in our society. Although they found children expressing positive affective feelings toward the elderly, the children held negative attitudes about the physical aspects of aging, character- izing the elderly as "sick," "ugly," and "sad." The children did not want to get old themselves, but the youngest children were most negative about the prospect of growing old. "I don't want to die," was the typical response to the question, "How do you feel about getting old?" "You have a better chance of not dying if you're brand new," reasoned one 4-year-old.

A curriculum designed to foster positive attitudes in children toward the elderly and aging process changed the attitudes of the experimental group (See- feldt et al., 1977). The curriculum provided accurate information about the elderly and the aging process by exposing children to an unbiased look at the attributes, behaviors, and characteristics of the elderly in a wide variety of roles.

Trade books and textbooks provide students with views about the elderly and aging. Fillmer and Meadows (1986), in a content analysis of the treatment of the elderly in five sets of basal readers published between 1975 and 1983, con- cluded that stereotyping of the elderly in basal readers is substantially reduced over that found by previous researchers. Today's authors portray the elderly as intelligent, capable, competent, skillful, hardworking, and physically well. In ap- pearance, the elderly are no longer shown in stooped positions and using canes but with normal postures. Their dress can no longer be described as dowdy and the ever-so-present apron has disappeared from the women's clothing. The per- sonalities of the elderly now tend to be active, and they display kindness, cheer- fulness, and friendliness. The 5 percent of the elderly portrayed negatively tended to be in stories from folklore. The researchers do claim that, although the por- trayals are more favorable than found by previous researchers, the settings need to be more reflective of reality, showing fewer white-collar professionals and more retired, widows, minorities, and divorced persons, who make up a large pro- portion of the elderly.

Those who are surprised or concerned about children's attitudes and lack of information about the elderly should think for a moment about a child's understanding and views about death. If a child is likely to hold mixed, negative, and confused concepts about the elderly, the prospects are dim for the majority of young children to find an adequate experiential basis for formulating concepts of death. Nevertheless, young children are curious and ask questions such as: "Grandma, are you going to die soon?" "What will happen to me when I die?"

"Can the bird come back to life?" Maurer (1974) suggests that questions such as these are a natural outgrowth of the child's need to know and an attempt to determine the life span of a human. What answers do you think a child would receive to these questions? A surprised grandmother may reply, "Goodness, I hope not!" How do you think a child would interpret such a response? What responses would you give to each question?

THREE LEARNING THEORIES CONCERNING CHILDREN'S UNDERSTANDING OF DEATH

Empirical research on the topic of death and children is extremely limited because of its sensitivity. The research that has been done is interpreted in three theoretical frameworks reflecting the views of the researchers.

Social learning theorists believe that children learn from elements in their environments. Mitchell (1967) points out that various stimuli might hasten a child's awareness of death. The television and print media are two she particularly mentions. Television has been criticized for its treatment of death and the linkage of death to violence and to the lack of realistic emotions and feelings by numerous critics. Children's books dealing with death vary in their quality. Davis (1986), in a content analysis of 57 books with death themes, concludes that since 1965 books for young children have a greater focus on death-related experiences, but are limited to death and the reactions of people to death. He concludes that books published since 1965 are more realistic than those published earlier, but many of the books grossly distort and misrepresent the experiences of dying and grieving.

The direct life experiences of children have changed over the years. Advocates for the study of death by children—whether in the home, church, or school—claim that children are no longer exposed to death at an early age because of advances in medicine. However, some social and economic groups do have a much higher death rate among their members, including the young. Variations in the acceptance of discussions about death by upper middle-class students and urban students are examined by Balkin, Epstein, and Bush (1976). They conclude that urban students did not want to discuss death because they believed the discussion would encourage unwanted emotions to surface and that bad things would happen as a result. Upper middle-class students were more inclined to believe that discussions of death are appropriate.

Children, as we have already seen, ask questions about death and interpret the answers they receive. Kastenbaum (1967) suggests that children tend to learn that people die under certain conditions. Death may be accidental or may occur because the person is very old. "The equally significant corollary assumption is that the child himself will not die. He is not very sick, he is not old, and he does not intend to become very sick or very old" (Kastenbaum, 1967, p. 100). Therefore, most children see death as a long way off.

Using a psychoanalytic framework for his explanation, Rochlin (1967) suggests that the lack of finality of death may be explained by denial on the part of the child. According to Rochlin, the young child learns rapidly that death means the absence of life. Despite this recognition, there is apparently no pragmatic or philosophic acceptance on the part of the child. In observing the "death play" of children, he confirms that planes crash with no apparent damage to the victims. He concludes that "death play" serves an important denial function. Apparently children realize, at a very early age, that death is inevitable, but very well-developed defense mechanisms are functioning to defend against the realization that life will end.

Researchers who use the cognitive-developmental theory to interpret their findings have identified patterns that they call stages or sequences in a child's understanding of death. Preschool children do not find death as final and inevitable, viewing it instead as a negative and unpleasant prospect (Nagy, 1959). Formanek (1974) found that children at the most immature level are unable to respond to probes about death. At the next stage, children give partial explanations based on information that they gather from here and there. Koocher (1973) notes that young children produce concrete or egocentric responses to questions about death, which include fantasy reasoning and magical thinking. Childers and Wimmer (1971) demonstrate a moderate relationship between increasing age and acceptance of the universality of death.

Several cognitive developmentalists suggest that a lack of acceptance of death on the part of the young child does not mean that children have no disagreeable sentiments concerning death. According to Nagy, the most painful thing about death may be the separation idea itself. Kastenbaum and Aisenberg (1972) have documented death discoveries in children under 2 years of age that were registered at an emotional depth that previous researchers thought impossible for such a young child. Galper (1978) suggests that the young child may well tie together aging and death in an unattractive package. She reports that the children in her study who were the most concerned about death were also the most negative about their own aging and the elderly. She speculates that the child with such a reaction may seek to avoid older persons as a way of avoiding stimuli associated with death.

Five major conclusions emerge from the research concerning children and death that should be kept in mind when dealing with young children:

1. Children do know about death. Evidence indicates that the primary existence of death is available to the child as early as 2 or 3 years of age.
2. Qualitative changes occur in the child's thinking about death as the child develops.
3. Psychoanalytic theory describes denial and the apparent need of young children to deny that they will die as an explanation for a young child's inability to recognize death as final. Denial may also be a strong defense mechanism for all ages.
4. Young children's ideas about death may be a reflection of learning from environmental influences, such as socioeco-

nomic class, media encounters, and parental explanations. Therefore, children within a single classroom from homes with various lifestyles may respond quite differently from one another to the topic of death.

5. All children view death as a negative and unpleasant prospect. Death stimuli evoke an intense emotional response at all ages, and that includes the teacher as a person as well as a teacher.

CAN'T WE LEAVE THESE TOPICS TO THE PARENTS?

All teachers, but particularly the primary teachers, perform several roles as they go about their daily tasks with children. Only some of the time do they formally instruct the students. However, children observe, imitate, and learn from them at all times during the day. Often the teacher will be viewed as a parent by the child. Primary teachers also do much more individualized teaching and talk more with individual students than do those at other levels. Very young children share and talk about things that older students will not mention. Sooner than beginning teachers think, they will encounter death or the fear of death with a child.

At least three plans of action are available. A teacher may refuse to deal with the topic of death with the children, but this sends a message that the students will understand in their unique ways and interpret by themselves. Given your educational goals and philosophy, consider whether the refusal to deal with the topic is an appropriate response. Another approach is to deal with the topic as an integral part of the curriculum. Still another is to deal with the topic when the opportunity arises because of a death or when the topic arises naturally from a student comment. The natural entrance from a situation is called a *teachable moment*. With either approach, the teacher must be prepared. Preparation includes, at a minimum, clear objectives and carefully thought out, instructional strategies. Individual teachers may also want to have learning materials and a written lesson plan readily available, even if they select the teachable moment option.

Confronting the Stereotypes. The topics of aging, the elderly, and death are emotionally charged for both children and teachers. Frequently heard comments among teachers include:

> "I'm not going to teach forever, like some of my teachers did. I'm going to retire while I can still enjoy life."
> "I was so stiff this morning, I must be getting old."

They reflect the stereotypes and fallacies prevalent in North America about the elderly and aging. Children need to learn the truth and to recognize the error of such common stereotypes as these:

- Old people share the same personality traits.
- Old people can't learn new things.

- Old people are forgetful and suffer mental loss.
- Old people have no sex life or interests.
- Old people don't do important things.
- Old people are in poor health and must be cared for by others.
- Old people move slowly, can't hear or see, and have lots of pain.
- Old people look bad—wrinkled, bald, and with poor posture.

The vast majority of the elderly are very productive. Many continue to work in their chosen occupations and others work as volunteers, making important contributions to their communities. The truth is that there is as great a diversity in personalities among the elderly as there is among any other age groups. Personalities do not change with age. A negative older person was in all probability a negative young person, whereas the older person who likes children has probably always liked children. Although we do hear much about the elderly ill and particular diseases that affect the elderly, few elderly are in need of care in full-care facilities. Baldness, deafness, and many physical problems are not limited to the elderly and are not necessarily caused by aging.

Overcoming Discomfort. The atmosphere in which the topics of aging, the elderly, and death are studied should reflect high standards in knowledge and respect for individuals and human dignity. This respect must be afforded to the subject being studied, the students doing the learning, and the teacher. Teachers should think about their ability to feel comfortable in teaching about these topics. If they are personally comfortable, teachers can do a better job in the tasks of teaching and classroom management associated with the lessons. Feelings about situations that might develop related to teaching these topics can be rated on the scale provided in Figure 14–1. One way to deal with uncomfortable situations is to avoid them if at all possible. Another way is to try to lessen the potential impact of the feeling through some plan. For example, teachers can try to anticipate the reactions of their students to questions and rehearse possible responses, saying them aloud to hear how they will sound to the students. Find a way to get to know your parents and to let them know what you will be teaching prior to beginning a study. Parents are usually willing partners in the child's school experiences if they are informed and asked to participate.

The remainder of this chapter is devoted to appropriate strategies, materials, and background knowledge that will assist the teacher in approaching the topics of death, aging, and the elderly.

CURRICULUM OBJECTIVES

The classroom atmosphere is important but so are the knowledge and experiences that students gain from lessons. The following are some goals that a teacher might wish to stress when teaching about aging, the elderly, and death:

Rate your feelings concerning how comfortable you would be in each of the class situations described. Circle the word that best describes your feelings.

1. A child is very unhappy and you think he/she may cry.
   Very Comfortable   Comfortable   OK   Discomfort   Uncomfortable

2. You don't know the direction the class discussion will go once you have asked your first question.
   Very Comfortable   Comfortable   OK   Discomfort   Uncomfortable

3. You think you might expose your feelings and emotions as you teach the lesson.
   Very Comfortable   Comfortable   OK   Discomfort   Uncomfortable

4. You might have to answer an embarrassing question.
   Very Comfortable   Comfortable   OK   Discomfort   Uncomfortable

5. You might be asked a question for which you do not know the answer.
   Very Comfortable   Comfortable   OK   Discomfort   Uncomfortable

6. A parent questions the appropriateness of what you are teaching.
   Very Comfortable   Comfortable   OK   Discomfort   Uncomfortable

7. You hear a student say something that is factually very inaccurate.
   Very Comfortable   Comfortable   OK   Discomfort   Uncomfortable

8. You hear a student say something that is prejudicial.
   Very Comfortable   Comfortable   OK   Discomfort   Uncomfortable

9. Students fail to give any response to questions you ask.
   Very Comfortable   Comfortable   OK   Discomfort   Uncomfortable

10. You have to say what you personally think or believe.
    Very Comfortable   Comfortable   OK   Discomfort   Uncomfortable

Use these questions to help you reflect on your responses and critically examine your answers to the Comfort Scale:

- What events did you think would make you very uncomfortable?
- Are there any of the uncomfortable situations for which some type of advanced planning could lessen your apprehension?
- Looking at the things you find very comfortable, ask yourself how often you provide the opportunity for students to display this type of activity as you teach?
- Do you think you would be rewarded as the teacher if such opportunities were available? Would the students be rewarded?
- Can you think of additional opportunities to provide these experiences to your students?

FIGURE 14–1
Comfort Scale

1. Provide emotional support for children by listening to their concerns, feelings, and fears about death, aging, and the elderly
2. Provide correct factual answers to students' questions about death, aging, and the elderly
3. Help students identify stereotypes, myths, and erroneous information about aging, the elderly, and death
4. Help students to learn that all living things die as part of the life cycle
5. Increase students' information about the elderly through exposure to a variety of elderly people in a wide range of situations
6. Promote students' respect for human dignity as an important value for all age groups
7. Provide opportunities for students to build skills in listening, self-expression, empathy, and valuing

The goals can be accomplished through different means. The teacher may plan units and lessons designed specifically to teach about aging, the elderly, or death (see Figure 14–2). Another approach is to examine the present curric-

FIGURE 14–2
Older people can help us learn new skills.

ulum and integrate ideas about aging, the elderly, or death where appropriate opportunities are available. Still a third method is to use the teachable moment approach. In this approach the teacher picks up on students' comments and questions that can be related to the goals he has for teaching about aging, the elderly, and death. Teachable moments can also occur during private conversations with individual students. Still other teachable moments occur in times of crisis.

Integration of the Topics Into the Existing Curriculum

Opportunities for integrating the topics of aging, the elderly, and death into the existing curriculum are numerous, as these examples suggest.

1. Select stories for oral reading with themes about elderly people or that express feelings and views about aging and death.
2. When studying occupations, include guest speakers from all age groups. Discuss which occupations, if any, might be limited to people of a certain age group. Discuss whether people should be forced to stop working or retire just because they reach a set age.
3. Invite community volunteers to come to the class to tell what they do to help make the community a better place in which to live. Include volunteers of all ages and people who work as volunteers with organizations that deal with people of all ages.
4. At show-and-tell time, encourage children to share things that they have learned from an older person or things that were made for them by older people. Ask the children how they feel about these skills or artifacts and how they feel about the person who taught them the lesson or made the item.
5. Have students celebrate Grandparents' Day by making cards or gifts for an older person or have a program or party with older citizens as the guests.
6. When studying history, begin as early as age 4 having students interview older people to learn about their personal experiences and memories of big events or to learn about social history. (See chapter 9 for detailed suggestions.)
7. When students encounter the elderly through class experiences, have them discuss what they learned from the older person that they could not have learned from a younger person. Ask the students to give adjectives that describe the older person.
8. Use older people as volunteers in the classroom. They can listen to children read, help with crafts, help with parties,

tell stories, and assist on field trips, to mention just a few possibilities.

9. Celebrate historical events in honor of great persons from the past. This will help children to identify with the history and continuity of people through many lifetimes. It will help them to see that, though the people are dead, the memory of them is still present and important to the living.

10. When giving writing assignments, ask students to write letters, essays, and poems about or to older people.

11. When celebrating birthdays, have the students tell things that they can do on this birthday that they could not do on their last birthday. Comment on the changes in their abilities as well as their size.

Special Lessons or Units

Expressing feelings and building empathy begin with an awareness of feelings. The full range of feelings, including sadness, happiness, anger, and fear, can be worked into lessons for children. Young children who may not yet be able to define a feeling may do very well in expressing an emotion through drawings, dance, dramatic play, or other art forms.

Instructional activities stressing feelings include:

1. The use of a sad picture or musical selection as a vehicle for discussion of feelings. One nursery school teacher played a rather slow and sad piano concerto and asked the children to move to the music and describe their feelings. Eric said: "This music makes me feel sad. I want to move slowly. I think the piano is crying."

2. Reading and discussing a book, such as *Annie and the Old One* by Miles, that deals with the themes of aging, death, and the life cycle from the perspective of a young Native American girl. "Annie was very sad when she thought her grandmother would die, she tried to stop her from dying, but it didn't work; we all have to die sometime," commented a 4-year-old after hearing the story. (See chapter 15 on resources.)

3. Drawing a picture that expresses a particular emotion or drawing a picture that reflects the mood of a musical selection.

A topic that examines the concept of change in both science and history is "Exploring the Life Cycle." It provides the opportunity to learn both the meaning of death and the continuity of all life, including families and nations. Children also begin to see that death is a natural part of the life cycle and that it is not unnatural or the fault of the child. Children are asked to look to the future by predicting changes or tasks that need to be completed in attaining a goal.

Activities that teach important aspects of the life cycle include:

1. Observing the growth and changes in plants. Children enjoy planting seeds that will sprout quickly. Focus attention on the changes that occur as the seeds sprout and grow, and on the conditions necessary for plant life to exist.

2. Walking through the neighborhood or a park. This provides a laboratory where children can observe the changes of the countryside in all four seasons. Students also observe the life cycles of individual species. They find the living, the dead, and the decaying. Discuss with the children the changes in the landscape and their feelings about the changes and the mood of the setting.

3. Reading and discussing books. Books such as *The Dead Tree* by Alvin Tresselt or *The Growing Story* by Ruth Krauss explain the life cycle in words and pictures.

4. Classifying objects into living and nonliving categories.

5. Ordering pictures of students themselves in the growth sequence. The teachers ask such questions as, "What happened to the babies that you used to be?" Students tell things that they can do today that they could not do when they were young. Students can also examine pictures of their parents or grandparents and look for the changes in their lives.

6. Gaining an idea of how much children have grown since they were born through the following tactile experience. Each child finds out his birth weight and length. Then each child is given a bag of sand that equals the birth weight, which he can hold and carry. The child also is given a tape the length of his birth length, which can be compared with his present height and those of other classmates.

7. Reading biographies. This helps children to see that certain characteristics and personal traits remain the same in persons as they grow older.

8. Matching pictures of baby animals with the adult animal of the same species.

9. Talking about what students would like to be or do in the future. Older students can research and identify tasks that must be completed to prepare for a chosen occupation.

Researching their own family's history helps children to see that they have a connection to both the living and the dead and that the dead may be gone but that their contribution to the family remains a part of the family (see Figure 14–3). Activities that can be used in studying a family history include:

1. Making a family album.
2. Interviewing parents and grandparents to see what they did when they were approximately the same age as the child.

FIGURE 14–3
Language experience stories can help us explore our feelings about the elderly.

3. Trying on old clothing worn by family members.
4. Looking at old pictures of family members and family's homes, cars, toys, and pets.
5. Playing with or looking at toys and games used by parents or grandparents.
6. Finding out the oldest thing that the family has and any story or information known about the item.
7. Listening to older people tell of their experiences when they were growing up.
8. Visiting a cemetery and seeing where members of their family are interned.
9. In second or third grade, reading their birth announcements and those of their family members from old issues of the local newspaper or a reel of microfilm. Children can use the

newspapers to see what important events took place in the year they were born or who was the president the year they were born.

10. Learning the origin and meaning of their names. Who selected the name for them? Why did they make that particular selection? In doing this activity students will find that some ethnic groups follow specific traditions in naming their children.

Teachable Moments Approach

Teachable moments are student- or event-initiated opportunities that a teacher seizes upon to instruct students about a topic. These may involve the entire class or individual students. A teacher who elects to use this approach may find that the topic is not considered in some years. This does not mean, however, that the teacher has not planned the lesson. There is a need for clear knowledge and attitudinal objectives appropriate to the grade and experience level of the student. The teacher knows that some topics will come up every year, given the interests of the children and the type of community. A teacher may keep lesson plans and teaching resources filed in an easily accessible place for use on a moment's notice for a topic such as tornado safety. The teacher might also wish to do this for a topic such as AIDS or the death of a pet, parent, or well-known person. Guidelines for teachable moment lessons include the following:

1. Accept the students' feelings and allow them to share their feelings.
2. Provide correct factual information as requested, but answers need not be long.
3. Use correct terminology in discussing the topic.
4. Be willing to get the correct information and tell the students that you will share it with them when you get it.
5. Take the time necessary to handle the topic and invite students to come to you if they have additional concerns.

FACTS AND GUIDELINES FOR TEACHING ABOUT DEATH

The subject of death is difficult for all ages and people to handle. Our own reactions often make it impossible or difficult to help others. Children are capable of handling this subject; however, the pre-schooler has more difficulty and requires more time to resolve the loss. For teachers, a death will almost always come as a surprise, which means that the teacher will need to work through the crisis for himself as well as try to assist the students. Parents too have the same problem, and often a child comes to the teacher because the parent is unable to help the child. Open communications with the parent will, of course, assist the teacher in helping the student.

Thus far, we have not given thought to death coming in our own classroom or school. Death seems to come at the end of a long lifetime. However, young people die. The children we teach, the parents of our students, and our teaching colleagues may die. Today we also hear much about the disease AIDS, which kills younger people, and the reality of young death is brought into the news and conversations that our students hear. The statistical probability of facing a situation in which the teacher must deal with a death of a young person is already greater than he may expect. "In a school system of 6000 students approximately 4 students per year will die and 40 will experience the death of a parent" (Smith-Martenz, Cooper, & Leverte, 1981, p. 6).

Erna Furman (1978), who counsels children, describes the needs of the child and the role of mourning.

> If the death is understood, if its cause is understood and the disposal of the body is understood, and if the bereaved child is reasonably sure of his or her own survival and of having bodily and emotional needs met to a sufficient extent, mourning will start of itself. It is a process that is not always visible from the outside.... Mourning is a mental process that consists primarily of two parts: on one hand, a very gradual and painful detachment from the memories of the deceased, and on the other hand almost the opposite, a taking into oneself some traits or qualities of the deceased. (p. 32)

In her excellent article, "Helping Children Cope With Death," Furman recommends that teachers do the following:

1. Help children understand death in its concrete manifestations.
2. Help students to realize that all living things die.
3. Do not give abstract or philosophical answers to students under age 6, because they will not understand and will interpret what you say in their own terms. This holds a strong possibility of negative attitudes toward religion or the internalization of false ideas.
4. Acknowledge and initiate the discussion of a death with the child by extending sympathy and giving the child an invitation to talk if the child wishes.
5. Tell the classmates about a death clearly and with few details and suggest that the students may extend sympathy, but should treat the child normally upon his return.
6. Empathize with each and every feeling a child expresses and help the child recognize and control each feeling.

CASE STUDY: A SCHOOL DEALS WITH THE DEATH OF THREE CLASSMATES

This is a true description of the events that surrounded an accidental death of three members of a third-grade class in a Western state.

At the beginning of the weekend three classmates went sledding in the mountains. All died in an avalanche. The story made the news and so the children in their third-grade class heard of the tragedy during the weekend. When they arrived in school on Monday, the three children's desks were empty. The classmates were told that the three children had died and that the classmates would be going to the funeral as a group, but that they were not going to talk about the incident or the three children and there would be no crying in class. Before attending the funeral the students were asked to wear good, Sunday-style clothing and told that they would all sit together at the funeral. If their parents were attending the funeral, they would still be expected to sit with the class. They were expected to be very quiet. After the funeral, the children who wanted to do so could go to the caskets and see the bodies of the three who died. Then all of the students returned to the school in the buses that brought them. On the bus and playground the children whispered about what they had seen and how the three children looked. When they entered the school, the third grade returned to regular class work and nothing more was ever said.

Critique the case study. Identify those things that were done correctly and those things that you believe should have been done differently. Explain your answers by relating your recommendations to the needs of the children and the general reading of this chapter. Explain how you think the teacher felt in the situation. Identify the concerns of the teacher in this case study. Tell how his concerns are similar or different from what your concerns would be if you were in a similar situation.

AIDS AND THE CHILD

Today the increase in the number of deaths associated with AIDS brings the topic of death into the news. AIDS is a fearful illness because it is terminal. Parents, of course, are worried about whether children carrying the AIDS virus should be allowed to attend schools, and their concern has received much national news coverage by the media. The U.S. Surgeon General has said that AIDS education should begin as early as possible for all children. He mentions that some children begin to ask questions about AIDS at ages 9 or 10. He stresses the need to put emphasis on the IV drug problem as related to the spread of AIDS. Because young children do not understand sex and are not personally interested in sex, it is recommended that explanations for the very young be related to something that they clearly understand. Most of the children worry about "catching AIDS" because they associate it with "catching a cold." Most of the questions the teacher will encounter about AIDS will be in the nature of fear about catching it and dying. Assuring children that they will not catch AIDS as they do colds is sufficient.

Even though the publicity has been vocal, very few children between the ages of 5 and 12 have AIDS. As of March 1, 1989, the Center for Disease Control reported 87,188 cases of AIDS. Less than 1% (only 243) were children between 5 and 12. The vast majority of them acquired AIDS from hemophilia and related disorders and blood transfusions. More children are being born with AIDS or HIV. A total of 1,189 children under the age of 5 are among this group. Some of these children may soon be entering the school population. C. Everett Koop, U.S. Surgeon General, has said:

> You can't morally censure the children who have AIDS. Right now, practically all the children with AIDS are hemophiliacs who got it through blood transfusions. And in five or six years, there will be children born to drug-abusing parents who will survive and go to school with AIDS. You simply can't blame any of these kids for having the disease.

School systems and states are writing curriculums for AIDS education. Those who wish to teach more about this can check the educational resources for accurate information and for teaching suggestions. Teachers should keep in mind that, with such an illness, the public is more accepting of medical experts' involvement with the class than an individual teacher. Teachers may consider asking a health official or medical doctor to assist in dealing with this topic.

TERMINALLY ILL STUDENTS

Leukemia, cancer, cystic fibrosis, muscular dystrophy, and AIDS are all illnesses that are terminal and that children have. The odds are very small, but teachers may someday find themselves teaching a class in which there is a student with one of these diseases. Because children may have these diseases for several years, they often return to school between treatments. They need to maintain a positive self-image and to take part in normal activities, rather than dwell on their illness. However, the teacher must be sensitive to special needs that such children and their families have. The teacher has a special role to play among the professionals caring for such a child and should know and work closely with others involved with the child. At the same time, the teacher needs to keep the student's role in class as nearly like that of the other students as possible. Because each case is unique, prescriptive behaviors listed in a general reference are of little help. The teacher facing such a situation should learn as much about the disease and the specifics of the child as possible. Of great assistance will be the general literature on dealing with the terminally ill. Two excellent articles specifically for teachers are "Death in My Classroom?" by Cathleen Postel and "An Unexpected Lesson" by Laurie Knowlton.

SUMMARY

Teachers have a vital role in focusing and framing experiences for children, including those related to aging, the elderly, and death. The teacher who treats children with honesty and dignity and is accepting of their thoughts and feelings can assist them to have faith in themselves. He can help them to understand the path of life that they will tread and help provide the positive self-concept that lays the foundation of joy and fulfillment in each stage of life's journey. In so doing he will be contributing much to the personal growth and development that enables children to look forward to completing a satisfying life filled with human dignity.

REFERENCES

BALKIN, E., EPSTEIN, C., & BUSH, D. (1976). Attitudes toward classroom discussions of death and dying among urban and suburban children. *Omega, 7,* 183–189.

CHILDERS, P., & WIMMER, M. (1971). The concept of death in early childhood. *Child Development, 42,* 1299–1301.

DAVIS, G. L. (1986). A content analysis of fifty-seven children's books with death themes. *Child Study Journal, 16,* 39–53.

FILLMER, H. T., & MEADOWS, R. (1986). The portrayal of older characters in five sets of basal readers. *The Elementary School Journal, 86,* 651–662.

FORMANEK, R. (1974). When children ask about death. *The Elementary School Journal, 75,* 92–97.

FURMAN, E. (1978). Helping children cope with death. *Young Children, 33,* 25–32.

GALPER, A. (1978). The relation of children's death references to grade level and attitudes toward the elderly and the aging process. Unpublished doctoral dissertation, University of Maryland, College Park, MD.

JANTZ, R. K., SEEFELDT, C., GALPER, A., & SEROCK, K. (1976). *Final report: Children's attitudes toward the elderly.* Washington, DC: American Association of Retired Persons.

KASTENBAUM, R. (1967). The child's understanding of death. In E. A. Grollman (Ed.), *Explaining death to children.* Boston: Beacon Press.

KASTENBAUM, R., & AISENBERG, R. (1972). *The psychology of death.* New York: Springer.

KNOWLTON, L. P. (1988). An unexpected lesson. *Learning, 16*(7), 110.

KOOCHER, G. (1973). Childhood, death and cognitive development. *Developmental Psychology, 9,* 369–375.

MAURER, A. (1974). Intimations of mortality. *Journal of Clinical Child Psychology, 3,* 14–17.

MCTAVISH, D. C. (1971). Perceptions of old age: a review of research methodologies and findings. *Gerontologist, 11*, 90.

MITCHELL, M. E. (1967). *The child's attitude to death.* New York: Schocken Books.

NAGY, M. H. (1959). The child's view of death. In H. Feifel (Ed.), *The meaning of death.* New York: McGraw-Hill.

POSTEL, C. A. (1986). Death in my classroom? *Teaching Exceptional Children. 18*(2), 139–143.

ROCHLIN, G. (1967). How younger children view death and themselves. In E. A. Grollman (Ed.), *Explaining death to children.* Boston: Beacon Press.

SEEFELDT, C., JANTZ, R. K., SEROCK, K., & GALPER, A. *Children's attitudes toward the elderly: A study of curriculum implementation.* Final Report submitted to the American Association of Retired Persons, National Retired Teachers Association, August 1977.

SMITH-MARTENZ, A., COOPER, J. A., & LEVERTE, M. (1981) *Creative consultant series loss.* Doylestown, PA: TACT.

TREBIG, D. L. (1974). Language, children and attitudes toward the aged: A longitudinal study. *Gerontologist, 14*(5), 14–75.

15

USING RESOURCES TO TEACH THE SOCIAL STUDIES

Sandra Bradford DeCosta
West Virginia University

Teaching the social studies to any age group requires a variety of resources. They may be in print form, manipulatives, pictures, or other typical classroom materials. They may also be in forms less ambiguous to the developing mind—that is, in concrete forms that are human, environmental, technological, or all of these in combination. Whatever is selected, the resource will likely enhance learning by appealing to a greater number of the senses: a demonstration that is seen is better understood. A film that is viewed together and immediately discussed combines the visual and auditory experiences with descriptive and explanatory talk about what was viewed. A computer game teaches, corrects, and generally assists in understanding mapping skills. An audiotape of someone sharing the excitement of a special event or reading a story can be replayed time and again to hear the messages and confirm the information. Any and all of these constitute effective ways to incorporate teaching aids or resources into a lesson.

A good teacher assesses what the children need and what is available, then incorporates the most appropriate resource. A good teacher remains current and informed about available people as teaching resources so that opportunities can be created to invite them to the center or school. This chapter describes some of those resources and ways in which they can be made to enhance teaching and learning. It encourages teachers to use the neighborhood and community to improve teaching and increase the likelihood of student learning.

THE GUEST SPEAKER

Young children are eager listeners to speakers and delight in having a guest speaker invited to the classroom. If a "local expert" might be willing to speak or demonstrate a skill or talent, by all means that person should be contacted. To make the visit as valuable as possible, supply your guest speaker with a "preparation packet." Include a little information about the children, indicate their ages, provide a general statement about their overall familiarity with the topic, and tell how you will prepare the children for the visit. Set some time limits so that children won't become tired and unruly. Provide your speaker with a few age-appropriate goals. Then in preparing your students, present an introduction to the content or the forthcoming speaker and some of your expectations regarding their learning. Indicate just how you expect the children to listen. Decide how they might keep track of new information. Consider whether the children might best ask their questions of the speaker or during a class discussion of the event. All these things need to be carefully planned and discussed so that children will have a sense of what will occur. They should be comfortable and confident in this experience and have a role in the proceedings.

You might want to video record the speaker's performance so that the program can be viewed again by the children, other groups in your school, or shared with parents. You must secure permission from the speaker but this is a wonderful record of important events. All the children can be incorporated into the film, making it even more personally beneficial.

Keep in mind, too, that parents are excellent resources and speakers. A survey sheet can be prepared and sent home at the beginning of the term. It should ask parents to list interests, hobbies, and skills and their places of employment. The survey will provide a wealth of community resources but also assures many parents that they are indeed valuable contributors to their children's education.

A guest speaker can be seen and heard in the school or even the classroom, but it is also possible to take the group on an outing away from the school to enhance learning. The teacher may choose to take the children to a dramatic performance, to hear a musician, or to visit an office. We have long known that the school is not the only place for learning. The value of the site visits should not be missed, although they do require careful planning.

THE FIELD TRIP

Field trips serve many purposes, but primarily they are concrete opportunities to see and experience. Trips may be day-long or may last an hour. They should be planned to achieve specific objectives. That is, a lesson plan must be developed for a field trip in much the same way as any other lesson or learning activity.

In advance, identify your needs—that is, what you hope to have the children learn from the visit. Then contact local businesses, agencies, and sites that are most likely to meet your requirements. Make an appointment to meet with the education guide or representative in charge of field trips. Prepare a list of your objectives and take a note pad. Go through the motions of a field trip: identify things to point out to the children, try to satisfy your own concerns and try to anticipate the questions of your students, determine the approximate time this trip will take, decide if you will need to introduce technical language or difficult concepts in advance, and look for situations that will warrant special safety precautions. Request a copy of any company printed information so that you can use it to extract relevant information to present to the children. When you decide if this will be a good place for the group to visit, mail out a confirming letter to the field trip contact person indicating date, time of arrival, length of time allocated for the trip, number of children, their approximate ages, and the grade level. Your full name, address at school, and phone number should appear in the letter as well as the total number expected on the trip. This figure should include you, the students, aides, other teachers, and parent volunteers. Ask that the representative confirm the trip by mail or phone.

You must now arrange transportation. Is this a walking field trip? Or must you arrange for the bus, the driver, and several adults to assist you? Are you in a setting that allows parent chaperones to drive students to the field site? Brainstorm your probable needs and make all the preparations necessary to assure a smooth trip.

Prepare the parent permission slips to be sent home well in advance of your trip. Some districts have a standard form whereas others allow or require teachers to develop their own. Include a brief statement that tells the parents where you are going and why and list individual needs for this trip such as fare, lunch, boots, a heavy sweater. Ask for parent volunteers to contact you at school. Do indicate that the signed form must be on file by a specific date in order for the child to attend.

Prepare name tags for the students that include their names and the name and phone number of the school. Establish cooperative seatmates or pairs and notify the children of your selections. Bring several jump ropes for the children to grip. This is an easy way to keep groups of five or six children together and in line. Notify the children in advance, and then repeatedly, of your expectations for their conduct and learning.

The following is an example of a field trip developed and implemented in a small town. Modify this trip to meet your needs.

LESSON PLAN

What Is a Summer or Part-Time Job? (A Field Trip for First Grade)

Children are often confused about the roles and responsibilities of employed teenagers. They wonder about the jobs available, what is required of a worker, the working conditions, and the pay. A number of concepts involving all the content areas can be taught and demonstrated through a unit of lessons on this topic.

By way of introducing the unit, the children and I developed a list of questions about teenagers' jobs that we wanted to answer. I brought in two upper-grade children from our school prepared to talk about the neighborhood jobs they had held. The jobs included:

- Caring for pets while neighbors were away
- Caring for plants while neighbors were away
- Collecting mail and newspapers for neighbors
- Raking leaves
- Cleaning garages
- Shoveling snow
- Going to the neighborhood grocery for someone
- Babysitting
- Cutting the grass

Implementation My students interviewed the older children to collect information. We all listened while specified teams engaged in the questioning. During an open question period, anyone was free to inject a question. Each child later illustrated the jobs that had been described and the new, important information that was learned. Each student entered the crucial information into her "Kids' Careers" notebook. We graphed our findings to provide another way of organizing them.

I arranged a number of local field trips. Some we could walk to and others required parent drivers or the school bus. Each trip was set for Friday morning and each was thematically developed to collect information and apply what was learned into designated content areas. For example, one theme of our trips was designed to focus on the amount of money earned each week and the kind of job involved. These visits combined math and social studies concepts. We visited the local newspaper office, Holiday Inn, a flower/nursery business, McDonald's, a supermarket, and a discount variety store. The businesses all employed some teenagers in summer and after school and paid different hourly rates for different jobs. General information was collected by the children—again in teams with clear responsibilities for data/information collection. The places we visited dictated the information we were seeking, and so question sets were different for each trip. After each visit we returned to the school to debrief and enter our findings into the folders. I usually took a camera so that we would have a pictorial memory of our trip.

Whether in a city or a small town, productive and meaningful field trips are possible. Museums, Disneyland, or a zoo are not necessary for an educational field trip. Possibilities exist in every community for learning outside the classroom. As is true in any teaching/learning endeavor, proper planning and organization on the part of the teacher are essential.

FAMILY INTERVIEWS AND ORAL HISTORY

Learning about oneself, the family, one's heritage, and the family history are all basic to the social studies. Opportunities for this kind of learning exist in each family. A special and ongoing assignment can be created to enable the children to engage in some family investigation. Children need only a little encouragement to learn more about themselves and the history of the family. The assignment often becomes an exciting event and leads other members of the family to become similarly involved. A little survey sheet put together by the teacher and sent home with the children would have them find out such things as: Where did Mom grow up? What did she do after school? What were her favorite games? What was life on the farm like for Gram? Was Gram really a pioneer or was that before even her time? How many states have my relatives lived in? Where did they live before they came to this country? Why did they come here? When?

As part of this assignment, encourage children to bring in copies of the family tree and trace back several generations. Help children use a tape recorder and devise a general interview form so that they can obtain their own interview information. Encourage them to place pictures in an album and connect the photos with taped information or written narrative. Help them see that members of their own families are valuable sources of information. All kinds of things can be learned through interviews. Send the children out to find cooperative members of their families. As part of a closing lesson, organize the findings into a bulletin-board display. A fine guide for activities of this sort is Weitzman's *My Backyard History Book*. Other sources are Mehaffy, Sitton, and Davis Jr.'s *Oral History in the Classroom;* Cutler, Wigginton, Gallant, and Ives' "Oral History as a Teaching Tool"; Thavenet's *Family History: Coming Face-to-Face with the Past;* and Nelson and Singleton's "Using Oral History in the Social Studies Classroom."

You might identify other local sources of information and, with your students, write the history of the town or recreate a model of the town as a village. Visit a nursing home and arrange for senior citizens to be interviewed by the children. Keep in mind that you are always surrounded by writing and by informed human resources to enhance children's understanding of the social studies.

PICTURES, FILM, FILMSTRIPS, AND RECORDS

For decades teachers have used pictures, film, filmstrips, and records as part of early childhood social studies activities. These media do not fully substitute for the real thing, but they give children an opportunity to learn about what might otherwise be completely unfamiliar. For example, a record can allow us to hear an elephant trumpeting. The recording combined with a picture of an elephant can develop some understanding of elephants when there is no zoo near enough for a field trip.

Preservice teachers should begin developing a picture file (Kenworthy, 1977). Pictures should be laminated or covered with clear contact paper so that they will not deteriorate quickly. When a teaching position is obtained and an annual teaching plan is developed, the teacher lists areas for which pictures will be needed and actively searches for them. Films are often preferable to pictures because they are closer to real life (Bryan, 1977). A filmstrip with an accompanying tape recording is somewhat less concrete than a film, whereas records and pictures are the least concrete because they utilize just one of the senses. Lists of appropriate films, filmstrips, and recordings should be developed. Chapter 16 provides a listing of items that might be included on these lists.

Before the film, records, or other media are used, a list of questions should be developed to guide discussion of the media and/or an activity planned that builds on the media (Cooper, 1981). Using media with no organized plan for discussion or activity wastes time and results in little learning. Media are a necessary part of the early childhood social studies but are worthwhile only if their use is planned. Table 15–1 lists good reasons for using audiovisual materials along with some temptations to be resisted.

TELEVISION AS A TEACHING TOOL

Television can be a fine teaching tool and an aid to education for all children if it is understood and properly controlled by the user. However, it is more likely

TABLE 15–1
Reasons we may use audiovisual materials

Temptations	Good Reasons
■ Unfilled last hour of the day	■ To motivate children
■ Antsy children	■ As an introduction to a lesson
■ A headache	■ As a review of a lesson
■ Lack of time to prepare a lesson	■ As a supplement to a lesson
■ Need to occupy children so teacher can do other things	■ To present material in several ways to help students internalize objectives
■ "It's easy"	■ To actively involve students in the process (use the equipment)
■ Tired teacher	■ To involve several senses of the children
■ "It's Friday"	■ To present ideas in a way that would be impossible without AV equipment (for example, seeing a volcano erupt)
■ Filler, because lesson took less time than planned	■ To give someone else's view on a topic
	■ For fun and excitement

to be used as an entertainment medium, dulling rather than heightening the senses. Few teachers, parents, or children understand the power and the potential of television. Fewer take television seriously enough to learn about it and explore its potential for teaching and learning. Too many children are watching too much television indiscriminately. Children and their families might, with the help of the teacher, develop a plan for television viewing. Typically, the set is turned on and abandoned; eventually another person passes by and begins to watch; the group grows until more are clustered around the set, viewing—but not with a purpose. Television viewing requires careful, thoughtful selection. It might result from a family discussion of programs and the idea of the week's family viewing. This could assure the presence of an adult to explain what is being viewed.

Television viewing is a part of the daily life of nearly every American child. The TV set is present in more than 98 percent of all American households and, according to Dorr (1986), the American television set continues to be more common than the telephone or indoor toilets. It is turned on for more than seven hours each day and directly viewed by children for 4.5 to 5 hours each day!

Although clear evidence exists that children engage in heavy television viewing, there is less evidence that the viewing is critical or purposeful. To demonstrate to students the need to plan and control television viewing, the teacher may read Byars' *TV Kid* to them. This book describes television in the life of a young boy. The television provides him with friends, family, and role models and has become his reality!

Steps to Train Critical Viewing

The following four steps may help in teaching children to be more critical viewers and users of television. The steps are also intended to help the teacher assist students to develop better viewing habits and inject more balance into the use of TV.

To Identify or Monitor

To Evaluate

To Direct or Guide

To Expand

Step 1: To Identify or Monitor

By means of:

- careful attention to a child's viewing habits and tastes
- systematic logging of viewing time
- talking to child about viewing behaviors
- documenting viewing patterns
- discovering child's "favorites"

For purpose of:

- becoming familiar with the amount and type of viewing the child engages in
- gathering data to be used in making future decisions
- learning about the child
- learning about how child "uses" television

Step 2: To Evaluate

By means of:

- watching television with the child; talking with child after viewing
- observing child's behavior during and after viewing experiences
- applying personal and professional criteria in determining program quality and worth
- considering programs in terms of family values

For purpose of:

- determining the viewing that is worthwhile and viewing that may not be worthwhile for the child
- developing a backlog of experiences on which to make intelligent recommendations
- knowing what to praise and what to condemn

Step 3: To Direct or Guide

By means of:

- taking responsibility for child's viewing behavior
- explaining, as appropriate, parental criteria to the child
- fostering the habit of discriminating viewing
- knowing about upcoming programs of worth

For purpose of:

- controlling child's behavior and encouraging selective, purposeful viewing experiences
- identifying programs consistent with family values
- establishing positive habits and worthwhile tastes in television programming
- not missing the best television may offer
- turning television *off* at the right times—and *on* at the right times

Step 4: To Expand

By means of:

- looking for ways to interact with and engage the child in formal and informal postviewing experiences
- seeking home and extended world connections to television experiences
- acknowledging growth potential for selective television viewing
- turning the set off after discrete viewing experiences

For purpose of:

- using television as a catalyst to expand the cognitive, emotional, social, affective, and physical development of the child
- fostering dialogue between parents and child
- providing, in advance, consistent purposefulness for the child's viewing

A Viewing Guide

To assure value in a viewing experience and/or to alert students and their parents to an upcoming and recommended program, a viewing guide is suggested. This is easily developed by the teacher and distributed to all students to be taken home. It serves as both an alert to a recommended program and an outline of purposes for the viewing experience.

A viewing guide can be developed from limited information—a *TV Guide* description of programs is sufficient. Some of what is provided in the viewing guide will come from the natural predictability of television story lines and some will derive from the teacher's personal knowledge. Teachers should prepare the guides and send them home periodically for cooperative student/parent use. Parents can use them to prepare themselves and their children for viewing a program.

A viewing guide should include the following:

1. What the show will be about: a preview statement
2. Why the show is worth watching: reasons students might— or should—be motivated to view
3. Some motivation for the viewing experience: application to the students' lives
4. Anticipated issues or themes for the students to think about prior to viewing
5. Questions, issues, and concerns to think about during the viewing
6. Expansion activities for postviewing follow-up: something to do, to think about, to read (a means of responding)

As an example, a recent *TV Guide* provided the following description for "ALF," a program that is a favorite of many young children:

> *Willie's promotion means the Tanners will have to move, but as*
> *Willie scares up buyers for the house, ALF scares them away*
> *with some mysterious mischief.*

This is very limited information, but anyone who had seen the program previously would be able to predict what is likely to occur. The viewing guide might include the following:

1. The *TV Guide* description tells us a little of what the program will be about. Those of you who have seen the program before will know what to expect. This week the program will be about . . . (insert the *TV Guide* description in this space).

2. This program is likely to be funny because Alf tries to be a human character. I think Alf will not want to move; therefore, I expect he will make it very difficult, in funny ways, for buyers to like the house. Watch carefully to see if I am right and be ready to discuss ways that Alf caused some problems for the buyers.

3. Some children in the classroom are likely to have participated in at least one move. This might be a time to ask if they recall how they felt about the move. They might reflect on insecurities, fears, sadness, excitement, anticipation—all the emotions that might surround a move. They might be asked to describe how they would react if they were to learn that they were moving.

4. I expect the characters in the program to demonstrate some of the emotions previously listed. I expect Alf to cause some chaos—the sort of thing that might make the family question the move. I think Alf will be motivated by his affectionate feelings for the family and that he will do things "for the good of the family."

   Find evidence to support my beliefs or examples that show Alf to be another kind of character.

5. Have you ever moved? Can you understand that while you may be excited about moving, you might also be a little afraid—afraid to make new friends, afraid others might not like you, afraid things won't be quite as good as they are here? And it might be sad to leave all your old friends.

6. Certainly view to determine whether the usual predictability of the program prevails. That is, some programs are much the same each week. There are little variations but mostly the programs consist of predictable events. Look for some books that deal with a theme of moving and finding new friends.

Read and write a little report about the ALF program and a comparison to your book. Take this a step further, and try to recall a new child in the school. That's just the child to invite over for lunch or to play next Saturday! Understanding the emotions of a move may make children more sensitive to the needs of others.

From your answers to the above, you and your students should be able to assess whether the ALF program is valuable or important enough to you to continue to see it. If the information you collected convinces you that it doesn't entertain and/or educate you, then you may wish to consider eliminating it from your viewing. While one of the goals is to make better and more educational use of television, another is surely to decrease the amount of time children spend with the television! A child who cannot provide his parents with legitimate justifications for his TV selections—justifications that match the family values—should not be given selection responsibilities.

Use the viewing guide to assure a single viewing experience in an evening rather than an evening of viewing. It will help assure less time spent in front of the tube and more use made of the viewing experience.

A Viewing Survey

In an effort to find out how much television viewing the children are engaged in, survey information can be collected. The most accurate information is usually derived when one interviews rather than asks for blanks to be filled. Figure 15–1 is a form that was used in a West Virginia University course on "Children's Television: Problems and Potentials." The form served the purpose of gathering meaningful information about viewing patterns and preferences.

The Power of Television

The current national average for daily television viewing by American children, ages 2 to 12, is approximately 5 to 6 hours. Even with the more conservative estimates, that translates to more time spent with the television set than in school. It translates to an electronic medium of powerful proportions training, teaching, convincing, and appealing to children with all its captivating power.

When we speak of the power of television, it is with reference to power as few have ever really known it. Consider that television has the *power* to:

inform as well as *misinform*

entertain at high or low levels

humanize or to *dehumanize*

but always to *educate*

1. When do you most often watch television? (select two)

   weekday afternoons _____   weekend mornings _____

   weekday evenings _____   weekend evenings _____

2. _____ is my favorite television night.

3. My three favorite shows are: _____

4. Listed below are some things that might make you want to watch television. Put a check by the ones that are true for you.

   _____ TV commercials that tell what is coming on

   _____ What my friends are watching and talking about

   _____ What my parents watch or suggest that I watch

   _____ What the *TV Guide* or newspaper says will be on

   _____ Earlier episodes of the same program that I liked

   _____ Whatever is on that the family is watching

5. How many hours of television do you watch in an average week?

   _____ 4–8 hours   _____ 9–15 hours

   _____ 16–25 hours   _____ 26–35 hours

   _____ more than 35   _____ less than 4

6. How often and under what circumstances do your parents set limits on the amount or type of television viewing you do?

7. Remember a time when a teacher or your parent encouraged you to watch something on television—and you did. Think what the program was and how many times this has happened.

8. Compared to other kids my age I watch:

   _____ less television   _____ more television   _____ the same

9. My favorite TV people are: _____

10. My favorite TV programs on PBS (Public Broadcasting) are: _____

    _____

11. If you could change one thing about television what might that be?

12. I usually watch TV with: _____

FIGURE 15–1

Informal television survey for children and adolescents

FIGURE 15–2
A child helps the microcomputer tell a story.

Television has the potential to shape attitudes and instill values. It teaches rules and provides examples of those rules in action. The values and rules inadvertently learned from television may or may not reflect those of the family. Therefore, it becomes essential that we teach children and their parents how to use television. Teachers who demonstrate knowledge of TV and recognition of its potential as a teaching tool are individuals in control of the medium. Recognition of the power of television means that we take it seriously: that we develop critical viewing skills, that we teach about it, and that we learn to control television.

COMPUTERS AND YOUNG CHILDREN

Technology in another teaching form has crept into the classroom. There has been a recent move toward the incorporation of computers into the early childhood setting (see Figure 15–2). In some schools, the presence of computers has been accepted as evidence of "progressive education," but in others some developmental considerations are occurring. IBM's "Writing to Read Program," designed primarily for kindergartners and first graders, has provided a new way of teaching reading, writing, and phonetics to children (Martin & Friedberg, 1986). Test results have been mixed, but there appears to be growing evidence that mainstreamed children and those thought to be difficult to teach are responding favorably to this method. Other groups are being tested and information is becoming more available. Other forms of computer education or computer-assisted education have worked their way into the early childhood curricula. Common among them are games, voice simulations providing directions and reinforcement, and activities for all the content areas. A listing of microcomputer programs appropriate for use in social studies education in early childhood is given in Chapter 16.

The real teaching/learning value or appropriateness of the computer in the early childhood setting is not certain. Hill (1986) issues an alert that we tread carefully before jumping on the computer bandwagon. She cites the concerns of behavioral optometrists regarding visual–tactile skill integration in young children; a need to determine the cognitive abstractness, therefore cognitive appropriateness, of computer tasks; and other developmental considerations that might lead to stress in the computer kid. Many programs are exploring the uses of computers with young children. At this time it appears to be important to use computers in a nonstressful setting as an additional tool that is an adjunct to learning. Much more research will need to be conducted before we decide on the best classroom uses of computers for young children.

SUMMARY

We are surrounded by teaching resources. They are plentiful regardless of the size of the community. They are parents, community leaders, and business owners; they are also the offerings of nature and the out-of-doors. Researching the community will yield a wealth of resources. The owner of the local bakery can help children better understand the world from a new perspective. The zoo, the airport, and the city park are all places run by and cared for by people who can describe their jobs and the uses/functions of their places of work. Through encounters such as these, the sometimes mysterious outside world begins to be a more meaningful place to the child learner. The television can, of course, be a fine resource but viewers must learn to control it before it takes control. Computers, too, can be fine resources but they must be used in appropriate, carefully planned ways. This chapter points out the easy availability of teaching resources but signals a clear alert that there are ways to plan for the most meaningful uses of resources.

REFERENCES

BRYAN, S. (1977). *Effective use of films in social studies classrooms. How to do it.* Washington, DC: National Council for the Social Studies.
BYARS, B. (1976). *The TV kid.* New York: Scholastic.
COOPER, B. (1981). *Popular music in the social studies classroom: Audio resources for teachers. How to do it.* Washington, DC: National Council for the Social Studies.

CUTLER, W., WIGGINTON, E., GALLANT, B., & IVES, E. (1973). Oral history as a teaching tool. *Oral History Review, 3*, 30–35.

DORR, A. (1986). *Television and children: A special medium for a special audience.* Beverly Hills, CA: Sage.

HILL, S. (1986). Beware of bandwagons: Young children may not need microcomputers. In D. Harper & J. Stewart (Eds.). *Run: Computer education* (rev. ed, pp. 31–33). Belmont, CA: Wadsworth.

KENWORTHY, L. (1977). *Reach for a picture. How to do it.* Washington, DC: National Council for the Social Studies.

MARTIN, J. H., & FRIEDBERG, A. (1986). *Writing to read.* New York: Warner.

MEHAFFY, G., SITTON, T., & DAVIS, O., JR. (1979). *Oral history in the classroom. How to do it.* Washington, DC: National Council for the Social Studies.

NELSON, M., & SINGLETON, H. (1975). Using oral history in the social studies classroom. *Clearinghouse, 49*, 89–93.

THAVENET, D. (1981). *Family history: Coming face-to-face with the past. How to do it.* Washington, DC: National Council for the Social Studies.

WEITZMAN, D. (1975). *My backyard history book.* Covelo, CA: Yolla Bolly Press.

16

A LISTING OF RESOURCE MATERIALS FOR THE SOCIAL STUDIES

Barbara Hatcher
Southwest Texas State University

This chapter includes selected books, magazines, and additional materials to complement a social studies program for young children. A bibliography of children's books is included on the following topics: understanding oneself and others, the young child and change, other places and cultures today, and our American heritage. An additional section includes professional references for teachers. Both practical and theoretical titles are provided. Movies, filmstrips, records, kits, study prints, games, dolls, and software, as well as useful children's and teacher's magazines, are highlighted in the chapter. All materials are developmentally appropriate and easily obtainable for classroom use.

UNDERSTANDING ONESELF AND OTHERS

Feelings About Self

HUGHES, S. (1978). *Moving Molly.* Englewood Cliffs, NJ: Prentice-Hall. Molly moves to the country with her family and eventually copes with her loneliness by exploring a hole in the fence.

JONAS, A. (1982). *When you were a baby.* New York: Greenwillow. A child looks at baby dependence and revels in freedom.

KERKEY, V., & KERKEY, B. (1979). *Robbers, bones and mean dogs.* Danbury, NH: Addison-Wesley. These excerpts from papers written by students about their scary feelings are cleverly illustrated and should help spark discussion about emotions and fears.

SIMON, N. (1976). *Why am I different?* Chicago: Albert Whitman. Child characters find themselves in situations in which they discover differences among themselves and others. Simon explores their feelings about these differences and their ultimate realization that all people are different from others in one way or another.

STONE, E. H. (1971). *I'm glad I'm me.* New York: Putnam. A small black boy finds joy in the world around himself, but the greatest joy is within himself.

ZOLOTOW, C. (1979). *Someone new.* New York: Harper & Row. In this thoughtful and provocative story, a child discovers that he is changing and, as he comes to terms with himself, realizes that this is what growing up means.

The Home and Interpersonal Relations

ADOFF, A. (1973). *Black is brown is tan.* New York: Harper & Row. A story about a multi-racial family.

ANRES, E. M. (1980). *Places I like to be.* Nashville, TN: Abingdon. In delightful short, rhymed verses a very young child describes the things he enjoys doing with family and friends.

CUNNINGHAM, J. (1981). *A Mouse called Junction.* New York: Walker. The many types of families are charmingly portrayed in this delightfully illustrated book. Although families differ in many ways, they all are units in which sharing and caring play an important role.

FLOURNEY, V. (1985). *The patchwork quilt.* New York: Dial. A story of multigenerational families.

JUKES, M. (1984). *Like Jake and me.* New York: Knopf. A story about step-parenting.

KEATS, E. J. (1967). *Peter's chair.* New York: Harper & Row. Sibling rivalry rears its head.

LEROY, G. (1975). *Emma's dilemma.* New York: Harper & Row. Emma must make many adjustments when her grandmother moves into the house.

LIONNI, L. (1986). *It's mine.* New York: Knopf. In this fanciful tale three quarrelsome frogs learn to cooperate and share.

NOLAN, M. S. (1978). *My Daddy don't go to work.* Minneapolis: Carolrhoda. A black girl tells of family problems caused by her father's unemployment.

ROY, R. (1981). *Breakfast with my Father.* Boston: Houghton Mifflin. This book conveys the importance of a young boy's relationship with his father during his parents' short-lived separation.

RYANT, C. (1985). *The relatives came.* New York: Bradbury. A funny, affectionate remembrance of a larger extended family.

SIMON, N. (1976). *All kinds of families.* Chicago: Albert Whitman. Conveys the idea that there are many ways families come together or choose to live.

WILHELM, H. (1986). *Let's be friends again.* New York: Crown. A charming book for teaching about emotions and values between brothers and sisters.

WILLIAMS, V. B. (1982). *A chair for my mother.* New York: Greenwillow. A story about single-parent families.

Aging/Death

ALIKI, A. (1979). *The two of them.* New York: Greenwillow. Tender words and bright, soft pictures tell of the love between a child and her grandfather through shared days until his death.

ALLEN, L. (1979). *Mr. Simkin's Grandma.* New York: William Morrow. Because children are so familiar and endeared to their grandparents, they can appreciate the zany antics of this fun-loving grandma.

BUSCAGLIA, L. (1982). *The fall of Freddie the leaf.* New York: Holt, Rinehart & Winston. Story about the life cycle of a leaf.

DE PAOLA, T. (1981). *Now one foot, now the other.* New York: Putnam. Five-year-old Bobby is frightened and saddened by his grandfather's illness. However, little by little, Bobby helps his grandfather regain his ability to walk and talk.

FASSLER, J. (1971). *My grandpa died today.* New York: Human Sciences. David is able to reconcile himself to his grandfather's death.

HOOPER, L. L. (1981). *Nana.* New York: Harper & Row. Details of feelings at the loss of a beloved grandma.

KESSELMAN, W. (1981). *Emma.* New York: Doubleday. Sensitive, beautifully illustrated story of a 72-year-old woman who begins to paint and finds life full again.

MILES, M. (1971). *Annie and the old one.* Boston: Little, Brown. Poignant, simply told tale of a Navajo child who learns to accept her grandmother's approaching death.

ROY, R. (1979). *Old tiger, new tiger.* Nashville: Abingdon. Delightful illustrations underline the charming tale of how old and young can live together and learn from each other.

TOWNSEND, M., and STERN, R. (1981). *Pop's secret.* Danbury, NH: Addison-Wesley. This book was initially assembled by a young boy in an effort to come to terms with his beloved grandfather's death.

VIORST, J. (1971). *The tenth good thing about Barney.* New York: Atheneum. Tender yet unsentimental treatment of a little boy's grief when his cat dies.

Children With Special Needs

BRIGHTMAN, A. (1976). *Like me.* Boston: Little, Brown. Rhyming text and beautiful photographs explain the concept of mental retardation for the young child.

CARRICK, C. (1985). *Stay away from Simon.* New York: Clarion. A story about retardation.

CHARLIP, R., & CHARLIP, M. B. (1980). *Handtalk: An ABC of finger spelling and sign language.* New York: Four Winds. Illustrated sign language with photographs in this book.

CLIFTON, L. (1981). *My friend Jacob.* New York: Dutton. A young boy's relationship with an older, retarded friend reveals that friends can help each other in many ways.

MACLACHLAN, P. (1981). *Through Grandpa's eyes.* New York: Harper & Row. John loves to visit his blind grandpa, who teaches him to see with his fingers, ears, and heart.

NEWTH, P. (1981). *Roly goes exploring.* New York: Putnam. Book about blindness. Versions in both print and Braille.

SOBOL, H. L. (1977). *My brother Steven is retarded.* New York: Macmillan. Eleven-year-old Beth describes candidly and unflinchingly her conflicting emotions about her retarded older brother.

WITTMAN, S., & YOLEN, J. (1977). *The seeing stick.* New York: Crowell. Ragged old woodcarving storyteller brings the world alive for the mind and touch of the emperor's blind daughter.

Career Awareness/The Child as Consumer

ARNOLD, C. (1982). *Who works here?* New York: Watts. Discusses how effective community life is based on people working in diverse occupations.

FIGURE 16–1
Learning through books is fun.

ASCHE, F. (1976). *Good lemonade.* New York: Watts. About a young boy who tries all
        types of gimmicks to sell his bad-tasting lemonade. He finally decides that the
        best way to do it is to have a good product.
FLORIAN, D. (1983). *People working.* New York: Watts. Shows people working in the city,
        country, and on the water.
HOBAN, L. (1981). *Arthur's funny money.* New York: Harper & Row. A hilarious account

of Arthur's attempts to earn money to buy a T-shirt and cap. Concepts of economics, advertising, consumer protection, free enterprise, and inflation are woven into Arthur's business.

KUNNAS, M. (1985). *The nighttime book.* New York: Crown. Author discusses the activity of people who work at night. Translated from the Finnish by T. Steffa.

PROVENSEN, A., & PROVENSEN, M. (1985). *Town and country.* New York: Crown. Large format book that portrays life in the city and on the farm. Useful to discuss economic concepts.

ROCKWELL, A. (1981). *When we grow up.* New York: Dutton. A good read-aloud book for children beginning to study the world of work.

ZIEFERT, H. (1986). *A new coat for Anna.* New York: Knopf. A delightful story about barter and ingenuity after World War II.

THE YOUNG CHILD AND CHANGE

BURTON, V. L. (1942). *The little house.* New York: Houghton Mifflin. Built in the country, the little house watches the cycle of the years pass peacefully until the city moves to engulf it.

COONEY, N. E. (1981). *The blanket that had to go.* New York: Putnam. Susi dreads leaving her blanket behind when kindergarten starts.

DELTON, J. (1980). *Lee Henry's best friend.* Chicago: Albert Whitman. After Blair Andrew moves, life is hard for Lee Henry until he develops a new friendship.

MCCLOSKEY, R. (1957). *Time of wonder.* New York: Viking. Study of seasonal changes.

SMITH, J. L. (1981). *The monster in the third dresser drawer and other stories.* New York: Harper & Row. A young boy copes with moving, a new sister, a new tooth, and other daily mishaps.

OTHER PLACES AND VARIOUS CULTURES

AARDEMA, V. (1977). *Who's in rabbit's house: A Masai tale.* New York: Dial. Rabbit finds his neighbor's help almost as bothersome as the threatening occupant.

AARDEMA, V. (1979). *Ji-mongo-mongo means riddles.* New York: Four Winds. A delightful collection of riddles taken from 11 tribes of Africa. Beautifully detailed illustrations bring Africa to life.

ANDERSON, J., retold by A. BENJAMIN. (1985). *The nightingale.* New York: Crown. Nightingale saves the Emperor of China in this classic tale.

BAKER, B. (1981). *Rat is dead and ant is sad.* New York: Harper & Row. A cumulative Pueblo Indian tale stresses the consequences of reaching wrong conclusions.

BAKER, O. (1981). *Where the buffalos begin.* New York: Warner. Tale of an Indian boy who seeks the magic lake from which the buffalos came.

BAYLOR, B. (1976). *And it is still that way: Legends told by Arizona Indian children.* New York: Scribner's Sons. These legends and folktales were told to the compiler. Collections of the oldest and best-known stories of Native Americans.

BEHRENS, J. (1978). *Fiesta!* Chicago: Children's Press. The fun of celebrating a Mexican-American family holiday, Cinco de Mayo, is the subject of this book.

BRANDON, W. (Ed.) (1971). *The magic world: American Indian songs and poems.* New York: William Morrow. The book is designed for adults, but could be used selectively with young children. It contains a comprehensive collection of Indian poetry and songs.

BRYAN, A. (1982). *I'm going to sing: Black American spirituals.* Vol. 2. New York: Atheneum. Words and music are complemented by woodcuts.

CLIFTON, L. (1973). *All of us come cross the water.* New York: Holt, Rinehart & Winston. Beautifully illustrated and told in rhythmic black prose. The poet describes a little boy's answer to his teacher's question about where his people came from and his conclusion that all Americans have "come across the water."

D'AMATO, A., & D'AMATO, J. (1970). *African crafts for you to make.* New York: Julian Messner. Directions on how to make a variety of crafts.

DE ARMOND, D. (1985). *Berry woman's children.* New York: Greenwillow. An Eskimo folktale told by a grandmother.

ETS, M. H. (1963). *Gilberto and the Wind.* New York: Viking. Gilberto learns to play with and understand the moods of the wind.

GILROY, T. (1979). *In Bikole: Eight modern stories of life in a West African village.* New York: Knopf. Through eight unforgettable stories, the lifestyle of a small West African village is portrayed. The book portrays the determination and the will of a proud people as they continue to survive supported by ancient tradition.

GREENFIELD, E. (1977). *Mary McLeod Bethune.* New York: Crowell. Bethune was the only one of 17 children in her family to go to school. Through courage and hard work, she became an educator of national importance.

HALL, E. (1975). *The Eskimo storyteller.* Knoxville: University of Tennessee Press. Folktale from Noatak, Alaska.

HARRIS, J. C. (1976). *Jump! The Adventures of Br'er Rabbit.* New York: Harcourt Brace Jovanovich. Five traditional black American slave tales of Br'er Rabbit.

HAYER, M. (1986). *The weaving of a dream: A Chinese folktale.* New York: Viking. Magical legend retold with lovely illustrations.

IKE, J., & BARAUCH, Z. (1982). *A Japanese fairy tale.* New York: Warner. A hunchback takes the disfiguration of his future wife, allowing her to be beautiful.

LEDER, D. (1976). *Why am I different?* Chicago: Albert Whitman. Book focuses on how differences enhance our lives and the uniqueness of each individual.

LEE, J. M. (1985). *Toad is the uncle of heaven: A Vietnamese folktale.* New York: Holt, Rinehart & Winston. Retold story of a clever toad who rescues the earth from drought.

LOBEL, A. (1982). *Ming Lo moves the mountain.* New York: Greenwillow. A wise man helps Ming Lo believe he has moved the mountain.

MARTEL, C. (1976). *Yugua days.* New York: Dial. Adam Rure visits his parent's homeland, Puerto Rico, for the first time.

MASON, J. (ed). (1977). *The family of children.* New York: Ridge Row Press, Grosset & Dunlap. Black and white photographs of children from around the world in a variety of settings and endeavors.

MCGOVERN, A. (1970). *Black is beautiful.* New York: Scholastic. A series of photographs showing various objects and natural phenomena stressing the fact that black is beautiful.

MORROW, S. (1968). *Inatuk's Friend.* Boston: Little Brown. Inatuk, a young Eskimo boy, moves with his family to Point Barrow. The family says goodbye to friends in a warm and sensitive way.

NEWTON, P. M. (1982). *The five sparrows: A Japanese Folktale.* New York: Atheneum. Kindness is rewarded and greed is punished in this Japanese folktale.

PARISH, P. (1970). *Ootah's lucky day.* New York: Harper & Row. Tale of an Eskimo boy on a walrus hunt who is met by a bear.

POLITI, L. (1973). *The nicest gift.* New York: Scribner's Sons. There are many Spanish words in the text and illustrations are of the barrio in East Los Angeles.

POLITI, L. (1976). *Three stalks of corn.* New York: Scribner's Sons. Chicano culture, including some recipes, provides the setting of this story about a girl and her grandmother.

SAN SOUCI, R. (1978). *The legend of Scarface: A Blackfoot Indian tale.* New York: Doubleday. A scarred young brave travels to Father Sun to ask for the hand of the maiden he loves.

SCOTT, A. H. (1972). *On Mother's lap.* New York: Dodd, Mead. A warm, tender story of an Eskimo family and of a young boy's realization that there is enough room on mother's lap for both him and his little sister.

SEEGER, P. (1986). *Abiyoyo: Based on a South African lullaby and folk song.* New York: Macmillan. African lullaby and folktale with accompanying musical refrain.

SPIER, P. (1980). *People.* New York: Doubleday. This book about diverse cultures is positively superb for young children. Spier matter-of-factly explains that we come in all sizes, shapes, and colors. He shares that people everywhere love to play games, keep pets, celebrate holidays, eat special food, use language, and live in homes.

STRETE, C. K. (1979). *When Grandfather journeys into winter.* New York: Greenwillow. The touching relationship between an American Indian boy and his grandfather.

WOLF, B. (1978). *In this proud land: The story of a Mexican-American family.* Philadelphia: Lippincott. Photographs and text follow a family from the Rio Grande valley to Minnesota for summer employment.

YARBROUGH, C. (1979). *Cornrows.* New York: Coward-McCann. Past and present mingle in this discussion of an unusual hairstyle.

YASHIMA, T. (1975). *Crow Boy.* New York: Viking. A shy introverted little boy gains recognition when an understanding new teacher arrives in his Japanese village.

AMERICAN HERITAGE

ANDERSON, J. (1986). *Pioneer children of Appalachia.* New York: Clarion. Photos of recreated Appalachian life in Fort New Salem, West Virginia.

BRENNER, B. (1979). *Wagon wheels.* New York: Harper & Row. An *I can read history too,* this beautifully written story is a delightful edition for children. A black family heading west to Kansas during the last century is helped by the Osage Indians during a fierce storm.

DELAGE, I. (1981). *Pilgrim children come to Plymouth.* New York: Garrard. Describes the Pilgrims' first year from the viewpoint of children.

JACKSON, L. A. (1977). *Grandpa had a windmill, Grandma had a churn.* New York: Parent's Magazine Press. Nostalgic photographs portray a young girl's symbolic memories of her grandparents and their lives on a Texas farm.

KALMAN, B. (1981). *Early stores and markets.* New York: Crabtree. This is part of the early settler life series. Interesting information and beautifully illustrated, this series will be popular with children and teachers.

KALMAN, B. (1981). *Early travel.* New York: Crabtree.

KALMAN, B. (1982). *The early family home.* New York: Crabtree.

KALMAN, B. (1982). *Early schools.* New York: Crabtree.

KALMAN, B. (1982). *Early settler children.* New York: Crabtree.

KALMAN, B. (1982). *Early settler storybook.* New York: Crabtree.

KALMAN, B. (1982). *Food for settlers.* New York: Crabtree.

KALMAN, B. (1983). *Early artisans.* New York: Crabtree.

KALMAN, B. (1983). *Early city life.* New York: Crabtree.

KALMAN, B. (1983). *Early health and medicine.* New York: Crabtree.

KALMAN, B. (1983). *Early pleasures and pastimes.* New York: Crabtree.

LEVINSON, R. (1985). *Watch the stars come out.* New York: Dutton. A story of immigration to the United States in the early 1890s.

ROOP, R., and ROOP, C. (1986). *Buttons for General Washington.* New York: Carolrhoda. Based on the true account of coded messages sewn on a young patriot's coat.

PROFESSIONAL REFERENCES FOR THE TEACHER

BERNSTEIN, J. (1983). *Books to help children cope with separation and loss.* 2nd ed. Ann Arbor, MI: Bowker. Selective, annotated list of children's books, films, filmstrips, and cassettes; books and chapters from books about bibliotherapy; and recent ERIC documents related to death and separation.

CANFIELD, J. (1976). *100 ways to enhance self-concept in the classroom: A handbook for teachers and parents.* Englewood Cliffs, NJ: Prentice-Hall. Contains a handbook of strategies for strengthening children's self-esteem. Not all activities appropriate for young children.

DREYER, S. S. (1981). *The bookfinder: A guide to children's literature about the needs and problems of youth aged 2–15.* Vol. 2. Circle Pines, MN: American Guidance Service. Useful topic reference book for educators seeking books for children on timely topics.

FASSLER, J. (1976). *Helping children cope.* New York: Free Press. Useful bibliography and reviews of books that assist children in stressful situations.

FREEMAN, J. (1984). *Books kids will sit still for.* Hagerstown, MD: Alleyside. Excellent read-aloud bibliography for levels K–6.

GREENFIELD, F. V. (1977). *Games of the world.* New York: Holt, Rinehart & Winston. Tells origin of games and how to make and play them. Special festivals included.

JONES, C. (1979). *Learning for little kids.* Boston: Houghton Mifflin. Excellent resources for books about alternative parenting roles, birth, death, divorce, adoption, moving, and lots more. Also materials, games, activities, and information.

LASS-WOODFIN, M. J. (1978). *Books on American Indians and Eskimos: A Selection guide for children and young adults.* Chicago: American Library Association. This bibliography is designed to help educators make intelligent choices among the many book selections now available on American Indians and Eskimos. Each review summarizes content, comments on possible uses, lists strengths and weaknesses in writing and accuracy, and estimates grade level. Books are rated as good, adequate, or poor.

LEE, N., and OLDHAM, L. (1978). *Hands on heritage.* Long Beach, CA: Hands on Publishing. Includes activities for art, cooking, and recreation with special section on festivals for China, Greece, Israel, Japan, Mexico, Native Americans, and West Africa.

MARQUEVICH, R., and SPIEGEL, D. (1976). *Multi-ethnic studies in the elementary school classroom.* Rico Rivera, CA: Education in Motion. Excellent resource with background information on Asian-American, European-American, Native-American, Afro-American, and Mestizo cultures. Covers holidays, people, art, cooking, games, and songs plus a bibliography for each section. Multiethnic calendar is included.

PAGANO, A. L. (Ed.). (1978). *Social studies in early childhood: An interactionist point of view.* Washington, DC: National Council for the Social Studies. Concise and ready conference explaining the nature of social studies experiences for young children.

PASTERNAK, M. (1979). *Helping kids learn multi-cultural concepts.* Champaign, IL: Research Press. This book provides activities to help students develop increased multicultural and multiethnic understandings.

PERL, L. (1975). *Slumps, grunts and snickerdoodles: What Colonial Americans ate and why.* New York: Seabury. Early Colonists' culinary favorites.

SARACHO, O. N., and SPODEK, B. (1983). *Understanding the multicultural experience in early childhood education.* Washington, DC: National Association for the Education of Young Children. This publication celebrates the unique contributions of each cultural group while fostering children's competence and flexibility.

SCHRIBER, J. (1984). *Using children's books in social studies: Early childhood through primary grades.* Washington, DC: National Council for the Social Studies. Extensive, annotated bibliography of books for younger children that deal with social studies themes.

MOVIES AND FILMSTRIPS FOR THE SOCIAL STUDIES

People and Places

BARR FILMS. (1975). *Taleb and his lamb.* Pasadena, CA (16 min., film, color). A young Bedouin shepherd grows attached to a lamb. To prevent the lamb from being sold, the boy runs away with it into the desert. An unusual film and an outstanding folktale. 4-star film.

EDUCATIONAL DIMENSIONS. (1976). *People of China.* Stanford, CT (2 filmstrips, 2 cassettes, color). A simply written script compares Chinese and American customs and lifestyles.

LEARNING CORPORATION OF AMERICA. (1975). *Miguel: Up from Puerto Rico.* New York (15 min., film, color). Miguel lives in an apartment in New York City, but harbors fond memories of Puerto Rico, his birthplace. Both Spanish and English are used in this film.

LEARNING TREE. (1976). *Children everywhere.* Boulder, CO (4 filmstrips, 4 cassettes, color). How children in different parts of the world are alike and different.

LIVE OAK MEDIA. (National Geographic Education Services). (1981). *People and the places where they live.* (Series). Washington, DC (14 min., 3 filmstrips and 3 cassettes, color). How people adapt to their environment and work together to form communities. Each filmstrip succeeds in portraying cultural diversity and similarity by providing examples of the various methods employed by each group to provide themselves with food, shelter, and clothing.

PIED PIPER. (1977). *I'm somebody special.* New York (8 filmstrips, 8 cassettes, color). Teacher's guide. Eight children discuss their families, background, school friends, and activities. Good introduction to multicultural study.

WESTON WOODS. (1981). *Whistle for Willie.* Weston, CT (6 min., animation, color). This story is about a boy who wants to whistle.

WESTON WOODS. (1981). *The fire stealer.* Weston, CT (8 min., filmstrip, 1 cassette, color). Adapted from the book by William Tope. The story relates how Nanobozho brought fire to the Indians of his tribe.

Family Life/Change

ENCYCLOPEDIA BRITANNICA EDUCATIONAL CORPORATION. (1981). *My family and me.* (Series). Chicago (7 min., 4 filmstrips, 4 cassettes, color). This series provides useful materials to supplement the study of the family. The series portrays many kinds of families.

GUIDANCE ASSOCIATES. (1974). *Brother, sister, feelings and you.* Circle Pines, MN (2 filmstrips, 2 cassettes, color). Dramatizes family situations and ways to cope with feelings.

WALT DISNEY EDUCATIONAL MEDIA COMPANY. (1980). *Family problems: Dealing with crises.* Glendale, CA (9 min., 6 filmstrips, 6 cassettes, color). This series deals openly and realistically with the problems facing many school children today: divorce, death, anger, fear, moving, and grieving.

Career Awareness/Consumer Education

CORONET. (1976). *Jobs and people.* New York: Random House. (6 filmstrips, 6 cassettes, color). Shows people providing goods and services. Coronet provides other series on career awareness.

EDUCATIONAL ACTIVITIES. (1977). *Career awareness.* Freeport, NY (4 filmstrips, 4 cassettes, color). A vocational awareness program to acquaint students with many occupations.

FILMFAIR COMMUNICATIONS. (1971). *Night people's day.* Studio City, CA (11 min., film, color). An unusual documentary about the people and machines that work at night: typesetters, mail clerks, hotel chefs and bakers, sanitation people, and repair people.

Death

BFA EDUCATIONAL MEDIAS. (1971). *My turtle died today.* Santa Monica, CA (8 min., animation, color). In this film, adapted from the book by Edith Still, a young boy tells about the death of his turtle.

Special Days

ENCYCLOPEDIA BRITTANICA EDUCATIONAL CORPORATION. (1976). *Holidays: Histories and legends.* Chicago (6 filmstrips, 2 records or cassettes). Explains the history of several American holidays and reviews present customs associated with the holiday.

LEARNING TREE. (1981). *Celebrating holidays.* (Series). Boulder, CO (17 min., 4 strips, 4

cassettes, color). These filmstrips describe the holiday to children while preparing for its celebration.

LIVE OAK MEDIA. (1984). *Thanksgiving Day*. Ancromdale, NY (cassette). Presents, simply,
the background for celebrating Thanksgiving.

RANDOM HOUSE. BROWN, M. T. (1985). *Arthur Celebrates the Holidays*. New York (vi-
deocassette, VHS or Beta, 5 stories in one cassette). Contents: Arthur's Halloween, Thanksgiving, Christmas, Valentine, April Fool.

RECORDS FOR SOCIAL STUDIES

CAEDMON. (1979). *Sing children sing: Songs of the Congo*. New York (#TC1644 for 12"
phonodisc, #CDL511644 for cassette). An unusual perspective on the Congo
(Zaire) sung by children of different areas and recorded in the field. Bilingual
lyrics included.

CAEDMON. (1979). *Sing children sing: Songs of Mexico*. New York (#TC1645 for 12"
phonodisc, #DCL51645 for cassette). Mexican children's chorus with mariachis
and violins.

CAEDMON. (1980). *Sing children sing: Songs of Israel*. New York (#TC1672 for 12" phonodisc, #CDL51672 for cassette). Recorded in Israel by children's chorus. Tri-
lingual lyrics included.

CANYON RECORDS. *Source of Indian music*. (write for catalog) 4143 North Sixteenth
Street, Phoenix, AZ 85016.

CMS RECORDS. *Folkways Records*. Folkways Records provides an extensive collection of
records for classroom use. Their "Ethnic" series, "Children's" series, and "Folk
Dance" series are extremely useful. Records may be obtained in 10" phonodiscs, 12" phonodiscs, or cassettes. Many items are recorded on site to ensure
authenticity.

Catalogues describing their extensive collection may be obtained by writing
Folkway Records, 43 West 61st Street, New York, NY 10023.

A number of useful titles are listed below; however, this is a small sample of
their collection.

#4401 *Music of the Sioux and the Navajo*
#4420 *Music of the American Indians of the Southwest*
#4444 *Eskimos of Hudson Bay and Alaska*
#6510 *American Indian Dances*
#7201 *Afrikaans Children's Folk Songs*
#7224 *Jewish Children's Songs and Games*
#7533 *Negro Folk Songs for Young People*
#7601 *American Folk Songs for Children* (Pete Seeger)
#7661 *Jambo-More, Call and Response Songs and Chants* (Ella Jenkins)
#7666 *We Are All America's Children* (Ella Jenkins)
#7738 *Holiday Songs of Israel*
#7777 *A Cry from the Earth: Music of the North American Indian*
#7844 *African Songs and Rhythms for Children* (Orff Schulwerk)
#7851 *Latin American Children's Game Songs for Mexico and Puerto Rico*
#8745 *Music of the Orient in Hawaii: Japan/China/Korea/Philippines*

INDIAN HOUSE. *Sounds of Indian America: Plains and Southwest*. #87557. Box 472, Taos,
NM 87571.

KITS, STUDY PRINTS, DOLLS, AND GAMES
FOR THE SOCIAL STUDIES

AMERICAN GUIDANCE ASSOCIATES. (1981). *My Friends and Me.* Circle Pines, MN (Kit contains books, puppets, cassettes or records, picture cards, and manipulatives.) Activity board, $50 extra. Without board, $209.50. Discusses cooperation, consideration of others, ownership and sharing, and dependence and help. Designed for preschool–kindergarten.

CHILDCRAFT EDUCATIONAL CORPORATION. Source of ethnic dolls. 20 Kilmer Road, P.O. Box 3081, Edison, NJ 08818.

DAVID C. COOK PUBLISHING COMPANY. (1978). *Safety.* Elgin, IL (12 prints, 11"x14", color, $4.95). Safety prints demonstrating safety rules to follow at home, play, and school. Grades preschool–3.

KAPLAN SCHOOL SUPPLY CORPORATION. Source of ethnic dolls. 5360 Eastgate Mall, Suite E, San Diego, CA 92121.

MCGRAW-HILL. (1975). *Free to be You and Me.* New York, NY (Kit contains 6 filmstrips, 3 games, poster and additional materials.) Grades K-4, $160. This kit is based on the original book and previous record and film. It uses a variety of stories and visual effects to teach young children to develop their individuality.

PIED PIPER PRODUCTIONS. (1980). *Everybody Has Feelings.* Verdugo City, CA (Kit contains filmstrips, prints, records.) Grades 1–3. Songs in English and Spanish are included in this kit, which explores anger, fear, and other emotions. Useful for development of self-concept and cross-cultural understanding.

SINGER/SVE. (1976). *Adventures in Self-Awareness: The Me I Can Be.* Chicago. (Kit contains 6 filmstrips, poster, activity cards.) Grades K–3, $150. Cartoons and dramatizations intended to motivate children to think about inquiry, motivation, and values clarification.

SINGER/SVE. (1976). *Lollipop Dragon World of Work.* Chicago. (Kit contains 6 filmstrips, games, prints, and a mural.) Grades K–3, $225. Introduces fundamental career concepts.

SINGER/SVE. (1976). *A World of Our Own: Primary Social Studies Learning Module.* Chicago. (Kit contains 5 filmstrips, 60 activity cards, 12 craft patterns, and additional materials.) Grades 1–3, $135. The kit considers basic needs, community services and resources, social change, and interdependence. This is illustrated in a city setting only.

CHILDREN'S MAGAZINES FOR THE SOCIAL STUDIES

The following magazines contain articles, short stories, make and do activities, games, puzzles, and creative ideas for young children. Subjects include holidays and special celebrations, important individuals and events in history, conservation and ecology, safety, character development, and people and places around the world. The scope of these publications is broader than the social sciences; however, teachers, parents, and children will find numerous resources for the social studies in these inexpensive journals. Many of these publications contain excellent color photographs and illustrations.

Chickadee. The Young Naturalist Foundation. 255 Great Arrow Ave., Buffalo, NY 14207

Children's Playmate/Humpty Dumpty Magazine/Jack and Jill. P.O. Box 10681, Des Moines, IA 50336

Happy Times. 5600 North University Ave., Provo, UT 84604

National Geographic World. National Geographic Society. P.O. Box 2330, Washington, DC 20013

Ranger Rick's Nature Magazine. National Wildlife Federation. 8925 Leesburg Pike, Vienna, VA 22184

Super Times Magazine. 5600 North University Ave., Provo, UT 84604

Turtle: Magazine For Preschool Kids. P.O. Box 10681, Des Moines, IA 50336

Wee Wisdom. Unity School of Christianity. Unity Village, MO 46065

TEACHER'S MAGAZINES FOR THE SOCIAL STUDIES

Social Education. National Council for the Social Studies. 3501 Wisconsin Ave., Washington, DC 20016

The Social Studies. 4000 Albermarle St., NW, Washington, DC 20016

Social Studies and the Young Learner. National Council for the Social Studies. 3501 Newark St., NW, Washington, DC 20016

MICROCOMPUTER PROGRAMS

"Conservation and Counting," Hartley Courseware, Inc., Dimondale, MI, 1984. Developmental activities to help children experiment with conservation using counting activities.

"Facemaker," Spinnaker Software Corp., Cambridge, MA, 1983. Teaches children fundamentals in using a computer and allows them to develop pictures of faces.

"Hey Diddle Diddle," Spinnaker Software Corp., Cambridge, MA, 1983. Favorite nursery rhymes.

"Kermit's Electronic Story Maker," Simon & Schuster, New York, 1985. A writing kit for beginning readers.

"Kidwriter," Spinnaker Software Corp., Cambridge, MA, 1984. Allows children to create their own storybook.

"Observation and Classification," Hartley Courseware, Inc., Dimondale, MI, 1984. Activities that encourage use of observation skills and using them to classify.

"Stickybear Opposites," Weekly Reader Family Software, Middletown, CT, 1983. Helps children identify and understand terms describing opposites.

"Tuk Goes to Town," Mindscape School Software, Northbrook, IL, 1986. Children choose different places in town that Tuk visits.

NAME INDEX

SUBJECT INDEX